DATE DUE

JX1965.F67 1989   6324

FOSTER
WOMEN FOR ALL SEASONS

Women for All Seasons

Women for All Seasons

The Story of the Women's International
League for Peace and Freedom

Catherine Foster

The University of Georgia Press

Athens and London

© 1989 by Catherine Foster
Published by the University of Georgia Press
Athens, Georgia 30602
All rights reserved

Designed by Kathi L. Dailey
Set in Mergenthaler Palatino and Eras
Typeset by The Composing Room of Michigan
Printed and bound by Thomson-Shore
The paper in this book meets the guidelines for
permanence and durability of the Committee on
Production Guidelines for Book Longevity of the
Council on Library Resources.

Printed in the United States of America

93 92 91 90 89   5 4 3 2 1

Library of Congress Cataloging in Publication Data

Foster, Catherine.
Women for all seasons: the story of the Women's
International League for Peace and Freedom / Catherine Foster.
p. cm.
Bibliography: p.
Includes index.
ISBN 0-8203-1092-1 (alk. paper)
ISBN 0-8203-1147-2 (pbk.: alk. paper)
1. Women's International League for Peace and Freedom—History.
2. Women and peace—History.   I. Title.
JX1965.F67 1989
327.1'72'088042—dc19   88-17516
                                        CIP

British Library Cataloging in Publication Data available

Contents

Foreword

The women who established the Women's International League for Peace and Freedom in 1915 advocated fundamental changes in economic and social conditions and relations, nationally and internationally, to minimize and manage conflicts before they erupted into war. They founded the league as a vehicle through which women could organize themselves and work effectively to bring about those changes. WILPF has by its nature always dealt with highly political issues: hence a need for discussion, analysis of the causes of conflicts, introspection, and policy development leading to action. To ensure the continuity of the organization, its pioneers set up a structure in which democratic processes were not only guaranteed but were made essential to the existence of the organization. With its ups and downs, the league has endured.

While for many years WILPF was one of the few if not the only international women's peace organization, in recent years more women's peace groups have sprung up, often in spontaneous response to a national development but reaching beyond borders to those with similar experiences for mutual support. These movements are national or transnational rather than international. Together they form a network with varied but related concerns. They do not replace international organizations. It is entirely possible for a multi-issue organization such as WILPF to cooperate with the single-issue movements of recent years.

We live in a world in revolution. There is increasing recognition that solutions to one social problem need to be sought in relation to others, while at the same time, the solution of one problem cannot be made hostage to that of another. This underlines the need for all in the peace movement to find ways of working together.

It is impossible to record WILPF's history fully, or to convey in a few pages the organization-wide actions undertaken in more than seventy years' time. Moreover, many of the records are missing or widely scattered. Yet as we approach our seventy-fifth anniversary, we take strength from our history in seeking new approaches to our work so that we can better respond to the challenges of our time: to rid our world of nuclear weapons, to replace exploitation with sharing, to preserve our natural environment—in short, to build a world in which all women and men can live in security. Catherine Foster's *Women for all Seasons* can help us in our reflections as we develop new approaches and think anew about how to work together to reach these goals.

Edith Ballantyne

WILPF Secretary-General
Geneva
February 1988

Preface

The Aims and Principles section of the constitution of the Women's International League for Peace and Freedom (WILPF) is printed below for readers who are unfamiliar with the league.

1. The League aims at bringing together women of different political and philosophical tendencies united in their determination to study, make known, and help abolish the political, social, economic, and psychological causes of war, and to work for a constructive peace.

2. The primary objectives of the League are the achievement of total and universal disarmament, the abolition of violence and other means of coercion for the settlement of all conflicts, the substitution in every case of some form of peaceful settlement, and the strengthening of the United Nations and its family of Specialized Agencies, for the prevention of war, a sustainable environment, the institution of international law, and for the political, social, and economic cooperation of all peoples.

3. Conscious that under systems of exploitation and oppression these aims cannot be attained and that a real and lasting peace and true freedom cannot exist, the League's duty is to facilitate by nonviolent means the social transformation which would permit the inauguration of systems under which would be realized social, economic, and political equality for all without discrimination on grounds of sex, race, religion, or on any other grounds.

4. The League sees as its ultimate goal the establishment of an international economic order founded on meeting the needs of all people and not on profit and privilege.

5. The work of all the national sections of the League is based on these aims and principles and on the statements and resolutions adopted by the International Congress and the International Executive Committee.

Acknowledgments

Although only my name appears on the cover, *Women for All Seasons* was truly a collaborative effort. The first acknowledgment must go to the Women's International League for Peace and Freedom, which provided the inspiration for this work and, later, tremendous technical and financial support through its affiliate, the Jane Addams Peace Association. Many thanks in this regard are also owed to Joseph Cimmino, who not only donated training, consultation, and access to his word processor over a three-year period, but also accompanied me to the WILPF congress in Zeist in July 1986, where he did my photographic work without pay. It is no exaggeration to say that without his help, this book would not have been completed. The help of Elizabeth Dearborn, Kay Camp, Edith Ballantyne, and William Van Wyke must also be noted: they voluntarily edited parts of the manuscript and gave encouragement and advice which kept this project moving along, particularly in its later phases.

I am also grateful to literally hundreds of WILPF members who have given of their time and knowledge. In particular I would like to thank, first, the forty-nine patient women who participated in the sometimes lengthy interviews I conducted; though not all of the interviews were used, each of the women contributed helpful information and further inspiration. Next, many women opened their files and allowed me to use their materials freely; thanks are particularly due to Judy Adams and the Women's Peace Oral History Project at Stanford University, Lucy Haessler, Elisabeth Stahle, and Alice Hamburg. Finally, special thanks to the women in the WILPF offices both in Geneva and in Philadelphia. These staff members and volunteers were consistently friendly and willing to lend a hand or an ear, and they generously entrusted me with precious original papers and photographs.

Most of the actual writing was done at my grandparents' farm in western Georgia, but I put pieces of the book together in a myriad of work settings—on the banks of the Rhone River in Geneva; in the Berkeley, California, foothills; and at the Swarthmore Peace Collection in Pennsylvania, to name but a few. Throughout the United States, Europe, and beyond, more friends, relatives, and associates than can be named in this short space gave of themselves to help make this project happen, and to them I am also grateful.

•

Women for All Seasons

Introduction

These pages tell the story of a daring group of women from twelve countries who came together in 1915 with the high goal of putting an end to war. The organization they founded, the Women's International League for Peace and Freedom (WILPF), has persevered for more than seventy of the stormiest years in history. A small organization geographically spread over twenty-three nations, the league has survived through the persistent loyalty of its members despite a host of obstacles—constant financial crises, vast geographical and cultural distances which separate its women, and a far from welcoming and often downright hostile political climate.

What also emerges here is a portrait of some of the individuals who have kept WILPF going these seven decades—their accomplishments, their dreams, the problems they as peacemakers have faced in a war-torn world. These are ordinary women whose lives are extraordinary examples of courage and determination. In particular I have tried to capture their amazing sense of optimism, for it is that spirit which makes them and their organization so noteworthy. An early American social worker and cofounder of WILPF, Jane Addams, once observed, "What after all has maintained the human race on this old globe despite all the calamities of nature and all the tragic failings of mankind, if not faith in new possibilities and the courage to advocate them?"[1]

Until recently, women's achievements have been glaringly absent from the pages of history. For instance, how many textbooks dealing with World War I include an account of the women who visited fourteen heads of state with a peace plan for a neutral na-tions' conference of mediation? This and other little-known actions like it are chronicled here, expanding the boundaries of traditional history.

The story is pieced together largely through conversations with women of WILPF, and much of it is told in their own words. I have chosen to expand on simple narrative to include oral history, the process of interviewing women to find out about experiences and impressions that may not be recorded (or noted) elsewhere.

As well as having interviewed nearly fifty women, I have used materials from their old journals, letters, and articles, believing that the actual participants can tell their story much better than I as an observer could. What comes through, then, is not just one per-son's perspective but that of many, weaving a rougher but richer and more varied tapestry. An obvious drawback is the use of the English language, since that is not the native tongue of many WILPF members. Readers should bear in mind the language dif-ferences when reading the words of women from non–English-speaking countries.

Becoming part of WILPF and working on this project have been profound, life-changing experiences in developing my identity as a woman and as a "world citizen" (in the words of Nobel Peace Prize winner Emily Greene Balch). Talking with, growing close to, and beginning to understand women who have spent decades ac-tively embracing the causes of peace and freedom have strength-ened my own commitment to those values and my resolve to work toward a world which incorporates them. Dorothy Hutchinson, a Quaker activist and at one time the WILPF international chair who spent her life promoting peaceful settlement of disputes, summed up the league very well: "We have kept alive in good times and bad our faith in the social value of conscientious dissent. We have dem-onstrated that an enlightened and courageous minority can be the seed of social progress by consistently opposing laws, institutions, and customs which glorify power and prestige above human val-ues. . . . we have thus enabled our members to exercise their right to be fully human. To express and to implement intelligent com-passion is a human right."[2] Part of my reason for wanting to write

Women for All Seasons has been a desire to share this experience with others, especially women who think seriously on the matters of peace and human rights and responsibilities in the world but who have little support or outlet for their views.

In recent years WILPF has increasingly been an organization of older women, although there are certainly many young members too in its ranks of thirty thousand.[3] Ever since World War II, in fact, the league has grappled with the problem of how to attract younger women. Nevertheless, the ages of WILPF members are more a strength of the organization than a weakness, and that virtue is what I have found most inspiring and wish to emphasize in these pages—for instance, the sheer tenacity of many members in their convictions and various campaigns, and the insights that come with having been internationalists for decades of political and historical upheaval. The continued optimism and vision of a more just world expressed by sixty- and seventy-year-old women who have forty years of activism behind them truly make those visions seem possible. And, finally, the values and qualities which led them to persevere in peacemaking make longtime WILPF women strong models for those who choose to carry on that peacemaking tradition into the twenty-first century.

This project was originally conceived as an update of *Pioneers for Peace*, a book written in 1965 to chronicle the first fifty years of WILPF. As a result, I have focused on the most recent twenty years of the league's history. But because I have included oral histories and other personal reflections of many WILPF women, you will find in this volume a very different approach from that of its predecessor. I chose to assume neither that readers know very much about the league nor that they have read *Pioneers for Peace*. This required sketching a portrait of WILPF from its inception, which I did by using the league's fiftieth-anniversary celebration as a lens through which to view the accomplishments of its first fifty years. Thus, the story opens in 1965 as the women return to the league's founding place, The Hague.

In the first section of the book I trace the organization's history in narrative form, inserting comments from the interviews to amplify and personalize the narrative. In its five chapters I examine the women's activities and philosophies not simply chronologically but also through a number of themes that kept cropping up in my research, both in conversations and in the hundreds of thousands of microfilmed pages of archives from the international office in Geneva.

On nonviolence: the balance struck between pacifist members and those who believed in taking up arms with just cause.

On feminism: the evolution of WILPF's founders' position of looking toward women's suffrage as a way of ending war, to becoming a group viewing themselves as peace-minded people who happened to be women, to—more recently—a search to understand the unique connection between women and antiwar beliefs.

On age: building on existing knowledge; bridging generational differences (an especially important topic during the youth movement of the sixties); outreach to young women.

On building a movement: how a vanguard of middle-class intellectual women remain true to their progressive views but gain acceptance by enough people to affect government policies.

On internationalism: the tensions between a global perspective and nationalism; between cooperative international projects and concentration on the policies of the individual governments of each section; between a First World and a Third World focus.

Each of the above themes is examined here in terms of the way the organization has resolved problems or is still dealing with them, the responses of individual members, and the social evolution of the topic itself.

The second section includes eighteen profiles of WILPF members from fourteen countries. These are actual edited conversations with a cross section of women who discuss their backgrounds, motivations, beliefs, and experiences in the league. The women range from well-known public figures to those whose achievements have received no public accolade. By giving the reader a close-up of a segment of its membership, the interviews bring the organization into focus from a personal angle and add perspectives to the themes mentioned above.

Of course the themes themselves are interrelated. A comment

one often hears about WILPF is that it is an organization which "makes the connections"—the connections between peace and freedom, between women's rights and human rights, between rights and responsibilities, between feminism and nonviolence, between communication and cooperation, between cooperation and internationalism—the list goes on.

Thus, one event can shed light on a number of these topics. For example, in August 1968, Soviet tanks rolled into Czechoslovakia at the same time WILPF was holding its seventeenth congress in Denmark. Yet despite the fact that Soviet, Czechoslovakian, and other Eastern European women were present as invited observers—and had intense and differing views on the crisis—the congress did not break down. On the contrary, the delegates, who suddenly found themselves the subject of local press attention, reached agreement on a resolution concerning the invasion, which some U.S. delegates then hand-delivered to Moscow. This incident is a prime example of peaceful settlement of dispute, albeit on a microlevel, and a testament to the feminist principles of cooperation and continuous open dialogue which have always guided WILPF. In these pages, many such incidents are recalled by the women who took part in them.

In the text, readers will also notice that many activities are described without reference to their impact or end result. Calculating the "outcome" of attempts to influence global policies is, at best, very difficult because these outcomes are cumulative and may take years to become apparent. For instance, at the United Nations, a country that took up an idea suggested to it for years by a nongovernmental organization (NGO) would not often credit that organization if the idea later became policy. WILPF has had that very experience on several occasions.

On the other hand, not all the results achieved by the league are so intangible, as in the case of Art for World Friendship, a project which in its first years exchanged one thousand pictures by children from schools in fifteen countries, was formally hailed by several foreign governments, and was promoted on Voice of America radio. Projects such as these—and their impacts—are also explored in the narrative.

From the suffragists of 1915 who risked public scorn in calling

themselves "internationalists" to the women of the 1980s who frequently risk imprisonment to denounce policies of hardened nationalism and militarism, the women and the experiences told of
here are more than simply interesting and thought-provoking
(though they are that too). The rebirth of the disarmament movement, and the abundance of peace groups as well as women's
peace groups that it has given rise to, make the lessons of WILPF—
and the organization itself—all the more valuable because it has
lasted so long and therefore encompassed such a range of experiences. Throughout the years, it has attracted far-sighted women
whose ideas and actions have kept alive the goals of peace and
freedom in even the darkest of times.

1. The First Fifty Years

July 26, 1965—The Hague, Holland

The three hundred women gathered in the conference hall had spent the last half hour greeting old friends, introducing themselves to new ones, and talking politics or family. Some of them had difficulty talking to each other at all, since they did not speak the same language. They had come to The Hague from twenty-two countries to attend the Sixteenth Congress of the Women's International League for Peace and Freedom, and although they shared a common purpose as peace activists, most saw one another only rarely. For some, this international conference was the first they had attended.

As the opening speaker stepped to the stage, the hall became very quiet. Each knew this was a momentous occasion: fifty years before, in the midst of World War I, another group of women had come, at great risk, to The Hague for a historic congress at which WILPF was founded. Now, half a century later, it was time to look back and to look ahead.

Established in 1915 to seek disarmament, social and economic justice, and an end to all war, the league had struggled persistently throughout its years in pursuit of those aims. Yet the women assembled in The Hague in 1965 were well aware that they were still a long way from their goals and were in fact facing large and potentially even more serious world crises. As Kay Camp, a U.S. participant, recalled, "That was my first Congress. It was very exciting just to meet women from the various countries, get to know them a little bit, to see who was behind those names I had heard about for so long. It was the beginning of the period of anxiety about Vietnam—that was very predominant in our discussions. There was a determination to work on ending the war, and in fact, the cooperation of the sections in that work was probably as great as it's ever been since the earliest years."[1]

Again the women were coming together in the early days of a war that would change the face of history. Their voices were some of the first to speak out about the Vietnam War, just as they had been among the few to condemn World War I. The WILPF had begun its first campaign against the escalating conflict in Southeast Asia two years earlier, in March 1963. But in 1965 what would later become public outcry was still only a whisper.

In her introductory report, WILPF chair, Else Zeuthen, a petite, cigar-smoking, former member of the Danish Parliament, warned of the growing seriousness of the Vietnam War, citing the first U.S. bombing raids into North Vietnamese territory earlier that year. Over the following six days the subject of the war came up again and again in nearly every discussion. In fact, on July 28, 1965, in the midst of the congress, the U.S. president, Lyndon Johnson, dispatched an additional 50,000 troops to the area, bringing the U.S. presence to 125,000. Drawing the links between U.S. injustices abroad and at home, Bayard Rustin, a black leader of the U.S. civil rights movement, well-known nonviolent activist, and keynote speaker at the congress, pointed out that Johnson was using the "increasing freedom for Negroes as an umbrella to hide the dastardly things that are going on in Vietnam."[2]

The women had no way of knowing that not only would the conflict in Vietnam rage on for eight more years but opposition to it would erupt, dividing the United States internally as has not been done since the Civil War. That opposition would also irrevocably alter the world's perception of U.S. power. But it was not so much foresight as a sense of urgency that drove the congress delegates to focus their future work on Southeast Asia.

The project the women decided on was called "An Appeal to American Women to Help Stop the War in Vietnam." It was a campaign to collect hundreds of signatures of prominent women from around the world to go on a statement to be published as an advertisement in the *New York Times* and other major newspapers.

Optimism, persistence, and hard, even risky, work for peace in wartime were not new to WILPF women. Their organization would not have lasted fifty years without those qualities. Although the women were cautious not to rest on the laurels of WILPF's early accomplishments, they were also careful to preserve their heritage and to remember the founding mothers for strength to carry on.

The Founding of WILPF

The early twentieth century, the time of the league's founding, was an era of social reform, prompted primarily by the Industrial Revolution, which had concentrated wealth in the hands of a few and created a mass of workers who were often exploited and had no collective-bargaining rights. They soon organized themselves into a labor movement to demand more humane treatment and decent wages. Meanwhile, writers such as Marx and Tolstoy, also responding to the injustices around them, produced works that began influencing intellectuals worldwide toward more progressive social thought and action. Well-educated middle-class women of the times frequently worked with the poor in settlement houses and other social reform institutions that had recently been established to respond to community needs.

Concurrently, half of the human race had begun organizing for a place in public life. As a result of their participation in antislavery, workers' rights, and other campaigns, women in the developed world had become increasingly aware of their own lesser status. By the first decade of the twentieth century, there was a well-organized movement of women demanding suffrage in the United States and most countries in Europe. The international organization that united them was the International Women's Suffrage Alliance (IWSA), headquartered in London. From this organization and movement, WILPF emerged during World War I.

As with many other social reformers, suffrage activists were not united in their reactions to the war that was suddenly declared in Europe on August 4, 1914. No well-developed peace movement existed in those years. The outbreak of World War I served to coalesce one, a significant part of which was composed of women who saw action for suffrage and action for peace as inseparable.

British socialist and suffragist Emmeline Pethick-Lawrence is one of WILPF's lesser-known founding mothers. An excerpt from her memoirs captures the growing antiwar sentiment many suffragists were experiencing in 1914:

> The woman suffrage movement (at least many sections of it) was split by the war. In our own and many countries the idea of the solidarity of women had taken a deep hold upon many of us: so deep that it could not be shaken even by the fact that men of many nations were at war. The principles that had inspired our great struggle for women's emancipation came back to remembrance. Had we not spoken and written of the solidarity of women whose main vocation in every nation was one and the same—the guardianship and nurture of the human race? Could the women of the world remain silent while men in the bloom of their youth were being offered up by many nations for sacrifice? Sacrifice for what?[3]

In the early days of World War I, Pethick-Lawrence embarked on a speaking tour of the United States. In several cities she shared the podium with Rosika Schwimmer, a colleague from the IWSA. Schwimmer, a Hungarian feminist and internationalist, was determined to spark U.S. suffragists' interest in persuading their neutral nation to take the lead in negotiations to end the war. The image of sisterhood evoked by these two women from warring countries galvanized feminine opposition to the war and helped to launch the National Woman's Peace Party in Washington in January 1915. The Woman's Peace Party later became the U.S. section of WILPF.

In Europe, sentiment within the IWSA was divided. A few notable IWSA leaders enthusiastically supported the war effort, and plans for the organization's 1915 international gathering in Berlin had been halted.[4] Yet elsewhere in Europe, in Amsterdam, a radical plan was emerging. Aletta Jacobs, president of the Dutch suffrage movement, balked at the idea of canceling the meeting.

But I thought at once, just because there is this terrible war the women *must* come together somewhere, some way, just to show that women of all countries can work together even in the face of the greatest war in the world. Women must show that when all Europe seems full of hatred they can remain united. I felt that the alliance had to do that and we should invite the alliance to meet in Amsterdam. But several of the allied countries voted against holding an international meeting during the war and therefore the invitation was not accepted.

I received, however, many letters of sympathy with the plan from individual women in belligerent and neutral countries, and from Miss Macmillan of England a plan for a meeting of individuals.[5] The other members of my board of the suffrage society did not agree on this plan of a congress of individuals, but I thought it a good plan and decided to do what I could personally.

I therefore invited as many women as I could reach in different countries to discuss together what the congress should be and to make up the preliminary program. When the answers came, so many were in favor that I thought, "Now I dare to do it."[6]

The International Congress of Women at The Hague opened on April 28, 1915—without the blessing of the IWSA. Nor was it viewed fondly by governments, particularly Britain. Although forty-two U.S. delegates, along with Pethick-Lawrence and Schwimmer, did arrive on time at the congress after setting sail from New York in early April, their boat was stopped by British authorities off the coast of Dover and held motionless for four days despite the pleas of numerous prominent figures aboard. Of 180 English delegates, only 20 were granted passports, and even those were not then allowed to depart, as all traffic between Holland and Britain was stopped at the time.[7]

As British delegate Pethick-Lawrence recalled later,

the Congress proceeded to hold its sessions in an atmosphere of sympathetic harmony. The preamble to the resolutions stated:

"This International Congress of Women of different nations, classes, creeds and parties is united in expressing sympathy with the suffering of all, whatever their nationality, who are fighting for their country or labouring under the burden of war. Since the mass of the people in each of the countries now at war believe themselves to be fighting not as aggressors but in self-defence, there can be no irreconcilable differences between them; and their common ideas afford a basis upon which an honourable peace might be established. The Congress therefore urges the Governments of the world to put an end to bloodshed and begin peace negotiations."

Thereupon followed resolutions which in general tenor were very similar to the fourteen points afterwards formulated by [U.S.] President [Woodrow] Wilson. But included in them was a provision that women should be made responsible citizens and be given a voice in deciding these vital questions of war and peace that affect them so deeply.

The Congress did much more than pass resolutions. It brought into friendly association the women from the belligerent countries and made them realize that their fundamental interests were one and the same.[8]

These memoirs of U.S. delegate Emily Greene Balch call further into focus the atmosphere and significance of the congress:

The women, 1500 of them and more, have come together and for four days conferred, not on remote and abstract questions but on the vital subject of international relations. English, Scottish, German, Austrian, Hungarian, Italian, Polish, Belgian, Dutch, American, Danish, Norwegian, and Swedish were all represented.

On the first evening, Dr. Aletta Jacobs expressed her appreciation of the courage shown by those women who had braved all the dangers and difficulties of travelling in wartime. The programme and rules of order agreed on from the first shut out all discussions of relative national responsibility for the present war or the conduct of it or of methods for conducting future war. We met on the common ground beyond—the ground of preparation for permanent peace. The two fundamental planks, adherence to which was a condition of membership, were: (A) That international disputes should be settled by pacific means; (B) that the parliamentary franchise should be extended to women.

One of the most warmly debated questions was on Madame [Rosika] Schwimmer's proposal, which was finally accepted, to send delegates to the different capitals, both belligerent and neutral, to carry to them the resolutions voted by the Congress.[9]

A very curious thing has been the attitude of the press. Most of them had apparently been sent to get an amusing story of an international peace gathering of women—"base and silly" enough to try to meet in wartime—breaking up in quarrel. Day by day they went away with faces long with disappointment. In many countries the meetings were reported to have been either practically unattended or to have closed in a row. Nothing could be further from the truth. The largest hall in The Hague was needed for the meetings, over 2000 often being present; and difficult as it is to conduct business with so mixed and differing languages, different rules of parliamentary procedure, and divergent views, Miss [Jane] Addams and the other officials carried on orderly and effective sessions, marked by the most active will for unity that I have ever felt in an assemblage.

What stands out most strongly among all my impressions of those thrilling and strained days at the Hague is the sense of wonder at the beautiful spirit of the brave, self-controlled women who dared ridicule and every sort of difficulty to express a passionate human sympathy, not inconsistent with patriotism, but transcending it. There was not one clash or even danger of a clash over national differences; on every hand was the same consciousness of the development of a new spirit which is growing in the midst of the war as the roots of the wheat grow under the drifts and tempests of winter. It must not be thought, however, that the congress was stagnantly placid. One's every faculty was on the stretch hour after hour.

In the distress of mind that the war breeds in every thinking and feeling person, there is a poignant relief in finding a channel through which to work for peace.[10]

The "channel" Balch referred to was the organization established by the congress, first known as the International Committee of Women for Permanent Peace. Reconvening in 1919, founding members changed its name to the Women's International League for Peace and Freedom. Conceived from the first as an international organization, it was set up with thirteen national committees, or "sections," as they came to be known.[11]

Presiding over The Hague congress was Jane Addams, one of America's leading women and one of its first social workers. Addams had long been involved in the social reform movement and in 1899 had founded one of the country's first settlement houses, Hull House in Chicago. With her strong support for liberalism and cultural diversity, Addams shaped Hull House into more than a place of refuge for the poor, becoming involved in statewide policy battles for immigrants' rights, child-labor laws, and trade unions. Later Addams turned her attention to the suffrage movement. A frail, soft-spoken, but insistent woman, Addams viewed all of these issues as intricately linked. Partly because of her work with poor people, Jane Addams believed strongly that there could be no peace without social and economic justice, and it was the influence of her and other proponents of broad social reform in the league's founding ranks which nudged WILPF to adopt that view as part of its original platform.

Addams's reputation both as a crusader and as a mediator made her a perfect candidate for president of the wartime women's congress. Once she accepted the task, she applied herself to it fully, encouraging a spirit of cooperation at the event itself and even leading a daring follow-up mission appealing directly to national leaders for a negotiated peace—a strategy she had not personally endorsed.

Two small delegations of WILPF women set out from the congress to present a peace plan to the heads of state of thirteen warring and neutral nations. Addams led the delegation that met with officials in eight warring European capitals, and in Washington, where she was personally received by President Wilson. The women's purpose was to assemble a panel of neutral states for continuous mediation of the conflict.

Addams wrote about their mission in *Women at The Hague.*

> Travelling rapidly, as we did, from one country to another, perhaps nothing was more striking than the diametrically opposing opinions we found concerning identical occurrences.
>
> Our message was a simple one. After discussing our resolutions we ventured to report to the men who are after all responsible for the happenings of Europe that the 1500 women who met in The Hague, coming in smaller or larger numbers from 12 different countries, urge that whatever the causes of the war and however necessary it may have been to carry it on for the past 10

months, that the time has come for beginning some sort of negotiations which must in the end take place unless the war shall continue year after year and at last be terminated through sheer exhaustion.[12] We implied that if Europe is in disorder because of deep-rooted injustices or because certain nations are deprived of commercial, political, or maritime opportunities, that the solution can be discovered much better by men who consider the situation on its merits than by those who approach it on the basis of military victories or losses.

It may be natural for the minister of a nation at war to say, "This country will never receive negotiations; we are going to drive the enemy out inch by inch," but it is difficult for him to repeat it to a delegation of women who reply: "If a feasible proposition were presented to you, which might mean the beginning of negotiations between your country and your enemies, would you decline to receive such a proposition? Would you feel justified to go on sacrificing the young men of your country in order to attain through bloodshed what might be obtained by negotiations, the very purpose for which the foreign office was established?" No minister, of course, is willing to commit himself to such an undeviating policy.

On the contrary one of them said that he had wondered many times since the war began why women had remained silent so long, adding that as women are not expected to fight they might easily have made a protest against war which is denied to men.

We went into the office of another high official, a large, grizzled, formidable man. When we had finished our presentation and he said nothing, I remarked, "It perhaps seems to you very foolish that women should go about in this way; but after all, the world itself is so strange in this war situation that our mission may be no more strange nor foolish than the rest."

He banged his fist on the table. "Foolish?" he said. "Not at all. These are the first sensible words that have been uttered in this room for 10 months."

Our mission was simple, and foolish it may be, but it was not impossible. Perhaps the ministers talked freely to us because we were so absolutely unofficial. "Without abandoning your cause and without lowering your patriotism," we practically said to the representatives of these various nations, "whatever it is which you ought in honor to obtain, why are you not willing to submit your case to a tribunal of fair-minded men? If your cause is as good as you are sure it is, certainly such men will find the righteousness which adheres within it." Responsible people in all the warring powers said that if the right medium could be found, there would be no difficulty in submitting the case.[13]

Although the women found several ministers sympathetic to their proposals, particularly in Sweden, they were unable to persuade any of them actually to begin a mediating process. Addams's several meetings with Woodrow Wilson also failed to convince him that America should take the lead as peacemaker. Despite Wilson's private antiwar sympathies, he yielded to public and administrative pressure; and the United States entered the war too in April 1917, wiping away pacifists' hopes for an early end to the conflict.

Jane Addams had never been afraid to face public criticism, and face it she did upon her return home. Although Addams herself saw her social reform efforts and her work for peace as one and the same, the American public was less progressive, and less forgiving. A strong stand against war was relatively unheard of at that time, especially by such a well-known personality.

Addams and the other peace women dared not only to speak out against war but to link their convictions to their gender. Addams held that as nurturers, women have a stronger sense of moral obligation than men and that, therefore, there must be equal participation by women in all levels of society for social justice ever to be realized. Most WILPF founders actually believed that women's participation in public life—which they equated with suffrage— would bring an end to wars. This comment made by Aletta Jacobs in 1915 summarizes that position:

> Women will soon have political power. Woman suffrage and permanent peace will go together. When the women of a country are eagerly asking for the vote and a country is of a mind to grant the vote to its women, it is a sign that the country is ripe for permanent peace.
>
> Yes, the women will do it. They don't feel as men do about war. Men think of the economic results; women think of the grief and pain, and the damage to the race. If we can bring women to feel

that internationalism is higher than nationalism, then they won't stand by governments, they'll stand by humanity.[14]

Emerging as it did from the women's movement, WILPF signaled the beginning of a mass peace movement that has grown and persisted throughout most of the twentieth century. However, the founders' notion that with suffrage would come peace was challenged almost as soon as the Great War ended.

In the Aftermath of World War I

As they had pledged to do, the peace women held their second congress concurrently with the Paris peace accords in 1919. Though sorely dismayed by the terms of the accords, they took the establishment of the League of Nations as a victory. While that organization of nations never effectively functioned in the way they had envisioned, its creation had been urged repeatedly to Wilson by WILPF women and other American peace leaders. At the end of the war WILPF chose Geneva as the site of its headquarters and mandated its leaders to work closely with that body. From 1919 on, women from many countries gathered at the Maison Internationale, a lovely two-story house, to plan their peacemaking strategies.

Shortly after the end of World War I, women in most European countries and the United States were given the right to vote. Because it had been organized almost solely around suffrage, the women's movement quickly began to lose momentum. As a broad social force, it was practically nonexistent from the 1920s through the 1960s.

Accordingly, WILPF began to lose its original strong feminist focus as its leaders suddenly realized that suffrage alone would not bring permanent peace. That realization brought disenchantment to many WILPF pioneers, whose very understanding of feminism linked it to a world without war. Many did not stop to reflect that suffrage was far from true equality, and that perhaps if a truly equal society were ever inaugurated, there would be no more wars.

Organizationally, the league took the advice of founder Aletta Jacobs seriously: "bring women to feel that internationalism is higher than nationalism." In practical terms, the league increasingly centered its work on peace and international relations with less attention given to women's rights.

Throughout the 1920s and early 1930s WILPF concentrated on its work with the League of Nations, sending missions to trouble spots around the world and developing its own theory and practice of nonviolence. The latter was seen as particularly important after Gandhi began his campaign for Indian independence in 1919, which WILPF enthusiastically promoted. Mildred Scott Olmsted, a member from the United States and an early organizer for WILPF, said of that period: "The idea of peace missions came very early to the WILPF and I expect it grew out of the international suffrage movement. The League believed in sending missions of women to meet with women of different countries, and if there were problems in one of our own sections, we would send someone to talk with the membership. Sometimes we would send an international group into an area of tension to talk with people of all sides to see if we couldn't head off conflict."[15]

In the United States, WILPF became in 1917 the first secular peace organization to establish lobbying headquarters in Washington, D.C., for the purpose of establishing ongoing relations with legislators in an attempt to influence policy.

During this period and for several decades to follow, the link between women's rights and peace continued to weaken in the league's discussions and literature. Many WILPF women were still staunch proponents of feminism, both as a social force and in their private lives, and they were not pleased with this trend. As early as the 1920s, Lida Gustava Heymann and Anita Augspurg—two cofounders of WILPF who had devoted their lives to feminism and peacemaking—lamented that the league was losing its feminist orientation. In 1934 there was even serious discussion of dropping "Women's" from the title. To its credit, however, the league did remain an organization of women, and it did continue to stress women's responsibility to work for peace.

"The Greatest Service"

After World War I, Jane Addams gave virtually the rest of her life to promoting peace and justice. She became the first president of WILPF and continued as an active or honorary president for the rest of her life. In spite of the fact that her work for peace had actually been frowned upon by much of the American public who held her social welfare activities in such high esteem, in 1931 Jane Addams became the first American woman to receive the Nobel Peace Prize. Her friend and colleague Emily Greene Balch described her as follows:

> Jane Addams enjoyed even more than most people approbation and love, and they came to her in almost unexampled measure, and she suffered proportionately from hostility and criticism from which she had no conceit to shield her. By far the most serious and prolonged [criticism], however, was the opposition excited by her work for peace. But neither praise nor blame swayed her action.
>
> She was so unlike anyone else that I have known—so utterly real and first-hand; so subtle, so simple and direct; so free from any preoccupations with self, as free from asceticism as from self-indulgence; full of compassion without weakness or sentimentality (though she grew up in a sentimental generation); loving merriment while carrying the world's woes in her heart—both the many which pressed upon her in an immediately personal shape at Hull House and those of the nameless, unseen millions whose fates are part of our own personal fate. A great statesman, a great writer, one of the world's rarest spirits.[16]

Nobel awards are granted for "the greatest service to mankind." The peace prize goes to one "who has done the most or best work for the brotherhood of nations, the abolition and reduction of standing armies, and for the formulation or popularization of peace congresses."[17] It had frequently been awarded to statesmen for specific achievements. However, private citizens serving the cause of peace could also be so honored.

In 1946, just after the Second World War, WILPF could again be proud that one of its leaders was given the Nobel Peace Prize. The award went to Emily Greene Balch, also an American and one of the founders of WILPF. Unlike Jane Addams, Balch was practically unknown as a public figure. After the outbreak of World War I, she too, however, had devoted her life to peacemaking and particularly to the work of WILPF. She too had crossed the Atlantic in wartime to attend The Hague congress and had participated in the mission to the heads of state. Shortly thereafter, after twenty-five years as a social science professor at Wellesley College, Balch lost her faculty position because of her antiwar activism. Upon leaving Wellesley, Balch served as the league's first general secretary in Geneva from 1919 to 1922 and again from 1933 to 1936. In 1926 Balch was one of a five-person mission to Haiti, which was then occupied by U.S. Marines. Her book *Occupied Haiti* first brought that country to public attention and helped to spawn an official U.S. investigation which resulted in the marines' withdrawal. Balch was the WILPF international president at the time of the award.

Mildred Scott Olmsted, one of the few WILPF elders who remembers the league's early days, recalled her association with Balch:

> I visited the Geneva headquarters of the League, where I met Miss Balch. I realized what a center that had become because of her work. Miss Balch knew nearly everybody, and people like Gandhi, liberal leaders from all over the world, would come to our center, where afternoon tea was an institution. They would gather and talk peace and freedom. Miss Balch was such a rare spirit. I would say that one of the things that impressed me the most about Emily Balch was that you could take people of absolutely diverse viewpoints, put them together, and under her guiding influence they would be reasonable and friendly to one another.[18]

Both Jane Addams and Emily Greene Balch, the only two American women ever to receive the Nobel Peace Prize, donated half of their award money to WILPF.

The World War II Years

Beginning in the early 1930s, the league turned its attention, as did much of the world, to the rising fascism in Europe. The Nazis were beginning to amass power in Germany, and in March 1933 the WILPF section office in Munich was raided. Documents were burned and some women were arrested for no apparent reason. Anita Augspurg and Lida Gustava Heymann, two of the leading members, fled to Switzerland, where they both died in exile in 1945.

A conservative mood had overtaken parts of Europe, and in July 1933 Swiss authorities announced that Camille Drevet, the WILPF international secretary, had nine days to leave the country: she was being denounced as a "revolutionary propagandist." A week later, amid a flood of international protest, the authorities rescinded the order, but the incident was a foreboding of the difficulties WILPF would face in the coming years.

In addition, what had always been a division within the league now threatened to become a gulf. From its inception, the league had never called itself a pacifist organization, though many WILPF women were and are strict pacifists. Some of its members had always felt that use of force in the cause of social justice should not be condemned. As an organization, however, WILPF had consistently counseled against violence from any side. This position left each national section to decide how absolute a stance to take against violence. As fascist movements gained strength in Europe, intense differences developed within the league as to how to stop their growth. Those with a rather reformist outlook found themselves increasingly at odds with others, who favored more intense action through alliance with radical movements, including the Bolsheviks of the Soviet Union. The latter point of view was more evident in the French and German sections, whose members were experiencing the tyrannies of Hitler earlier and much more directly than those in Scandinavia, Great Britain, and North America.

Infighting over such ideological and tactical differences plagued the organization throughout the 1930s, but the league managed to avoid a split by allowing sections a large degree of autonomy. For instance, from the very early days of fascism, some members consistently called for economic measures such as oil embargoes and trade boycotts to contain Germany and Italy. Yet because the organization as a whole never focused on such proposals, its effectiveness was weakened by internal disagreements. The same phenomenon was evident in most peace groups during that period. Membership declined, with some members thinking WILPF was too pacifist and others critical of it for not being more so.

By September 1939 Europe was technically at war, and contacts among the national WILPF sections became increasingly difficult. Gertrude Baer, the WILPF representative who monitored the League of Nations' Economic Council, was sent from Geneva to the United States for both her own safety and that of the work she was doing, as the council had temporarily relocated to Princeton, New Jersey. Throughout the war, Baer was the primary force that kept the league together, assembling and sending out quarterly international circular letters which were the WILPF's main source of wartime communication.

Although entire sections went into exile during the war, not all WILPF groups were disabled. Most outstanding was the Danish section, which managed to get through the war with its membership of twenty-five thousand intact. Even after the German invasion of April 1940, this section met frequently and continued to sell small white peace flags, which a number of German soldiers wore hidden on the back of their lapels. In Norway, too, the WILPF section played a leading role in resistance to the Nazis. A Danish member, Rigmore Risbjerg Thomsen, recounted the experiences of her section in those years:

> We couldn't work regularly because we had Gestapo in our office sometimes and the vice-chair was imprisoned at times and many of the members were in the resistance movement. But one

month before the German troops arrived, we succeeded in getting three hundred Jewish children out of Vienna and had them brought to Denmark and placed in Danish homes. But a few months after the German soldiers came, we had to help most of them escape to Sweden. We also helped the Danish Jews to escape once the persecution really set in. On account of that, twenty-five years later, in 1965 the league of Denmark was listed in the Golden Book of Jerusalem.[19]

As it had done in 1919, WILPF held its first post–World War II congress simultaneously with the Paris peace talks. Two hundred members from fifteen countries gathered in Luxembourg in August 1946. For some of them, the mere sight of their worn, war-scarred friends from central Europe was a wrenching shock. Other members had died in concentration camps or in exile. In the wake of such destruction, wrought first by fascism and then by the devastating use of atomic weapons, could the women hold onto their ideals and pursue their work for peace? They spent a good part of the congress agonizing over that question and concluded that WILPF must continue.

The Postwar Years

The women were to learn that the war had done even more to the league than claim WILPF lives and cause ranks to dwindle. The travesties of fascism had impaired the organization's functioning, particularly in Europe, seriously enough so that even in 1965, twenty years after the war ended, WILPF had still not fully recovered. The experiences of Eleonore Romberg, a German member who joined after World War II, reveal some of the subtle but staggering long-term effects of the Hitler era.

> Especially in countries which were very strongly under fascistic rule, they [the Nazis] destroyed so very much, every notion and energy and self-confidence . . . [every bit of knowledge] about the rights of civilian people, especially women, to take part in political decisions. It takes years and years to rebuild this. The young women of the 1980s are little by little getting this feeling

again. A lot of women from my generation were, as we say, burned children. It really strikes you in these countries: it was difficult to get women into the parties, into the trade unions. They very often said after the war, "We will never join any organization; we don't like to be involved in any politics." Now at last we begin to get them in. I think it's so terrible that twelve years really destroyed the whole impression or consciousness of what a democratic situation is.

It was ten years after the war when I came in the WILPF. After half a year or maybe a year, I suddenly was chairwoman of the Munich branch. The first time I had to chair a meeting, I really didn't know how to do it. So, the elders said, "You first have to ask the audience to accept the agenda." Even such simple things I did not know. So I had to have them teach me. To make a decision and bring it to a vote—I didn't know how to handle these situations. So I just give you the idea that even the slightest elements and instruments of democracy we didn't know. And at this time I was more than thirty years old. If you take me as an example, you really could say that the German people had to be trained again to build up democracy—and still we have difficulties.

A short time before I came in, there were about eighty to a hundred members, but rather old ones, and one by one they died or went away to live with their children so they couldn't be active any longer. The next years it was very difficult to get younger women. All the others were about seventy, coming from the time before. And there I was, sitting like a child to get told fairy tales. I listened and listened; I'd never heard about this part of history. And more and more I got involved.

In the first ten years I was a member, there was in the German section a discussion, "Should we quit?" By this time I already had a lot of information about how our first sisters worked. So it was very strongly me who said, "We are not allowed to quit. We have to keep the tradition and we did not reach the goal yet." I was so full of all the experiences I had heard about that I worked hard to keep the German section going, even if our Munich branch was growing smaller.[20]

The problems Romberg cited in drawing in younger women were not unique to Munich. Through the postwar period, the league as a whole found it increasingly difficult to attract young women, often because of a reluctance to get involved in anything political. By the time of the 1965 congress, the vast majority of attendees were over forty. However, there was at least one university student at the congress; twenty-three-year-old Adrienne van Melle of Amsterdam attended almost by chance, and remembered the event quite vividly: "I had read about it in a magazine and decided to attend, since it was quite near my home. I was by far the youngest person there, and I must say that I as a student didn't feel that at home there. When I first saw the gray hair, older faces, and nice dresses, I didn't expect such progressive discussions. Yet, I was already a bit involved in peace work and was greatly impressed by their knowledge."[21] Van Melle chose to work with other groups but remained a member and maintained her contact with the international WILPF, primarily through Gertrude Baer.

Even the antiwar movements which were to sweep the 1960s and 1980s failed to boost WILPF's membership greatly. The league still faces this dilemma today. WILPF had never seen itself as a mass movement, and had instead tried to attract cadres of progressive-minded women who were ahead of their time. But after World War II it was no longer a choice: in the forty years since, the league has not again reached its pre-1945 membership of between 50,000 and 60,000.

In 1946 the women's task was to rebuild and refocus their organization. They had at least one cause for optimism: public support for the newly established United Nations (UN), and there they turned their sights. WILPF had in fact been monitoring the negotiations which created the UN, and the league was delighted that others shared their enthusiasm. Gertrude Baer, having kept the league together and maintained the League of Nations contacts throughout the war, relocated to Geneva and became WILPF's first UN consultant, a post she held until 1972.

In March 1948 WILPF was one of a growing number of groups to be granted consultative status as a nongovernmental organization (NGO) to the Economic and Social Council (ECOSOC) of the UN.

In 1949, as part of an NGO advisory panel, the league recommended that the UN institute a permanent agency for child welfare. The United Nations International Children's Emergency Fund (UNICEF) was given this status in 1950. During the same period WILPF was also one of the groups that pushed for creation of the UN High Commissioner for Refugees post and the passage of the Universal Declaration of Human Rights.

In 1948–49 WILPF took a highly unpopular stand in opposing the formation of the North Atlantic Treaty Organization (NATO). This position drove away some members, particularly in the Scandinavian countries. From the league's point of view, any such regional military alliance could only harden the divisions which were already in place through the rapidly developing cold war. However, fear of a return of fascism and of Soviet expansionism was rampant in Europe, even among peace-minded people, and the WILPF did not get much support for its campaign against NATO. The agreement was signed by twelve nations in April 1949. A Norwegian member, Mari Holmboe Ruge, recalled her section's experiences during that period.

> Our country joined NATO in 1949. And the Norwegian WILPF actually was the group that took the initiative to make a popular opposition against joining NATO. The political development that led to Norway deciding to join NATO was very fast, it was over in two or three months or something. The Alliance was created at the same time as the change of power in Czechoslovakia: since that had always been the most westward-looking of the eastern countries, a lot of fear was generated, and the media pressed hard on this kind of thing. There were negotiations going on for a Nordic Defense Treaty between the Nordic countries as an alternative to the NATO. They broke down and Norway said that it would join NATO: just after that Denmark decided that if Norway joined, then it would have to do the same. I was a schoolgirl at the time, I don't really remember the details, but there was a very heated atmosphere, and the renewed cold war surely didn't help to improve things. But there were some meetings and protests, and the WILPF section organized the first one. And it was not unanimous within the league that they should take a stand against NATO. So the membership split and they lost almost half of their members. The membership had already started to go down after the first postwar enthusiastic figures, but I think I'm

not too wrong if I say there were about 2,000 in that year, and the year after they had maybe 1,200. So that was a blow. Of course it also coincided with the general cold war and two-bloc thinking. It was a hard time for working for peace, anyway, so it may not have only been connected with this stand against NATO.[22]

Work in the early 1950s centered on the Korean War, which had begun in June 1950. This conflict alerted the world to the hideous threat of atomic weapons. For WILPF, it pointed up the need for seating the mainland China government at the UN. The league pushed for that action from 1949 until 1971, when China was finally seated.

In 1953 WILPF appealed for a "World Truce," a forerunner of the Nuclear Weapons Freeze proposal which was to revive the disarmament movement in the United States nearly thirty years later. The truce called for a two-year pledge by nations not to produce or use armaments and to prepare for a Disarmament Conference during the pause. The truce was circulated among UN delegates but did not gain acceptance.

The World Truce was more far-reaching than the freeze of later years, because it linked nuclear weapons with nonnuclear ones, stressing the need for total and universal disarmament. After March 1954, when the United States first conducted a nuclear test on the island of Bikini, a large international movement sprang up in protest of nuclear testing and weapons. However, WILPF remained one of the few groups to couple consistently its protests against nuclear explosions with calls for a substantive and strictly monitored decrease in *all* armaments.

Meanwhile, Gertrude Baer was working hard at the UN to get the World Health Organization to investigate the radiation effects of atomic tests. It began to do so in 1956. As early as 1955 she also proposed a study of utilizing solar rather than atomic energy.

By 1960 more and more women in the United States and Europe had become alarmed by revelations of radioactive strontium 90 getting to their children through milk contaminated by fallout from atomic tests. Out of their fears came an activism that for many was a first, and in 1961 a small handful of housewives in Washington, D.C., founded a movement called Women Strike for Peace

(WSP). Those women's frustrations demanded a kind of immediate expression not always present in WILPF's approach of study, writing, and lobbying to effect change, and some who had worked with the league found its structure too bureaucratic to allow rapid action in a crisis. The movement they launched was characterized by its spontaneity, aggressiveness, and lack of hierarchy. Within months Women Strike for Peace had mobilized hundreds of thousands of women to leave their jobs and homes and take to the streets on November 1, 1961, to call for an end to atomic tests. While Women Strike for Peace began as a spontaneous initiative which was most vehemently not an organization, the women continued organizing and ultimately did form an organization, the purpose and membership of which are similar to those of WILPF. In many places WSP and WILPF were composed of the same women; in other cases, they were separate groups which cooperated with one another. Public pressure generated in the November 1 strike and other actions, as well as in the ongoing work of the league, created the climate in which the Partial Test Ban Treaty was concluded in August 1963.

In the Third World

Since the 1920s the league had had several groups at work in Palestine, but it was not until 1953 that they actually became a section in what had by then become Israel. In 1956 the presence of a young Arab woman attorney at the Birmingham congress convinced WILPF that, in keeping with its tradition of fact-finding missions, it should send an envoy to the Middle East. The league chose Madeline Bouchereau, an active member and the wife of the Haitian counsel in Hamburg. During her trip to seven Middle Eastern nations in the spring of 1958, she found many Arab women interested in cooperating with WILPF in seeking a regional peace settlement.

This opening dialogue with Arab women paved the way for the formation of a Lebanese section, which was formally recognized in 1962. Also, Bouchereau's firsthand experiences with the oppression of the Palestinian Arabs in Israel as in other parts of the region prompted her to point out to other members the extent of the Jewish-Arab conflict—a mere foreshadowing of the controversy over this topic which continued in WILPF for years to come. The league had and still has a sizable Jewish membership; and for Jewish and non-Jewish members, memories of the experiences of Hitler fascism were very deep. That fact, together with little personal knowledge of Arabs as a people, made league members loath to be too critical of Israel at that time. A decade later, some of their views had evolved, however, and by the mid-1960s, WILPF would begin to study seriously the problems of the Middle East and to question its manner of relating to them.

It was also in the 1950s and early 1960s that colonialism began to crumble at last. The Korean War, the Cuban Revolution, the French disaster in Algeria, the decline of British influence in the Middle East—all illustrated the demise of the old order, when Europe and the United States had been clearly in command. By 1959 the number of member states in the UN had exactly doubled since its creation in 1945. WILPF women were uneasy about the unequal development among these nations: it seemed the gap between the haves and the have-nots was growing even wider—or at least becoming more apparent.

These occurrences would also have long-term organizational implications for the league, whose members were primarily haves in a world of have-nots. Up to now, the word "international" in the name had largely meant European/North American, even though there had traditionally been a few sections outside those two continents and WILPF had always had scattered contacts in a number of developing nations and a small but steady group of nonwhite members. But the emergence of the Third World as an independent force in international relations soon made the league examine how to become more truly international, that is, more relevant to the concerns of Third World women—a dilemma which it still grapples with in the 1980s. In early 1966 the international president, Dorothy Hutchinson, wrote of the new section forming in Colombia: "I think we must recognize the fact that in the developing countries (as is true of the developed countries as well) our membership will be drawn largely from the intellectual elite with whom we'll work in order to achieve the political, social, and psychological change needed for the development of the country and the interests of the people in it, which will be different from those in the more developed countries. . . . I strongly suspect that for a long time, the actual membership will not be drawn from the peasant class."[23] In the next two decades those assumptions would be seriously challenged from within the league itself and from the social and political forces happening around it.

In the late 1950s the UN was also trying to address the problems of economic and social injustice. It proclaimed 1959–60 World Refugee Year, primarily to call attention to the miserable refugee camps which still existed in Europe at that time. Then, in June 1960, the Freedom from Hunger campaign was launched with education, increased food production, and more efficient distribution as its goals. After Gertrude Baer suggested a plan for rural education by means of farm broadcasting (an idea she received from the league's Australian section), WILPF agreed to provide transistor radios to a region of India, the Kaira District Milk Cooperative of 250 villages. The UN's Food and Agriculture Organization then broadcast improved farming techniques to the cooperative. Nine national sections participated in the project and $3,200 was raised.

WILPF also undertook another major project for World Refugee Year. Under the leadership of its UN representative in New York, Adelaide Baker, the league was instrumental in establishing the Jane Addams Refugee House in Spittal Drau, Austria, to accommodate the large number of European refugees remaining from World War II.

In December 1961 the UN proclaimed a Development Decade to raise the standard of living in poor countries. Finally, it appeared, world leaders were beginning to acknowledge what WILPF had stressed for nearly half a century: the interrelation between peace and economic justice.

Seeds of Change

Thus, when the league convened in July 1962, it was with a certain atmosphere of optimism, particularly since the United Nations had only a few months earlier declared "general and complete disarmament" as its ultimate goal and set up the Eighteen-Nation Disarmament Committee in Geneva to discuss ways of realizing that goal. A statement by the French section in its report to the fifteenth congress summed up the flavor of the times: "Despite the arms race, perhaps because of it, there has never been so much talk of disarmament."[24]

Yet, in three short years, that optimism was darkened by the specter of Vietnam. As the U.S. role there became increasingly aggressive, WILPF members could predict the dismal course the war would take. In fact, on March 26, 1965, exactly four months before the league met in The Hague, Alice Herz, an eighty-two-year-old refugee of Hitler's Germany and an active member of a WILPF group in the state of Michigan, became the first person outside Vietnam to set herself on fire as an extreme act of protest against the American presence in Southeast Asia. Herz died ten days later in a Detroit hospital, leaving behind a note appealing to U.S. youth to take action against the war. The extreme nature of her act placed it outside the bounds of the league's approach and WILPF leaders were too stunned to respond publicly to it. As a result, organizationally, the league reacted more with sympathy than with support, though this was not the case with many of Herz's colleagues in her local WILPF branch.

Herz's dramatic plea came on the eve of a youth rebellion that would sweep the late 1960s and have a profound and lasting impact on Western culture. Some of those youths, especially black ones in the United States, had already started taking action against the injustice around them through the civil rights movement. Enormous progress was made during the early to mid-1960s toward the rights of blacks; however, there was still far to go in that regard both in and outside the United States. The most abominable example was South Africa, where the apartheid regime stood firm despite consistent internal pressure from the African National Congress and international appeals generated by WILPF and other groups similarly concerned.

So, even though the women who came together in The Hague in 1965 were celebrating their organization's fifty-year landmark with a "Jubilee" congress, their mood was rather somber.

In looking ahead, they were choosing a new leader. Else

Zeuthen of Denmark, once her country's UN delegate, stepped down after nine years as international chair. She was replaced by Dorothy Hutchinson, a U.S. leader known as a skilled conciliator and a dedicated pacifist.

The women were also seeking new organizational direction. Determined to continue their efforts against war and suffering, they were also entering a period of organizational evaluation, a process prompted by dwindling ranks and the advancing ages of many members, as well as a vague sense by some of having drifted away from the fiery spirit of their foremothers.

For one thing, the league had moved significantly away from its feminist roots. Shortly after the achievement of women's suffrage, WILPF's emphasis on women's equality had begun to fade because it was no longer evident that such equality would bring or even increase the likelihood of peace. Later, with the onset of fascism and the most basic of human rights at stake, progressive women had been increasingly drawn into campaigns where they worked side by side with men, first to resist fascism and later to counter the conservatism of the cold war era.

Slowly the league had evolved into being a peace organization whose members happened to be women, however proudly. WILPF members still felt most comfortable in the company of other women working for peace. Yet, most of them no longer gave much study or thought to the special relationship between gender and peacemaking that had been so important to WILPF founders, and in 1965 there was virtually no women's movement to bolster such thinking.

One member who did consistently keep the issue of feminism alive in the league was Gertrude Baer, the outspoken UN representative who had been an active leader since 1919. Even before the fiftieth-anniversary congress, Baer had become so frustrated with members' lax treatment of the topic that she severely berated them:

> The greater part of our own members pretend that equality as between men and women has been acquired in most countries and that the WILPF should leave aside what is not essential in their fight for abolition of war and its causes and establishment of a durable peace. Certain members even assert that they are not

feminists. Personally, I am proud of having had a mother who was a militant feminist and of having been a feminist myself for as long as I can remember. I shall continue to help bring about full equality—social, economic, legal, political, cultural—for every woman in every area of the world until her dignity as a free and independent human being is recognized and safeguarded in law and practice on every territory around the globe.[25]

As had often been the case with Baer, her remarks showed a foresight that even she herself was unaware of at that moment. And other WILPF leaders might have taken advice from her comments had they known that the following decade would give rise to a new women's movement and that by the 1980s the existence of a connection between women and peace would be obvious to activists once again, requiring new thought and direction by the league.

But in 1965 many WILPF women were tired and not quite ready to reexamine their basic philosophies on this matter. Not only had WILPF struggled for fifty years to be taken seriously, persistently delving into the predominantly male world of international relations. It had also seen its own goals of peace and social justice become ever more remote with the passage of two world wars, the terrifying development of atomic weapons, and the hardened ideological lines between East and West as manifested in the cold war.

As always, the very act of gathering internationally generated renewed fervor, and members left the gathering reinvigorated to work not just on stopping the war in Vietnam but on eliminating chemical weapons, securing passage of a nuclear nonproliferation treaty, promoting the UN, and working more intensively for more just economic relations between rich and poor countries. With this latter aim in mind they decided to sponsor a community-development seminar in India for the coming Appeal to American Women campaign.

Yet the women were still fighting an uphill battle for peace. In that half century the world had changed significantly, and WILPF was feeling a need to change too. Although the women did not know it at the time, the social and political upheavals of the next two decades would cause even more intense changes to both the world and their small but determined league.

2. A New WILPF Decade

On February 2, 1966, five women trudged through knee-high snow in one of the severest blizzards ever to hit Washington, D.C.[1] They were headed for the White House to deliver the Appeal to American Women to Help Stop the War in Vietnam to "Lady Bird" Johnson, wife of the president of the United States. The women were finally greeted, not by Lady Bird herself, but by an official from the National Security Council, who defended thoroughly Mr. Johnson's continued support for the war and discussed the situation in Vietnam with them for two and a half hours (an uncharacteristic length of time for any White House interview).

In addition to that meeting and the *New York Times* advertisement that appeared on April 3, 1966, WILPF members hand-delivered the appeal to the heads of more than one hundred prominent U.S. women's organizations. Thus culminated seven months of cooperative work, coordinated by Lorraine Moseley of the Australian section. Besides giving broad public focus to WILPF's antiwar efforts, the appeal increased international contacts and solidarity within the league, since most of the twenty-six sections had worked together to contact women in more than eighty countries.

Meanwhile, the war in Vietnam continued to escalate: 1,361 U.S. servicemen were killed in the first three months of 1966—nearly as many as had lost their lives in the previous three years combined. U.S. bombing of North Vietnam intensified, as did antiwar and anti-U.S. uprisings by Buddhists and students in South

Vietnam—this despite the fact that the regime of Nguyen Cao Ky had recently decreed the death penalty for those publicly advocating peace.

The signature campaign was only one of the forms of anti–Vietnam War protest undertaken by WILPF women. In 1966 and 1967 large springtime demonstrations took place all over the United States, Europe, Australia, New Zealand, and Japan; and WILPF women were among the planners and attendees. Especially in Australia and New Zealand, two of the strongest allies of the United States, antiwar sentiment was building rapidly. In February 1966, when the U.S. vice-president Hubert Humphrey and his wife visited Australia, WILPF members there presented them with this letter:

> What can we women do to stop the war? We can say that we do not win people's affection nor make them appreciate our way of life by bombing crops, dams, villages, schools, hospitals, and facilities they have labored so hard to produce; that we want our sons taught to serve their fellow men, not to kill them; that we want our tax money used for productive development, not destruction; that hungry children need bread, not bombs; and with thousands of American clergy, we can say, "Mr. President, for God's sake, stop the war!"[2]

Much of the international work was coordinated with the U.S. section, as this comment from Fujiko Isono in Japan illustrates.

> Every day in Japan there were reports in the newspapers from Japanese correspondents who were in Vietnam. So we wrote to the U.S. section to make known to the American public certain facts that were not necessarily coming out in the U.S. press. Once I was asked to write a sort of message on a Christmas card to U.S. wives and mothers. So I did that, and then we made a photo message card together with other Japanese organizations working for peace in Vietnam. And all these groups sent their cards to their contacts in the States. But in most cases the groups looked to WILPF to distribute things in the United States because they were only national groups and didn't have any sort of effective international channels.[3]

Toward Peace in Vietnam

Dorothy Hutchinson, the new international chair of the league, was influential in guiding the organization's policy on Vietnam during her tenure, 1965–1968. Hutchinson was a Quaker from Philadelphia who had devoted herself to the theory and practice of conciliation since World War II, when she pleaded for an end to the suffering by means of negotiations. Though disabled by poliomyelitis since her teens, Hutchinson traveled and spoke widely in promoting peace. During the 1960s she wrote extensively on the subject of an honorable peace settlement in Vietnam, and in 1967 she coauthored a book, *Peace in Vietnam*, which sold 73,000 copies.[4] In the early years of Vietnam, unlike many other WILPF women, she was adamantly not in support of unconditional U.S. withdrawal, but instead stressed the importance of a ceasefire coupled with negotiations. This position was similar to that of the UN secretary-general, U Thant, with whom WILPF often found itself allied in its search for peaceful settlement of conflicts.

But other sections within the league were pushing for a stronger stance: immediate withdrawal. Throughout the 1960s this same conflict plagued the entire peace movement in the United States: the public was growing more disenchanted with the war but was not yet willing to acknowledge the country's mistake in being in Vietnam in the first place. Thus, antiwar organizers were hesitant to say "Out now!" for fear of alienating potential supporters.

This was not Hutchinson's reasoning: she truly believed in negotiations as a prerequisite to the "honorable" peace that many North Americans still believed possible. She pursued that path in the halls of both the U.S. Congress and the UN. With her as chair, the positions that came out of WILPF international in those years were nearly always a compromise between Hutchinson's convictions (and those of others like her) and the more radical calls of "Out now!" and "Set the date!" from European, Australian, and other members. As Aja Selander, a Swedish woman who was at that time a vice-chair, said of Dorothy Hutchinson, "She has gained great respect at the U.N. Secretary-General and in some circles of the U.S. government with her proposal for an honorable peace in

Vietnam. I must admit that seen with my eyes from this arctic distance, the word 'honorable' at first seemed out of place, but I understand that it is essential for the Americans and that it might make some sort of discussion possible."[5]

Hutchinson's proposals called for an end to U.S. bombing of North Vietnam; a ceasefire unless fired upon; negotiations involving mutual withdrawal by North Vietnam and the United States and its allies; and international supervision of the agreement reached.

However, by 1969, in the wake of the 1968 Tet Offensive and President Richard Nixon's secretly ordered bombings of Cambodia, both Hutchinson and WILPF had become firmly convinced that the U.S. government's position was morally bankrupt: a halt to U.S. military efforts and a prompt withdrawal were now in order.

Disarmament and the Peaceful Settlement of Disputes

Of course, Vietnam was by no means the league's only concern during the 1960s. In other areas, too, Dorothy Hutchinson's leadership was nudging WILPF in certain directions. A lifelong concern of hers was setting up mechanisms for the peaceful settlement of international disputes, through the UN it was hoped. Hutchinson strongly believed in the necessity of creating the machinery for peacefully resolving international conflicts before disarmament could be possible, and she did much in the peace and United Nations community to legitimize that idea, convinced that most scientific, political, and military analyses of disarmament prospects overlooked its importance. Her pioneering speeches, publications, and actions on the topic—mostly carried out under the auspices of WILPF—encouraged the league to give heightened priority to peaceful settlement, already one of its long-term goals. A special committee was set up to deal with the subject.

At its fiftieth-anniversary congress, the league decided to work on formulating some constructive proposals for peaceful settlement machinery. Ironically, just after that, the British UN representative Lord Caradon proposed that the UN appoint a panel of experts for just that purpose. So, WILPF put its efforts into supporting Caradon's resolution.

Other WILPF leaders, too, had some excellent ideas on the subject. Else Zeuthen, for example, proposed the following set of international regulations:

1. no incursions across national boundaries by armed or unarmed invaders
2. no arms shipments across national boundaries
3. no inflammatory propaganda beamed across national boundaries to incite internal or international violence.[6]

As history has shown, most governments have yet to take such suggestions seriously.

Another disarmament concern during this period was a nuclear nonproliferation treaty. While negotiations on this matter were under way at the UN, WILPF designed its own draft for a treaty, one that would have been much more meaningful in controlling nuclear proliferation than the treaty that was actually signed in 1968. There were many significant differences between the two, but those that could have changed the course of history if adopted were a pledge by the nuclear powers not to use nuclear weapons on nonnuclear states and a freeze on nuclear arsenals at present levels, coupled with a commitment to reduce and ultimately eliminate the existing stockpiles. The league continued to push for a stronger agreement, but the treaty that was finally signed was so weak that it was actually opposed by the U.S. section of WILPF.

The Civil Rights Movement

It was difficult to rally the public on disarmament concerns because of more immediate threats. As antiwar sentiment was growing in relation to Vietnam, the civil rights movement had already taken off in the United States. The league's traditional emphasis was on actually stopping wars. Yet its broad interpretation of peace and the freedom referred to in its title made the civil rights movement a natural focus for U.S. members eager to encourage this public challenge to racism and injustice, and for years WILPF had been one of the few groups in many southern communities to challenge segregation. Carloads of women headed south for the Selma-to-Montgomery march of 1965, and in 1966 the U.S. section had a full-time staff person working on the Poor People's Campaign with Martin Luther King, Jr.

To address racism internally and to broaden its constituency, the section was especially interested in doing multiracial outreach. Amelia Boynton, a prominent black woman in racially tense Selma, Alabama, had been defying the city's white power structure since the 1940s by registering blacks to vote. She became affiliated with the league during the 1960s.

> The WILPF was having a regional meeting here in Tuskegee [Alabama] and I was asked to speak. We were then not in the thickest of the civil rights fight, not yet, but there were already some demonstrations on a small scale. Somehow—why I said this, I don't know—I said, "One of these days I might just run for the U.S. Congress." And I was applauded. I didn't think any-thing of it until one of the WILPF members gave me a check and said, "This will be your first campaign contribution." I went back and I started working. I thought to myself, well, I'll have to run for Congress now. And I kept in touch with several of the WILPF members. They were so supportive of what I was doing that it was a motivation for me to continue. [She did run for the U.S. Congress in 1965 but was defeated.]
>
> Then I got a letter from them saying that a group of WILPF women wanted to come and help with our struggle in Alabama—in fact, they asked me, "What can we do? We want to do some-thing." I realized that these people lived in places where the things that were going on in the South were like fairy tales or like something that might have happened hundreds of years ago, way off somewhere. So I made the statement, "What I would like to see you do is to come to Selma, live among the Negroes (as we were called then), eat with them, work with them. Then you can build your bridge and go across on the other side of the tracks to

talk with the whites." I felt as though that would be the best way because so many people just don't know what happens in the South—it just doesn't register unless they become part of it. And that's what they did. Those women were among the first of a group of whites to come down and actually work with the situation. That was before the civil rights bill was passed. And when they came, they were very serviceable. They lived with me in and out from 1963 to 1965. Many of them went back home and then came down again for the Selma-to-Montgomery march. Some were not able to walk the whole fifty miles, but they walked part of the way.[7]

WILPF activity on civil rights for blacks was not confined strictly to the United States. As Sheila Young, a Canadian WILPF member, recalled, "Many Vancouverites sent group or individual wires regarding Selma. The public seemed to be very alert on this issue, though apathetic about the stationing of nuclear weapons on our soil."[8]

Women's Liberation

Interestingly, unlike its role in most social movements, WILPF was not at the forefront of the new women's movement that was being painfully and slowly reborn in the mid-1960s. When it became clear that women's suffrage had not put an end to or even diminished wars, the league's feminist identity waned and by 1965 it saw itself as primarily a peace organization rather than as an organization for women's advancement. And few younger members entered the ranks to challenge the elders' sometimes traditional notions about women.

The women's liberation movement did not truly come into its own until later in the decade and was not fully addressed by the league until even later. But in 1966 seeds were sown; that October, for example, a number of international women's nongovernmental organizations held a seminar in Rome, entitled "The Participation of Women in Public Life." In a vote by international WILPF leaders, however, the league decided not to cosponsor the seminar but

merely to send observers. Gertrude Baer was one of those observers, and in her speech she reminded participants of the connection between equal rights and peace, urging them to support
Vietnamese self-determination. In her characteristically flamboyant manner, Baer, a strong feminist herself, gave a speech that
was almost eerily prophetic of the spirit of the international wom-
en's decade, still nine years in the future: "[Women's] collective
collaboration will show a growing sense of world-mindedness and
lead toward an increasing presence of women in our world today,
so full of grave and challenging problems. Do help us, friends, to
reintroduce into this man-made world the spontaneity of the heart,
the spontaneity of action for the benefit of humanity in building a
new society, well-balanced politically, economically, socially, and
culturally."[9]

While it was not to embrace feminist rhetoric again for more
than a decade, WILPF was articulating the links between international violence and domestic violence such as rape and battering,
soon to become prime feminist concerns. This was the theme of a
conference held in Pennsylvania in February 1967 by the U.S. section, entitled "Women's Response to the Rising Tide of Violence."

In keeping with its emphasis on development during this
period, WILPF international in October 1966 sponsored a seminar
held in India, "Women's Education and Community Development." The seminar was cosponsored and partially funded by the
United Nations Educational, Scientific, and Cultural Organization
(UNESCO) and brought together thirty-seven participants from
sixteen nations.

Questions about the Middle East

Vietnam was not the only place in which a civil war was aggravated
by the intervention of larger nations. While trouble had been brew-
ing in the Middle East for decades, it erupted in the Six Days' War
of June 1967 between Israel and the Arab states of Egypt, Syria,
and Jordan. In less than a week, hundreds of Israelis and thousands of Arabs were killed, and Israel tripled its territorial size,

annexing all of Jerusalem and capturing Syria's Golan Heights, the Egyptian Sinai and Gaza, and Jordan's West Bank, lands which it still holds today. Almost overnight, the one million Palestinians in the West Bank and Gaza became an occupied people. The capture resulted in a stream of 200,000 refugees, mostly into Jordan, only 18,000 of whom were allowed by Israel to return to their homes.

Coincidentally, two WILPF women were on a mission to the Middle East just before the war broke out and were able to witness the chain of events that led up to it: Johanne Reutz Gjermoe of Norway, who had been the league's Middle East reporter for years, and Ingrid Lindstrom of Sweden. Though critical of the roles of the Soviet Union and Syria and acknowledging the legitimacy of Israel's fear for its security, Gjermoe's report on the mission also fueled the league's growing disenchantment with Israeli policies, particularly on the questions of refugees and full-scale military attacks. Other writings among members during this period also reflect a budding suspicion about the Israeli WILPF section's increasing unwillingness to "rise above nationalism" (in the words of Dorothy Hutchinson) in keeping with the league's tradition. Thus, while there were no monumental policy changes on the Middle East, an internal debate on the subject was beginning that would trouble WILPF greatly over the coming fifteen years in its search for meaningful Middle East peace proposals.

Internal Reevaluation

WILPF was also beginning a process of self-examination concerning other organizational questions during this period. "Looking back" at the fiftieth-anniversary congress had consisted mainly of commemorating the league's early heroines. However, the new chair, Dorothy Hutchinson, felt a need to "reassess WILPF's role in the world and in the currently expanding peace movement," as she explained in an article in the league's quarterly publication, *Pax et Libertas*.[10] In it she solicited member input and later set up a committee for discussing the league's future, headed by another brilliant scholar and leader who would succeed her in 1968 as chair, Elise Boulding.

This introspection was prompted partly by declining membership and increasing age of the members (especially the leading ones), as well as passage of a fifty-year landmark. In addition, WILPF was planning an official move in mid-1966—an abrupt change to a modern high rise across from the Palais des Nations after forty-seven years in the old Maison Internationale.

In her article, Hutchinson characterized WILPF as an organization whose policies "express a balanced combination of moral and practical considerations. The WILPF has always approached government with persuasion rather than strident condemnation," she wrote. "[We] work with rather than against government departments and maintain cordial relations with official representatives even where strong differences over policy occur." The result, she said, was "a rather unique combination of the spiritual and intellectual approach to issues of public policy." In conclusion was a plea for WILPF not to blur its identity or its views in an attempt to be part of a bigger peace movement but to continue cordial relations with Communist and non-Communist countries and a number of diverse groups.[11]

Hutchinson's conclusion still holds true for WILPF today, despite numerous attempts to discredit the league. However, her emphasis on persuasion rather than condemnation was challenged almost immediately. She received a quick, angry response from at least one member, who had already withdrawn from section work because she felt the league was not strong enough in condemning U.S. policy in Vietnam. Even Phoebe Cusden, the British editor of *Pax et Libertas*, spoke up for a more condemnatory statement on the subject of Vietnam, although she agreed with the league's "general approach to government."[12]

This period of introspection was to last for the remainder of the 1960s, and the league reaped some long-term changes in its approach. But most members were too busy doing the actual peace and freedom work in their communities to puzzle over organizational problems for very long. As Mildred Scott Olmsted, who has been active in the league for more than half a century and was executive director of the U.S. section for forty-three years, observed, "Everybody in the WILPF was so interested in spreading ideas, they weren't the least bit interested in building an organization."[13] This was true from the league's founding to the present, according to Olmsted.

The Jeannette Rankin Brigade

As the decade continued, organizing against the Vietnam War consumed more and more of WILPF members' time, particularly in the United States.

Activists were getting frustrated and looking for new strategies, and WILPF women were no exception, having worked in numerous antiwar coalitions since the movement's inception. Many of them had at first been reluctant to take part in the street protests which, increasingly, were organized by youthful student groups. Instead, they had focused more on letter-writing campaigns, lobbying of elected officials, conferences, and small community vigils.

But in late 1967, an idea emerged for a large nationwide demonstration of women against the war to converge on Washington, D.C., when members of Congress returned to their opening session of 1968. This was the brainchild of Jeannette Rankin, a pacifist, suffragist, and longtime WILPF member, who in 1917 had been the first woman ever elected to the U.S. House of Representatives. She had cast the lone congressional vote against U.S. entry into World War II. At eighty-seven, Rankin was frail and living in semireclusion but still driven by a fiery spirit.

Frances Herring, a member from northern California, recalled how the idea was developed: "She [Rankin] had said in May, 1967 that if 10,000 women—the same number of deaths in Vietnam— would be willing to go to prison if necessary to protest the war, the war would stop. She received thousands of letters from women willing to act on her suggestion. She didn't know what to do with them. When the news reached the West Coast, Vivian Hallinan [another WILPF woman from the San Francisco Bay area] proposed that we should have a march on Washington with Jeannette at the front. On her own money, Vivian travelled around the country to see if people would be interested."[14]

People *were* interested. Although the original notion of 10,000 women committing civil disobedience never really materialized, 5,000 women—most of them dressed in black—marched through several inches of snow in Washington, D.C., on January 15, 1968, to greet the Congress with demands for immediate withdrawal of all U.S. troops from Vietnam, reparations for the ravaged lands there, the healing of a sick U.S. society, and refusal of the "insatiable demands of the military-industrial complex."[15]

WILPF was instrumental in the coalition that brought together a medley of women from all parts of the United States—young, old, black, white, wealthy, and poor. At the head of the march was Rankin herself, who was finally allowed inside the Capitol to present the women's petition to the Senate majority leader, Mike Mansfield, of her home state, Montana.

One participant, Lucy Haessler, who had first joined WILPF as a girl in Washington in 1919, recalled the event:

> There were about ten of us who traveled together from Michigan. I decided to take part in it because of having heard Jeannette Rankin speak in Congress so many years before. Since then she'd been not exactly in seclusion, but not public at all, so to know that she was still going to lead this thing was just wonderful. Nobody had heard much of her in years.
>
> It was very well organized and if the National Park Service and President Johnson hadn't interfered, it would have been even better. We got down to the station before the special train came in from New York and there we were, meeting all these women with all their banners. And we all wore black. We were to march to the Capitol steps and then we were to be received. But they wouldn't let us do it. They changed the line of march: we had to march to a different point. They did let Jeannette, her sister, and Coretta [Scott King] into the Senate Office Building, but Senator Mansfield would only receive Jeannette and her sister, not Coretta. We rallied at the Capitol and Judy Collins [a well-known folk singer] sang to us. Then we regrouped and as many of us as could went

to the Sheraton Hotel for an afternoon meeting, and Jeannette made a wonderful speech there. It was a long day: it was cold and it was snowy. The reason it was done on that date was it was the opening day of Congress, and traditionally that is the day when people with grievances have a right to petition the Congress. That's what we were doing.[16]

The Jeannette Rankin Brigade did not end the war, obviously, but it received major press coverage all across the United States and Europe. And, it was an appropriate opening for 1968, which historians now look to as the year that tipped the scales against the U.S. war effort in Vietnam.

3. A World in Turmoil

Nineteen sixty-eight was designated Human Rights Year by the United Nations, and indeed, by the dawn of that year millions of people in developing nations were crying out for basic human rights and enforcing their claims through more and more liberation struggles. As the civil rights leader Martin Luther King, Jr., had said prophetically only three years earlier when he accepted the Nobel Peace Prize, "All over the world, like a fever, the freedom movement is spreading in the widest liberation in history. The great masses of people are determined to end the exploitation of their races and lands. They are awake and moving toward their goal like a tidal wave."[1] Not surprisingly, as colonialism was finally collapsing and the demand for human rights was growing, the powers-that-be held on even more tightly, resisting change with their awesome military might.

Nowhere was this conflict more evident than in Vietnam, where the war continued unabated in spite of the fact that by early 1968 the United States had already exploded as many tons of bombs over that country as it had in all of Europe, Asia, and the Pacific during World War II.[2]

Yet the United States was now ripped by internal dissent: antiwar and civil rights protests, youth rebellion, and political turmoil. In March 1968 the nation and the world were stunned by the assassination of Martin Luther King, Jr., outside a motel in Memphis, Tennessee. In addition to leading the struggle for rights for U.S. blacks and championing the cause of oppressed people everywhere through nonviolent action, King had been an outspoken opponent of the Vietnam War and a longtime supporter of WILPF. His wife, Coretta Scott King, had been an active league member since 1960.

"The past two weeks have been of enormous emotional tension in this country and for me individually. I have never been more surprised than by Johnson's announcement that he doesn't choose to run, and never more shocked than by Martin Luther King's death. Coretta was with me exactly one week before the tragic occurrence speaking at a national press conference put on by the WILPF."[3] Dorothy Hutchinson wrote those words to the Geneva office, summarizing the turbulence that seemed to be seeping into every fiber of U.S. society, a trend that would not soon reverse itself. In June the nation was stunned again when Robert Kennedy was gunned down as he campaigned for the presidency.

Conflict and Opportunity

Social and political unrest were in no way confined to the United States. In the summer of 1968, WILPF women once again came together for an international congress, this time held in Nyborg, Denmark. The leadership was already expecting a stormy gathering, both because of the tense world situation and because of difficult internal questions of policy and direction that the league had raised for itself during the past three years. But an unforeseen and potentially devastating crisis shadowed even these important concerns when, on the third day of the congress, Soviet tanks rolled into Czechoslovakia. Fujiko Isono of Japan said of that day:

> All of a sudden one morning, the news came that Soviet troops had invaded Prague. Of course the situation had been precarious before that but it was still quite unexpected for the Soviet army to go in there. And we had observers at the congress from almost all of the Eastern European countries, including the Soviet Union and Czechoslovakia. So we had a meeting in which a resolution was proposed, deploring the Soviet intervention. And then the Soviet delegation said they couldn't stay in the hall where such a

resolution would be taken against their country. People were trying to make them stay.

I was the one who said, "Let them leave, because it's too much to expect them to stay in the conference hall." So they went out and then after the resolution had been voted, we went out and talked to them and managed to persuade them to remain for the rest of the congress. We thought the very fact that they stayed and listened to our point of view was important. And we listened to their point of view. They appreciated our way of doing things, though it wasn't their way. It was a difficult position for them.

And for one of the Czechoslovakian women, it was very difficult; she had lost a husband during World War II and now she had family in Prague and felt she couldn't get back there.[4]

Barby Ulmer of the United States recalled additional details of those days:

> It was a very sad time. It was a test of women being able to work out how we could continue talking, because the immediate response of the Soviet delegation leader was, "We are leaving tomorrow." And we finally convinced her that if we as women could not talk with each other and try to work toward understanding and solutions, then how could we expect nations to do it? So we convinced them to stay, and we had the beginning of productive discussions. She only knew what she got on the phone from her government and we only knew what we got on the news. But I had had the experience of being in Czechoslovakia just two or three weeks before this happened. It was a real opportunity to step into someone else's shoes and try to understand what the problems were like from their perspective, and until we can do that, we cannot hope to work toward solutions. Clearly, the Soviets were paranoid, but they saw a threat to their own security. If they didn't show tight control over what was going on in Czechoslovakia, the Czechs would be overwhelmed by western influence, because it was the most westward-looking country historically and even in terms of trade. The Soviet Union had been blockaded when they first won their revolution; they lost 20 million people during World War II. So they're paranoid but they've got good reason to be.

We have to take into consideration where the people we're negotiating with are coming from, and that's what we're not doing
in superpower negotiations today. And that is what we *had* to do
at that congress in 1968 or we could have lost those people [the
Soviet Women's Committee]. Consequently, we have an ongoing
relationship with them based on years of trying to understand
each other so we can live together.

All of us went back to our own communities with some understanding of why the Soviets felt they had to go into Czechoslovakia. It's not that we approved of it, but we could explain some
of the background. What it said to us was how necessary it is to
work to decrease international tensions and the need is even
greater today.[5]

What could have been a disaster, then, became instead an example of careful diplomacy and conflict resolution in practice. All
of the congress participants stayed on and a resolution was passed,
stating: "The WILPF is deeply disturbed about the crisis that has
arisen in Czechoslovakia; reaffirms its belief in the principle of self-
determination and its firm conviction that military intervention in
the internal affairs of another country for whatever reason is never
justified; expresses its sympathies with all people concerned; and
urges withdrawal of all foreign troops as a first step toward a
peaceful settlement through negotiation."[6]

Unlike many other American peace groups, which abandoned
Soviet contacts after the invasion, the U.S. delegation of WILPF
left the congress for Moscow as planned, continuing the U.S.
WILPF-Soviet Women's Committee seminars begun in 1961. The
delegation hand-delivered the resolution to their hosts and found
the Soviet women defensive but regretful about the Czechoslovakia
occupation.

Many of the women who attended the congress remembered
that Cornelia Weiss of the British section, at that time vice-chairwoman
of the league, had been a prime source of comfort to the anguished
Czechoslovakian women during those troubled days. The women
did return to their country, despite the occupation; and two
months later, in October, Weiss visited them in Prague. She found
a tense but calm atmosphere. By that time the Czech government

had signed the Moscow Treaty legalizing the stationing of Soviet troops in their country. Trude Sekaninova, who had attended the WILPF congress, was one of four government officials to vote no to the treaty.

Vietnam

Over the following months, Weiss and others coupled their protests against the Czechoslovakia invasion with protest against U.S. policy in Vietnam, the topic that was still the number one priority for the organization. Particularly in the United States, anti–Vietnam War activities were the section's primary focus. By 1969 the intensified U.S. antiwar movement represented a real threat to its government's policy of escalation—so much so that newly inaugurated President Richard Nixon later gave it as one of his reasons for keeping secret the bombing raids into Cambodia which he had begun ordering in March of that year. Although there were few large-scale protests in the early part of 1969, WILPF women joined other peace leaders in mobilizing an estimated ten million Americans in various antiwar activities across the nation on October 15, 1969—Vietnam Moratorium Day. The event was the largest national protest in U.S. history, galvanizing both seasoned activists and small-town moderates.

At about that same time, the U.S. section of WILPF had begun its "Tuesdays in Washington" series. These were weekly symbolic acts, such as dramatizing the war dead by a procession of coffins with actual names on them and street theater in front of the White House illustrating the chaining of industry to the U.S. military. Even though the participants were often small in number, the dramatic nature of the Washington actions made the press eager to report on them.

Between 1969 and 1971 the U.S. government began to take the antiwar movement seriously, starting a campaign of harassment, prosecution, and infiltration. Harsh sentences were meted out for acts of civil disobedience, and government agents were planted in antiwar groups. Many organizations suffered public and private attack during this period. WILPF was not lucky enough to avoid the crackdown. In the early morning hours of March 24, 1970, the president of the U.S. section, Kay Camp, got a call from the police, notifying her that Jane Addams House, the league's national headquarters in Philadelphia, had gone up in flames. "I went rushing down there," she recalled. "It was still smoldering, black, with hoses all over the place. We thought we had a pretty good case for arson but couldn't get anybody to take it up because we had been harboring conscientious objectors, draft resisters. . . . even the Black Panthers were permitted to use some of our facilities. We'd met with Ben Spock and other 'notorious dissenters.' There was a good bit of publicity and much evidence of arson, but all the evidence was circumstantial."[7]

The U.S. government saw fit to try to derail the antiwar movement, and it would still take years for it to begin heeding what the protesters were saying. Yet the movement was making itself heard all over the United States, as well as in other parts of the world: for example, WILPF sections in Mauritius, Japan, France, Great Britain, Scandinavia, and elsewhere held or joined numerous vigils and campaigned actively for U.S. withdrawal.

Youth

As the war in Southeast Asia raged on, much of the Western world had its grisly realities brought into their homes on the daily newscasts. Middle-class youth in Europe and the United States, children of the post–World War II baby boom, saw the filmed footage of the atrocities in stark contrast to the relative material comfort of their own lives. By 1968 the Vietnam War, the U.S. civil rights movement, and the revelation of suffering and injustices around the globe had given rise to a countercultural movement of youth who were rejecting the "establishment" values of materialism, power, and personal success that their parents' generation held dear. The young people were endlessly analyzed by the media for their interest in drugs, rock music, and long hair; and they were, admittedly, rejecting existing social structures without concretely building an alternative. Yet their concerns were most coherently expressed in antiwar protests, and this was their main point of contact with WILPF.

The very entry of masses of young people into the public eye by way of the antiwar movement forced the league to examine more closely than before its own lack of young members. At the league's 1968 congress, the question of "youth unrest" was alluded to only briefly, by the international chair, Dorothy Hutchinson, who said in her opening address: "War is the ultimate illustration of the lack of completeness [in our society] and youth are revolting everywhere against this. WILPF philosophy bids us always to counsel methods of nonviolence both for those who demand needed social changes and for those called upon to respond to this change."[8]

Her remarks and a report on nonviolence from the same congress reflected anxiety on the part of WILPF women about the ostensible violence in the student protests. Kay Camp recalled later that this was indeed a concern:

> Having worked so long with WILPF, when Vietnam came along I was kind of amused by the fact that the students got all the attention and obviously felt that they *were* the antiwar movement. This didn't bother me since they certainly deserved a lot of credit and were very active, very vocal, much needed. As far as relating to the students, I had no problem with it. I think there was a difference in style, in coalitions and such. [In WILPF] there *was* a strong fear of [student] violence. I think we were probably taken in by much of the government and media attitude toward the demonstrations at that time. I was very much on the other side; I thought that if there were any violence it would not be caused by the students and that they needed our support. But by and large our branches did cooperate with them.[9]

WILPF tried to dispel the notion that the concerns of youth could be easily dismissed. "Our organization of 12,000 women is proof that the peace movement is truly representative of middle

America as well as of unenfranchised youth. . . . Listen to us!" This was the message of the U.S. section in a telegram to President Richard Nixon on Moratorium Day in October 1969.[10]

By that year, the organization's discussion on student unrest had intensified and become more concrete. The Japan section inaugurated its Asian Student Seminars. Some WILPF women were trying hard to understand the young and to figure out how to bring them into the organization. As Gertrude Baer charged: "We must reach those *outside* the political parties, *outside* the churches, and particularly those unorganized young ones who are disgusted with their institutions but often have no aims, no objectives, no constructive proposals."[11]

But a "youth panel" held at the Executive Committee meeting in July 1969 was a disaster because of sheer inability to bring in a real cross section of youth representation, according to follow-up correspondence. That same year, a young woman named Sue Galloway, who had done fieldwork in the U.S. office, traveled through West Germany and Austria to organize new WILPF groups. But her dismal reports to the international vice-chair, Ellen Holmgaard, describing the old as unwilling to cooperate with the young, confirmed the existence of a "generation gap" even within the peace movement.[12] It would take years of discussion before the league began to discover meaningful ways to draw in young people, and even today this remains a dilemma in many WILPF groups.

During the Vietnam era, declining membership was a problem for some sections and not for others. A membership report to the 1968 congress found "sadly diminished numbers in some cases, steady holdings in others, and a welcome increase in Australia, the U.S., New Zealand and Italy." And of international associate memberships (then optional at the time one became a member of a WILPF national section), the current general secretary, Elizabeth Stahle of Sweden, reported to the congress a vast increase, which she attributed mainly to an influx from the U.S. section. She also noted, however, a "tendency of a greater international consciousness." In that "tendency" lay the seeds of a new international women's peace movement that did not finally come to flower until the 1980s.[13]

Questions about the Women's Movement

In fact, in the late 1960s the league was questioning its very role as a women's peace organization. WILPF's founders had looked to women's political power (which they thought would come with the vote) as the key to ending war. When the vote was won in most Western nations and still worse wars occurred, the rationale for being an organization exclusively of women was weakened. A British member, Margaret Tims, wrote in 1968:

> The women's peace movement, which grew out of the First World War, was a force largely because women as a whole were still outside "politics"; and above all, outside the system of "power politics" which was believed to have been mainly responsible for that war. It was, therefore, easier for women both to criticize the system and to offer constructive alternatives.
>
> Now women have been part of the system for 50 years and have a joint responsibility both for its failures and its achievements. They are concerned with peace and freedom as citizens and electors. As women, they may and should be concerned with the particular rights and freedoms which affect the status of women. But the two causes—of peace and freedom in the general sense and of women's freedom in the particular sense—are no longer synonymous and should be treated separately. By continuing to link them together, the WILPF is falling between two stools and being effective in neither cause.
>
> The WILPF should therefore decide whether it is to concern itself specifically with women's freedom, or, as it is now called, the status of women, with a much greater emphasis on the needs of women in the under-developed countries; or whether it is to go on pursuing the general aims of peace and freedom, from a broadly political viewpoint.
>
> . . . There is little or no evidence that women care more than men to preserve life on principle. . . . from a logical and common-sense viewpoint it would appear obvious that to limit to one sex the membership of an organization concerned with general problems is to make it exactly one-half as effective as it might be.[14]

Although neither of the directions she suggested was fully accepted by the league, the Danish section did drop "Women's" from its title in mid-1969 and was congratulated by the international chair, Elise Boulding, for doing so. "Perhaps our sisters are right and it's time for women to become people," she wrote in a November 1969 circular.[15] Many women, however, did not agree with Tims's notion that women had obtained political power and had thus become part of the system.

Ironically, at the same time WILPF women were thinking of opening their membership to draw in more men (it was up to each section to decide whether it would allow men equal participation), young women in the United States who had become social activists in the mixed groups of the civil rights and antiwar movements were beginning to exclude men. Having grown tired of making the coffee and having their opinions taken as second-rate, they began meeting to discuss their own oppression in all-female "consciousness-raising" groups. Though the groups began as "personal" and not as "political," they soon blossomed into the women's liberation movement, the rebirth of the women's equality movement.

By this time, most of the league's founders, themselves active in earlier feminist movements, had died or become less active. Having long identified themselves with the peace movement, many older and middle-aged WILPF activists were uncertain how to relate to the new feminists. Their attitudes ranged from supportive to skeptical to defensive.

An article in the March 1970 *Peace and Freedom* magazine of the U.S. section described the relationship between WILPF and the women's liberation movement as follows: "WILPF was born of the suffrage movement and has endorsed the Equal Rights Amendment, even realizing that for us this includes taking on massive resistance to women being drafted if it is enacted. WILPF has long supported the repeal of abortion laws. Our criticism is that some feminists equate equality and similarity—the idealization of masculine attributes."[16] The article ended with a call for feminists to give more attention to the values of reconciliation and compassion, illustrating again the far-sighted quality that has always characterized WILPF. That call predated by several years the body of feminist theory which pointed out the need for traditionally "feminine" values to be equally respected, taken out of the private atmosphere of the home and family and incorporated into the public arena of political and social activities.

The league's relationship to organized feminism remained ambiguous until well into the 1980s, with some of its members, branches, and sections active in the women's movement and others keeping their distance from it. As it had done since its founding, WILPF continued to promote women in leadership positions and to build women's skills in the political arena.

Alternatives

The youth, antiwar, women's, and minority rights movements of the late 1960s and early 1970s had something of a common thread joining them: a search for a new society which incorporated (instead of defeated) the "outsiders," that is, those who had been excluded under the old system. Methodologies, however, were often not clearly outlined for how to achieve the sought-after ends. To a lesser extent, that same lack of positive alternatives has remained a weakness, or at least a common criticism, of contemporary progressive movements.

WILPF women recognized early on the need for concrete proposals toward a new or whole society. Sybil Morrison, then chair of the British section, expressed frustration over this question in a letter: "If we don't know how to solve the problems of peaceful settlements; if we don't know how to see that it is not only material things that have changed in the last 50 years; not only that armaments have moved from gunpowder to nuclear annihilation; not only that Leagues of Nations, United Nations, Conventions, and Councils have failed to solve this problem but that we ourselves have failed even to consider what is needful to promote a new society, then we might as well give up."[17]

From its founding, the league had a vision of a world without war, and reconciliation and the peaceful resolution of conflicts had always been elements of that vision. During this period, when positive proposals were needed, WILPF again emphasized mechanisms of reconciliation. It did this, as in the past, mainly in terms of world affairs and conflicts between nations rather than work settings, interpersonal relations, and social structures—the priorities of many emerging women's groups.

International Outreach

More and more the league recognized the need to expand its membership, especially to develop a more meaningful Third World base, but it lacked the resources to carry out this task effectively. For one thing, the costs of hiring field organizers to travel thousands of miles were simply too high. As a result, contacts were often made by word of mouth in international circles, or even more casually through chance meetings by traveling members. Follow-up correspondence between the international secretary and one or two contacts in an entire nation was difficult at best and often bore no fruit. Situations like this occurred in Kenya, Nigeria, and elsewhere in the late 1960s. Although these were worthy efforts, they were not a sustainable way to expand membership to new countries.

The very idea of WILPF organizers going into the Third World was a contested one. As Dorothy Steffens—a WILPF member from the United States who lived in Nigeria and worked with women there for several years—advised in 1969:

> Take a lesson from the Black Revolution in the U.S. and "do our own thing." Black Americans have asked whites to give encouragement and moral support but to work with our own people in our own communities to help change their perceptions and attitudes. Aside from a very few highly skilled "outsiders" who are invited to give technical assistance for a limited time only, the Africans should be left alone to discover their own relevant needs and assisted to meet them with their own relevant programs. We cannot march into Africa carrying the torch of enlightenment. Intelligent and able Africans are able to do that for themselves. We weaken and confuse with our multiplicity of projects. The best

we can do is to keep channels open to individuals wherever we can gracefully do so and press our governments to keep hands off.[18]

A WILPF project with great potential for reaching out to Third World countries, but which ultimately yielded little in the way of building the organization, was the Congress of Women of the Americas, held in Bogotá, Colombia, in July 1970. This conference was the brainchild of Kay Camp, who had conceived the idea during a U.S. WILPF trip to South America the previous year. One of its goals was to provide an open forum for women's "exchange of ideas in the areas of nonviolent action, leadership techniques and educational tools."[19] The event gathered 125 women from twelve nations to talk openly about issues of concern to the region, including literacy, such women's rights as civil marriage and family planning, U.S.–Latin American relations, and militarism.

A second objective, "furthering the development of a group of activist women who will work to implement the goals of the congress in their home communities," was not so clearly reached.[20] The league had a fledgling Colombian section and a reliable contact in Lucila de la Verde, a coplanner of the congress who had belonged to WILPF for years. But de la Verde's sudden death just four months before the congress was a huge setback in the planning. And Phyllis Sanders from the U.S. section, who pulled the event together almost single-handedly from her home in New York, had a host of other difficulties—lack of money, visa problems, and a turbulent political situation in Colombia that erupted into a state of siege during the congress.

Although it was cosponsored by the international and the U.S. WILPF, the conference received little follow-up from either, primarily because of the distance and the distraction of many other commitments. Only one-third of its attendees were WILPF members, and although ten Latin American nations were represented, not a single new WILPF section emerged as a result of the congress. In fact, the burden of hosting it effectively crippled the Colombian section.

Yet during this same period, WILPF leaders began the important process of self-criticism regarding their organization's Euro–North American perspective and lack of consistent Third World input. In the summer of 1970, they took a small step toward remedying this by appointment to the Executive Committee of regional coordinators for Africa, Asia, the Middle East, Latin America, and Europe to facilitate better communication.

From the early 1970s on, the international office in Geneva grew in both responsibility and stature under the leadership of Edith Ballantyne, who had become international secretary in 1969. By 1972 she had assumed responsibility for coordinating the league's UN work in Geneva and was cultivating a greater role for WILPF among the UN's nongovernmental organizations. In 1973 Ballantyne was elected secretary of the NGO Subcommittee on Racism and Decolonization, where she became a chief organizer for the NGO Conference against Apartheid and Colonialism, which was held in September 1974 to mobilize awareness of conditions in southern Africa. In the coming years Ballantyne would become even more involved in the UN's NGO community, giving the league an increased presence and transforming its headquarters into the thriving international center it had not been since World War II.

Disarmament

Even though WILPF members were busy working against the Vietnam War and for freedom in developing countries during this period, there were always those in the league who kept their focus on the long-standing goal of disarmament. One of the central efforts during the late 1960s was the Nuclear Non-Proliferation Treaty, which was signed in July 1968. Before that date, Gertrude Baer and others had worked to include in the draft treaty an assurance by the superpowers to forego the use of nuclear weapons. When that failed, however, the WILPF international office continued its efforts by helping see that the requisite number of states (forty-three) ratified the treaty and by lobbying for its passage in the UN General Assembly, which finally saw success in 1970.

Another important disarmament initiative was the International

Conference on Chemical and Biological Warfare held in London in November 1969. The conference was a project of WILPF international and the British section, and it culminated nearly fifty years of WILPF work on this issue. Its purpose was to publicize U Thant's proposal that all nations abide by the 1925 Geneva Gas Protocol condemning the use and stockpiling of all such weapons, including tear gas. The conference brought together two hundred representatives from twenty nations and eighty peace and scientific organizations. Its papers were later published as a booklet, *The Supreme Folly*, distributed by the British section.

The Australian section was also focusing on chemical warfare during this period, publishing a booklet of statements by prominent Australian scientists on the topic. In the Scandinavian sections, the push was on for a zone that would remain free of biological and chemical weapons. Initiatives such as these helped to provide the climate in which the United Nations Convention Banning Bacteriological Weapons was negotiated and ratified (December 1971).

In the Third World

The league's eighteenth congress, held during December 1970 and January 1971, broke new ground in being the first ever to be held in a Third World country. As the WILPF international chair, Elise Boulding, said in her introductory address, "Being here is an affirmation that we mean to be a truly international organization in fact, not only in intention."[21]

Held in New Delhi, India, the congress was preceded by a seminar, "Nonviolence and Revolution," which was designed for young persons interested in or belonging to the league. Funded by UNESCO and generated by the much-publicized youth turbulence that seemed to be sweeping the globe, the seminar instructed eighty-eight participants from thirteen countries in Gandhian nonviolence techniques through discussion and visits to "Gandhian constructive work institutions" under way in India.

A post-congress study tour and seminar on women's education gave its participants a more in-depth view of the country and the work of the league's small Indian section. The section, headed by Dr. Sushila Nayar, had been largely responsible for organizing the congress and seminars.

The study tour made the congress's discussions on oppression in the Third World less abstract for at least one member, Edith Ballantyne of Switzerland.

> Both [the tour and the seminar] helped give us some idea of the problems of a developing country. Of course, three weeks is too short a time and one gets only a stream of impressions. However, the misery, the filth, the resignation of an immense body of humanity made most of us thoughtful about the prospect of a peaceful change. Indira Gandhi, who spoke to us for a good 20 minutes, sounds confident. But there is much violence everywhere, and I had the feeling that beneath the people's peaceful and loving eyes, hatred and violence could easily be aroused. The "Gandhigram" we visited was paradise—yet not one new Gandhian village has developed since the original seven were founded some 25 years ago. I'm afraid these will not be adopted as the solution. I myself have left more muddled and troubled than when I arrived.[22]

Nonviolence

Ballantyne was not alone in her musings. By 1970 the league's internal debate on nonviolence had resurfaced and intensified, brought on partly by the explosive and complex conflicts in Vietnam, the Middle East, and southern Africa. A *Pax et Libertas* article by a British member, Elsie Simmons, in April 1970, "What Price Freedom?" typified the dilemma felt by many members. Summarizing a discussion held in the British section's Annual Council, Simmons described recent stymied UN efforts to mobilize world public opinion against South Africa's repressive apartheid regime. She then raised the key question: "what about when all peaceful means have been exhausted?" In fact, that was the same question plaguing a large number of WILPF women and, like many others,

Simmons hedged a bit in her reply: "As members of the WILPF, we must remember that in our present world there are times when it appears peace can only be preserved at the cost of freedom or freedom won only at the cost of peace. If we 'clear our minds of can't' and face the stark realities of that choice, it may spur us to new, urgent, even painful solutions—trade boycotts, a UN peace force."[23]

Just as the British WILPF was composed of a large number of absolute pacifists, the U.S. section held a great many supporters of progressive armed liberation movements. In 1970 the section prepared a resolution on the subject to submit to the league's congress that December in India. The theme of the congress, appropriately, was "Economic and Social Justice: Prerequisite to Peace and Freedom." After a painful three days of debate, the international organization adopted a carefully worded resolution:

> A society that is military and exploitative generates movements for rapid change towards social justice. It is a human right to resist injustice and be neither silent witness nor passive victim of repression. Although we reaffirm our belief that violence creates more problems than it solves, we recognize the inevitability of violent resistance by the oppressed when other alternatives have failed.
>
> The WILPF has a duty to study and work towards developing methods for the effective use of nonviolent means; to make the public aware of the problems of the oppressed and the exploited; to analyze the structure of power in society and the use made of it; to engage ourselves actively in nonviolent movements for change.[24]

Members had a variety of reactions to the discussions held in New Delhi on this subject. Fujiko Isono of Japan said:

> I was on the committee to draft the statement. At the time there was a very big commotion—riots of students and blacks in the United States and other places. So there was a long discussion and also a seminar there about this problem. When we put in the statement that we have to understand people who have no other way but to resort to violence, it caused quite a row. Older members—many of them Quakers—said that while the League was

not condoning violence, it was very much against our principles to even say we understand its use. [The word "understand" was changed in the course of the debate.]

Yet if you condemn violence by the oppressed, then the oppressor can do anything. I personally think that it might have been all right in the olden times, but these days to condemn violence in any case, under any circumstances, would be too smug.[25]

And Erna P. Harris of the United States voiced this sentiment:

I support liberation, all kinds of liberation. And one of them is liberation from the notion that you can release violence on the world and not reap what you sow. It didn't occur to me that we [the U.S. section] could be so rude as to go to the seat of successful nonviolent resistance and get the International to change its policy. Thank goodness the original resolution was not the one we ended up with.[26]

Sections were left to interpret the statement as they saw fit, and the debate in New Delhi led many of them to explore more deeply the implications of both violence and nonviolence. The group from Hamburg, Federal Republic of Germany, for example, held a seminar in November 1971, and came to the following conclusions: "Uncritical, idealistic pacifism could never offer a serious, permanent challenge to individual or collective violence—and even less to structural. This doesn't mean that arms must necessarily be used against structural violence . . . but that every tactic, from collecting signatures, to demonstrations and strikes, forms part of the strategy of political movements. Peace means bread for the hungry, liberty for the oppressed, and for the liberation movements, the means to obtain their freedom."[27]

While the debate on nonviolence has never been laid to rest within the league, the New Delhi statement has remained the meeting ground for the various points of view on the subject.

The Middle East

Not only did the India congress awaken some WILPF women to the realities of the Third World; it produced what three previous years of meetings and extensive discussions had not: a concrete statement on the Middle East. More than three years after the UN adopted Resolution 242, WILPF finally called for its implementation and made a plea for resumed negotiations. The resolution urged withdrawal by Israel from territories occupied since the Six Days' War in June 1967; respect for the sovereignty of every state in the area; free movement through international waterways; just settlement of the refugee problem; establishment of Demilitarized Zones; and designation of a special UN representative to the Middle East.

In its desire to mediate between its own Lebanese and Israeli members, the league was slow in addressing the problem of a Middle East peace settlement. WILPF took no positions unless a representative from both the Israeli and Lebanese sections were present. And when positions had been taken, they tended to be so general as to be virtually without meaning. Yet, here was a statement containing at least some specificity; an addendum detailed how each of the two disputing sections viewed such a settlement. Although for years it had been one of the only peace organizations willing to discuss the issue, not until the New Delhi congress did the league take real steps toward a meaningful position. This was due in part to WILPF members' growing disenchantment with Israel—that is, with the disparity between its professed ideals and its actual policies. Also, members outside Israel were finding it harder as time went along to justify the nationalistic fervor of the Israeli WILPF section, whose women were nearly always defensive of their government's positions and unwilling to see its contribution to the conflict. As section chair, Hannah Bernheim-Rosenzweig asserted in 1970: "We find good reason to be proud of the government's actions, as well as the attitude of the people, especially the army. . . . whenever we feel the section should react to any step by the government, they themselves make amends so swiftly that we are left without reason to express our dissatisfaction."[28]

By the time of the eighteenth congress, even the Middle East rapporteur Johanne Reutz Gjermoe, who had long been hesitant to criticize Israel sharply, was concerned about the section's lack of objectivity. Her report to the congress noted: "If the Israeli section could say something like this: 'We do not agree with the annexation people in our country but we are for secure and recognized borders. . . .' There *are* groups in Israel who say exactly this, openly."[29]

The coming four years would see an even further deterioration of the situation in the Middle East with the most explosive episode being, of course, the war in October 1973 between Israel and Egypt and Syria. Feeling again constrained by the nationalism of its Middle East sections, the league called for an immediate ceasefire and negotiations. By that year, however, a number of WILPF groups, particularly in the United States, had begun to tackle the thorny issue of the Middle East by convening study groups and hosting speakers. Always at issue for the league were a fear and suspicion of the Palestinians, particularly of the Palestine Liberation Organization, but that fear was beginning to wane with more personal knowledge of Palestinians through the Lebanese section. From international headquarters, the idea of a Middle East mission—originally planned to leave from the New Delhi congress in 1970—finally began to coalesce. When that mission finally took place in 1975, it significantly altered the league's stance on that region, as we shall see.

Southeast Asia,
1971–1975

Continuing the WILPF tradition, one fact-finding mission did materialize in 1970, and the New Delhi congress successfully dispatched a team of six women to Vietnam. The U.S. section president, Kay Camp, led an international team of four who traveled to Saigon, where they found turmoil, overcrowding, anti-American dissent, and brutal police reprisals. Eight days later, Camp went north to Hanoi, accompanied by two U.S. WILPF members.[30] There the conditions were slightly less oppressive: at least there were signs of reconstruction and industry, though the city was obviously braced for an invasion. And out in the countryside, suffering was as evident as it had been in the south. Camp wrote later: "Profoundly moving were our talks with victims of U.S. bombardment, defoliation, and search-and-destroy. What does one say when, followed by the entire village, one is led to a small thatched hut where a woman lifts her wide trouser to show the stump of her leg? Or to two mothers who had been sprayed with defoliants during their second month of pregnancy and sit patiently waiting to show you their obviously deformed babies? What can you say when you know that 137 hospitals, 1500 schools, 475 churches, 420 pagodas, were systematically destroyed by U.S. planes?"[31]

Camp, a petite salt-and-pepper-haired Quaker from Philadelphia, had been working with the league and in the U.S. antiwar movement for years. But she was particularly distressed by what she saw in Vietnam and particularly inspired by the boldness of the women's peace group in Saigon, who coordinated the delegation's stay there. Frequently jailed or tortured for their actions, the Vietnamese women continued to speak out, and they enthusiastically signed a peace agreement with the WILPF visitors pledging to resist the war and calling on Nixon to "set the date" for withdrawal of all U.S. and allied troops by June 1971. They agreed to work with the league and to join in WILPF's set-the-date postcard campaign.

Kay Camp had no way of knowing at the time that her connection with Ngo Ba Thanh, cochair of the Vietnamese women's group and a graduate of Columbia University Law School, would be an intimate and fairly lengthy one. In September 1971, Camp's zeal got her appointed as coordinator of all WILPF anti-Vietnam work. That same month Mme Thanh was arrested and held without bail or charge for her forceful statements against the Thieu government and her pacifist activities. Thus began a two-year campaign, spearheaded by Kay Camp, to free Mme Thanh, with whom she corresponded as closely as possible. Not only did all WILPF sections and U.S. branches make written and personal appeals to U.S., South Vietnamese, and their own government officials to free Thanh; the league also mobilized other bodies such as the International Council of Jurists, Columbia University, and Amnesty International to take up the case.

During the two years of her imprisonment, Thanh was moved several times, her health neglected. In April 1973 she went on a hunger strike to protest her continued incarceration, whereupon the Thieu government offered to release her to the Viet Cong. She refused both that and an offer to leave the country as a visiting scholar to Columbia University (personally arranged by Camp), insisting that her place was in South Vietnam working for peace. She was finally released in September 1973.

Meanwhile, the league was engrossed in a number of other activities against the war. The U.S. section's International Women's Day action at the White House in 1971 assembled women carrying "Set the Date" and "Out Now!" signs in a multitude of languages. They delivered to President Nixon 8,000 hand-written postcards from members in fifteen countries (800 of which came from South Vietnam). Internationally, the WILPF raised several thousand dollars to contribute to the Hanoi Maternal and Child Health Center, a fledgling facility administered largely by women which the WILPF delegation had visited and characterized as "lacking in everything."

The ecological destruction wreaked by sophisticated U.S. weaponry had long been a focus of the Swedish section's antiwar efforts, and that aspect of the damage was the content of WILPF's contribution to the UN Conference on the Human Environment held in Stockholm in 1972.

Finally, in January 1973, Nixon announced that an agreement on ending the war had been reached, and the Paris Peace Accords were signed on January 27. Two U.S. WILPF members, guests of the North Vietnamese Women's Union, were the only North Americans present in Hanoi for the celebration.[32] But a true peace was still a long way off. Despite an immediate U.S. ceasefire and a gradual withdrawal of all troops, North Vietnamese soldiers and the dissenting portion of the South Vietnamese population were still fighting the Thieu government, which continued to be armed and aided by the United States. In fact, Nixon's assurances to Thieu at that time constituted a blatant invitation to ignore the terms of the Paris accords—which Thieu was only too willing to do.

So, the antiwar movement turned its attention to ending U.S. military aid and calling for release of the civilians held prisoner and tortured for their political activities. Of course the league could rejoice when Mme Thanh was released in September 1973, but there were still between two thousand and three thousand political prisoners in South Vietnam in 1973 and 1974.

By that time, however, the Nixon administration was less concerned with Southeast Asia than with its own salvation. The Watergate scandal was made public in 1972–73, and impeachment hearings began in May 1974. Yet the Vietnam War managed to rock on for another year, and so did protest against it.

For Kay Camp and others like her, frustration with the U.S. government had nearly reached the breaking point.

> It seemed so awful. President Ford had just requested another $500 million from Congress for the Vietnam War. I knew that an antiwar group had written to ask him for an appointment to discuss this, but I don't remember exactly how I got involved because it was a Catholic group. But I knew some of the leaders and I knew the Berrigans were involved. It seemed like a very good and clear action to take. First there was a rally; then we went with all the tourists in for a tour of the White House grounds. We sat down in the driveway and asked to see the President. [White House personnel] gave us no response—no deputy to talk to or anything. There had been many other trips to the White House in those years when we crossed the boundaries and could have been arrested. But this time they actually did it. We were in jail for just one day, and I remember they put seven of us in one small cell. One woman was eight months pregnant. Most people, maybe sixty, just paid the fine, but nine of us decided to go to trial. It was a real courtroom and was indeed "trying" in many ways. But I thought we made a pretty good case. There was a hung jury so we had to go through it all again, which brought another hung jury. That time the case was dismissed. At least it seemed to say that all those fines had been unjust.[33]

Finally, in the spring of 1975, North Vietnamese troops pushed deep into the south. In April, Thieu resigned and fled the country; less than a week later, Saigon fell and was renamed Ho Chi Minh City. With relief, President Gerald Ford proclaimed May 7, 1975, "the last day of the Vietnam era."

His statement was true for the United States, perhaps, although even there the war had deeply penetrated the nation's conscience, turning upside down its people's image of themselves as guardians of world freedom. But in Southeast Asia the war's vast human and environmental consequences will reach into the twenty-first century.

Chile

For the peace women, an end to the Vietnam War, though a relief, by no means represented a stopping point. In fact, sparks from that liberation struggle were turning into fires all over the world.

In 1972 a WILPF group had formed in Chile, the result of contacts established when Kay Camp and two other WILPF members went to South America in 1969.[34] So the stage was set for WILPF action when the democratically elected leftist government of Salvador Allende was overturned in a 1973 coup backed by the United States. The resulting military junta imprisoned, tortured, and executed thousands of people.

While nearly all WILPF sections were publicizing these events, mounting campaigns for the release of political prisoners—particularly women—and urging their governments to admit Chilean refugees, WILPF international was appealing to the UN to take action and trying to get Chile to admit a fact-finding team.

In February 1974 a WILPF mission of six women was finally allowed into Chile, but not through the channels that anyone had expected.[35] The Chilean UN ambassador in New York issued a personal invitation to the league to visit Chile and investigate for itself the human rights situation there. He was responding to a resolution sent to him by the U.S. section's national board, accusing Chile of "a program of mass executions, torture and arrests that has totally denied the political, economic, and civil rights of the people."[36] Ambassador Bazan probably never expected a reply from the league, since he took the liberty of making inaccurate claims that Amnesty International had given Chile a clean human rights report. However, the WILPF international vice-president, Kay Camp, took him at his word, accepted the invitation to Chile, and persuaded him to provide a letter authorizing government and diplomatic cooperation with WILPF in its human rights inspection.

Thus, the women were able to spend more than seventy hours talking with ministers and supporters of the new military government, as well as to meet with many victims of torture and relatives of disappeared or murdered citizens. They gained access to the Chile Stadium, which had been converted after the coup into a prison for some ten thousand Chileans who had served in or had been sympathetic to the Allende government. Stunned by what they saw and heard, the returning WILPF delegates testified before both the UN Human Rights Commission and the U.S. Congress about their impressions:

> The evidence we have obtained impresses upon us that Chile today is an extremely polarized society influenced by hatred and fear. The new ruling military elite, basing law on their own decrees, seem determined to achieve total control of the population. They are working to eliminate leftist and sometimes even liberal ideas and even persons to a point that constitutes a form of political genocide. We have concluded that five months after the forcible seizure of power by the junta, human rights in many areas continue to be flagrantly violated. Thousands are being detained without charge or due legal process. Hundreds have disappeared and are presumed dead.[37]

The extreme abuses by Chile's new military dictatorship abated only slightly in response to public pressure. The country has continued to be in a chronic state of repression despite the efforts of WILPF and other organizations around the world.

New Directions

At its nineteenth international congress, held in Birmingham, England, in July 1974, the league selected a new international president. Its outgoing chair, Eleonore Romberg of West Germany, was unable to accept a second term as a result of harassment from her employer, a Catholic university in Munich. Here is the sequence of events as she recalled them later:

> I almost lost my faculty position because of my political activities so I didn't run for office again. It just so happened that at the same time as a WILPF international meeting, there was a big reception at my school for the visiting cardinal. I had to excuse myself from it in order to attend the meeting. Later I was told I was the only professor absent. The head of the school called me in and asked me questions for hours and hours: how many times I'd been to Moscow, why I had gone to Israel, things like that. I'd never kept it a secret. They made me write a long explanation of why I'd done those things. My defense was "Why I think peace work is crucial in Catholicism." Then I was presented with my discharge papers. So instead I signed a statement which said that I wouldn't distance myself from my activities in WILPF but that I wouldn't continue in such an open way. There was strong psychological pressure on me at that time. In Germany this procedure is called *berufsverbot*, which translates "forbidden to be in one's profession," and it's not uncommon. But through this I found many more colleagues who were interested in peace work and a student peace group began [which evolved from a support group for Romberg against the harassment].[38]

WILPF selected Kay Camp as Romberg's successor. In Camp, the league had for the first time in years found a president with enough time to do full-time international organizing work. This she began immediately after the congress with a month-long expedition, visiting WILPF sections and contacts in Africa, Australia, New Zealand, and Mexico. At the end of her trip she wrote: "There could not have been a more meaningful initiation for this League official. Reassuring, it was, to see firsthand that WILPF members worldwide are outstandingly warm-hearted, creative and committed to basic social change. . . . What stands out is this: we are great people, doing splendid things. But we are totally ignorant of organization and finance!"[39]

Indeed, in 1973 and 1974, WILPF was in a financial crisis that exceeded even its ordinary teetering predicament. Before assuming the chair, Camp had designated 1973 as International Headquarters Year and had written to all sections urgently requesting funds to support and build the international work. And her schemes, though often rash, usually seemed to pay off.

The league could not have found a leader more zestfully committed to internationalism, or to feminism. Yet, Camp's travels to Vietnam, South America, and Africa had convinced her that feminism as it was evolving in the United States was not encompassing enough. After leaving Nigeria on her 1974 tour, she wrote: "We saw more square miles of 'inhuman' living conditions than I'd seen before. The faces of women piggy-backing their babies in slings seemed to reflect a misery which I could not help contrasting with their smartly dressed sisters of the U.S. demanding their version of women's liberation."[40]

In the coming decade, Camp would push the women's movement to address the importance of disarmament and economic justice, just as she would push WILPF to examine its own relationship to feminism. Circumstances would help in that task. With the arrival of the International Women's Year in 1975, its themes designated as equality, development, and peace, WILPF would find itself in a unique position to bring concerns about peace and freedom to an ever-widening audience of women—and to establish again within its own ranks the intimate connection between women and peacemaking that had been the vision of its founding mothers.

4. The United Nations Decade for Women

"While women represent 50 percent of the world's population, they perform nearly two-thirds of all working hours, receive only one-tenth of the world income and own less than 1 percent of world property."[1] If this statement, taken from a UN report, was true in 1975 and still true ten years later, what then was the point of the UN international women's decade? Those ten years saw world tensions escalate through new ideological battles between capitalist and socialist, white and colored, rich and poor, as powerful men increased world arms expenditures by several billion dollars, expanding nuclear stockpiles in both number and deadly sophistication.

But the decade also gave rise to a worldwide movement of women determined to change the very nature of power. These women mobilized the largest number of people in modern history to call for an end to injustice and the senseless arms race. From the more than twenty thousand Greek Cypriot women who marched on April 20, 1975, demanding that Turkey return all Cypriot refugees to their homes, to the fourteen thousand women who gathered in Nairobi in 1985 to relate their experiences and collectively demand peace, development, and equality, those ten years raised the consciousness, if not the standard of living, of women and men all over the world.

With increased literacy and access to media came a growing

awareness by oppressed people that resources did exist to transform their lives. This was also the era of large UN "issue" conferences which furthered that awareness. As Inga Thorsson, the Swedish UN disarmament delegate and a longtime WILPF member, recalled:

> The 1970s were the time of UN special issue conferences—women, the environment, racism, you name it. There was an intellectual awakening in those years that was remarkable. People complain that nothing comes out of all these conferences, but it takes time to create political will to implement action. That's what happened, and still is happening. Now it's the obligation of people to make governments understand that it's high time to follow up politically. So the 1970s stand out to me as an extremely interesting decade, and it has continued through the 1980s. It's a process that can't be stopped, in my view.[2]

The process Thorsson described is well illustrated in the developments that occurred during and because of the UN international women's decade. With peace designated as one of the themes for the decade, WILPF women saw a prime opportunity to take their concerns about the arms race and economic injustice to a much larger body of women. Beginning in 1975, a focus of the league's work was to ensure that the theme of peace was adequately addressed in the decade's activities. Official UN events often made the achievement of this goal difficult.

A case in point was the UN conference to celebrate International Women's Year, held in Mexico City in July 1975. There, a handful of WILPF women was largely responsible for giving the issue of disarmament what small attention it did receive. The women gave out literature stressing the impossibility of achieving development or equality without a climate of peace in which to do so. Meanwhile, disputes arose between First World feminists and poor Third World women on the meaning of equality as related to class and gender, highlighting the need for women as a group to address the theme of peace. But when Kay Camp and a few others attempted to include a call for disarmament in the "World Plan of Action" (the official conference document), several influential government delegations, headed by the United States, insisted that such matters would unnecessarily "politicize" the decade. There were few references to the need for peace in official conference proceedings.

Disarmament

To kick off International Women's Year, WILPF hosted its own seminar in May 1975 at the UN in New York: "Women of the World United for Peace: Disarmament and Its Social Consequences." The event, cosponsored by the Women's International Democratic Federation (WIDF), brought together 250 women from twenty-seven countries to discuss routes to disarmament.[3] The conference summary contained the following statement: "It is significant that International Women's Year coincides with the thirtieth anniversary of the end of World War II. In the intervening years, a new climate of international understanding and detente has developed which has helped make this seminar possible."[4]

That observation was certainly true. In the United States, the seminar was the first event in which an official representative of Cuba was allowed to attend a nondiplomatic function since the Cuban Revolution in 1959, and women from many socialist nations were granted visas to meet with WILPF branches across the United States. In the tumult of the 1960s and early 1970s, cold war hysteria had died down considerably. Among the world powers, the climate was fairly cooperative. Nixon's trip to Peking in 1972 vastly improved relations between the United States and China. In the U.S.-Soviet sphere the SALT I Treaty was concluded in 1972, and in 1974 SALT II talks opened.

Outside the halls of the UN, however, there was still very little public activity for disarmament in North America and Western Europe during the mid-1970s, even though WILPF and a few other groups like it kept the issue alive. In parts of Europe, for example, many WILPF groups held Easter marches calling for disarmament, and in 1976, the New Zealand WILPF section sent two thousand individual letters to French citizens cautioning them against their government's continued nuclear tests in the Pacific.

Public awareness of the nuclear threat began to increase a little in 1977 during the early days of the administration of President Jimmy Carter in Washington. Carter's attempts to involve the West German government in the decision to deploy the neutron bomb in NATO countries resulted in a public outcry in the Federal Republic, the Netherlands, and most of Europe. The result was an indefinite postponement in developing this menacing new weapon which would destroy people but leave buildings unharmed. That small disruption to "business as usual" in the arms race planted some seeds for a larger movement but reaped no immediate change.

In fact, when WILPF convened for its twentieth triennial congress in Tokyo in August 1977, the women were more or less resigned that the sweeping World Disarmament Conference they had hoped the UN would convene had now shrunk to a Special Session on Disarmament (SSD 1) of the UN's General Assembly.

That event took place in New York in 1978. WILPF representatives from some thirteen countries attended and the league was one of twenty-five NGOs allowed to address the session. After WILPF campaigned vigorously for her appointment, Kay Camp was selected as special disarmament adviser to the U.S. governmental delegation.

Probably the most concrete outcome of SSD 1 was its acknowledgment by consensus that humanity "is confronted with a choice: either to proceed to disarmament or face annihilation."[5] By setting forth an unprecedented program of action toward this end and by transforming and strengthening UN disarmament mechanisms already in place, SSD 1 helped to create a climate in which controlling the nuclear arms race was at least seen as vital and do-able. But in 1978 there was still no real mass movement for disarmament, and the continued efforts of WILPF and other small groups like it were simply not enough to make governments feel any pressure to act.

WILPF work in the UN and NGO community in Geneva had been considerably strengthened, however, with the election in 1976 of Edith Ballantyne to head the Conference of Non-Governmental Organizations (CONGO). Ballantyne was the first representative of a peace organization ever to hold that post, and her position gave the league a more central role in NGO work on disarmament as well as in other matters.

In Western Europe, public complacency would change dramatically after the December 1979 "two track" decision by NATO to install 572 new U.S. cruise and Pershing missiles in five European countries. The West Germans were particularly alarmed by the Pershing II, a new ballistic missile capable of hitting hard targets in the Soviet Union within seven to ten minutes of launch. Pershing deployment was planned for the Federal Republic only: the one NATO country which under the terms of the treaties signed in 1945 had no national authority to resist the new weapons. As the German member Eleonore Romberg recalls: "It was not until 1979 with all the news from NATO that people realized that Germany was so full of arms. We got the first maps out, and it was still a shock for a lot of people. So there was a big movement coming up again."[6]

Not surprisingly, women were at the forefront of the new wave of disarmament activists. In the first six months of 1980, Women for Peace—a new, loosely knit, nonhierarchical network of women peace activists—sprang up, beginning in the Nordic countries. Originators of these groups were often WILPF members, working side by side with young women who had never before taken a political stand and with others who had been working actively in the women's liberation movement.

Copenhagen: The Mid-Decade Conference

Peace as a theme of the international women's decade began to generate more widespread interest. In early 1980, Scandinavian women launched a petition appeal to stop the arms race, an idea that quickly spread to women in other NATO countries. In only a few months' time, half a million signatures had been collected, and in July 1980 the appeals were presented to Secretary-General Kurt Waldheim at the opening session of the UN mid-decade women's conference in Copenhagen.

As a result of this and other factors, the Copenhagen conference and NGO forum accompanying it had a much more activist flavor than had the Mexico City event five years earlier. Kay Camp described it. "Edith Ballantyne was president of CONGO and therefore chairwoman of the program for the forum, and she had pushed for a much broader kind of program. It impressed me as a great 'free university' with all kinds of workshops. . . . there was much more emphasis on peace, whereas in Mexico [the few WILPF attendees] felt we were doing it all by ourselves. There had been about 4,000 women who came to Mexico City, while in Copenhagen there were 8,000 registered and another 1,000 who showed up."[7]

Because of Ballantyne's leadership role in the forum, WILPF was a visible force in Copenhagen, and out of contacts established at that event, two new sections later emerged: French Polynesia and the rebirth of a group in the Netherlands.

Though it energized thousands of women, the conference itself was not fully successful in that it deadlocked over the final document. Ironically, the issue in dispute was the same one which had hampered WILPF for years: the Middle East. Palestinian women had spoken in workshops and plenaries of their bitter suffering under Israeli occupation. Out of this came a reference in the final document to Zionism as a form of oppression. Government delegations from the United States, Israel, Australia, and Canada balked at this inclusion, preventing the document's unanimous acceptance.

The Middle East

By that time, WILPF had more or less pulled itself out of the mire of internal struggle that had plagued it for years over this matter. In April 1975 the long-awaited Middle East mission bore fruit, and Edith Ballantyne and the United States section's Middle East committee chair, Libby Frank, toured Lebanon, Syria, Israel, and the West Bank for discussions with the Lebanese and Israeli sections and first-hand observation of conditions in the area.[8] After her return to Geneva, Ballantyne wrote:

It would be pretentious to think that we could break new ground, change the path of history, or succeed in reconciling official government positions where more important and powerful organizations have failed. But I feel the time has come to pull out of the paralysis we have suffered over the Middle East and begin to work to promote discussion and thinking which can create the conditions in which peace can be achieved. . . . such a discussion cannot be between the members of the Middle East sections alone with the rest of us sitting on either side or in the middle, but it must be among all members with equal responsibility and keeping in mind the aims and purposes we are committed to as members of the league.

In Israel the members want the league to concentrate on actions against terrorism and to help develop friendly contacts between Israelis and Arabs. In Lebanon, the members thought that the league must defend human rights in the occupied territories and take a position on the political options for settling the conflict. As important as the issues of human rights and the elimination of terrorism are, they are basically a result of the conflict rather than the cause, and any attempt to deal with them would only lead to a deadlock.[9]

Sure enough, at the league's Executive Committee meeting in Hamburg that fall, a Middle East seminar and discussion resulted in a substantive resolution with the following points:

· withdrawal by Israel to its pre-1967 borders
· recognition of the right of both Israel and a Palestinian state to exist
· negotiation for dispute settlement among Israel, the bordering Arab states and the Palestinians, including the PLO—under the joint aegis of the U.S. and the Soviet Union and in a UN context
· a halt to all arms sales to the region
· all aid to be channeled through UN agencies.[10]

Local WILPF groups, particularly in the United States, increased their study and organizing on the issue of the Middle East and their tours to the area. As a result, the league further refined its position over the next few years. One of the casualties in that process was the Israel section. In January 1979 the international

Rosika Schwimmer, a woman of Hungarian origin, was a powerful figure in the international women's suffrage movement and instrumental in drawing feminists' attention to the question of peace. She was known for her feisty demeanor and radical tactics. In 1914 Schwimmer toured the United States speaking against the war to feminist groups. Later, it was she who proposed that women visit heads of state to present the peace plan forged at the Hague congress. (WILPF)

Now a revered figure in Dutch history, Aletta Jacobs was the first woman physician in Holland. She was also a founder of the Dutch suffrage movement. Once characterized by her British colleague Emmeline Pethick-Lawrence as a "commanding personality," Jacobs originated the idea for the International Congress of Women at The Hague and was a primary force in making it happen. (Swarthmore College Peace Collection)

Swedish diplomat Inga Thorsson, a well-known figure at the United Nations, was the first woman to chair the UN Conference on Disarmament. She has been a member of Swedish WILPF since before World War II and in recent years has served as the league's special adviser on disarmament and development. (Photograph by Joseph Cimmino)

Thousands of disarmament petitions for the 1932 disarmament conference arrived at the league's Maison Internationale, a center for international peace activities. (Swarthmore College Peace Collection)

In 1917 Jeannette Rankin of Montana was the first woman ever elected to the U.S. Congress. Rankin voted no to United States entry into both world wars. A lifelong WILPF member, she served on the U.S. section board from 1924 to 1927 and was field secretary briefly in 1925. (WILPF)

A mild-mannered Boston social science professor who lost her post because of her antiwar activities, Emily Greene Balch dedicated the remainder of her life to the service of peace via the Women's International League of Peace and Freedom. In 1946 she received a Nobel Peace Prize. (WILPF)

Dedicated feminists and lifelong companions, Lida Gustava Heymann (*right*) and Anita Augspurg were founders of the German suffrage and peace movements and were among the world's strongest proponents at that time of women's involvement in politics. After helping to establish WILPF, they gave to the organization the bulk of their time and talents. Augspurg was the first woman lawyer in Germany.
(Swarthmore College Peace Collection)

Else Zeuthen, once a Danish delegate to the United Nations and a member of Parliament, was international chair of WILPF from 1956 to 1965. (WILPF)

In the league's first years, young Gertrude Baer of Germany became its youth referent. Later, she was named to the post of United Nations representative, which she held until 1972. A most influential personality in WILPF, Baer devoted virtually her entire life to the league's service. (Courtesy of Reine Seidlitz)

After World War II, Yvonne See joined the league in her native France and later became the WILPF representative to UNESCO. For more than forty years, she was a leader at the international level as well as in the French section. (Photograph by Joseph Cimmino)

Fujiko Isono has worked with several WILPF sections and has served on WILPF's international executive committee. Here she is addressing the WILPF Twenty-third International Congress in 1986. (Photograph by Joseph Cimmino)

At the height of the cold war in 1961, the U.S. section of WILPF initiated this seminar with the Soviet Women's Committee. Held at Bryn Mawr College, it was the first of eight joint meetings between the two groups over the following twenty-five years. Joining executive director Mildred Scott Olmsted (*second from right, seated*) and other WILPF leaders was the author Margaret Mead, a WILPF sponsor (*center, seated, in print dress*). (WILPF)

Dorothy Hutchinson became president of the U.S. section in 1961 and international chair in 1965. Her activism began during World War II when she wrote the Society of Friends pamphlet *The Call for Peace Now*. (Courtesy of Ethel Jensen)

In 1978 Kay Camp was selected as special adviser to the U.S. delegation of the United Nations Special Session on Disarmament in New York. (WILPF)

Phoebe Cusden of Britain, editor of *Pax et Libertas* (1955–69), was once mayor of the city of Reading. From a conservative Anglican background, she became a member of the Society of Friends and a socialist active in the British Independent Labour party. (WILPF)

Edith Ballantyne has headed the league's international headquarters since 1969 and has coordinated its United Nations work in Geneva since 1972. In 1976 she was elected president of the Conference of Non-Governmental Organizations of the United Nations (CONGO). (WILPF)

In the summer of 1964, the U.S. section turned its attention to the civil rights movement. Here, the Marin County, California, WILPF branch organized letter-writing drives demanding federal protection for civil rights workers in the South. (WILPF)

One week before her husband's murder on April 4, 1968, Coretta Scott King (*right*) joined WILPF leaders Kay Camp and Dorothy Hutchinson (*seated*) in Washington, D.C., asking the U.S. government to stop the violence in Vietnam and heal the nation's domestic injustices. (WILPF)

Organized by the U.S. section of WILPF and Women Strike for Peace, this 1965 Mothers' Lobby against the War in Vietnam included a picket in front of the White House. (WILPF)

On January 15, 1968, an aging Rankin (*center, with glasses*) led the Jeannette Rankin Brigade of five thousand women to greet the U.S. Congress with a demand to stop the Vietnam War. Coretta Scott King (*second from left*) also headed the march. (Courtesy of Ethel Jensen)

Sushila Nayar was WILPF's international vice-president at the time of the 1970–71 congress in New Delhi. Nayar, a dedicated follower of Gandhian nonviolence, was once Mahatma Gandhi's personal physician and was the first minister of health in independent India. (WILPF)

During the New Delhi congress, a WILPF delegation met with the Indian prime minister Indira Gandhi (*right*) to discuss the nation's process of social change. At left is international chair Elise Boulding. (WILPF)

A distinguished U.S. sociologist, Elise Boulding was WILPF international chair from 1968 to 1971. Her well-known book *The Underside of History* chronicles four millennia of women's achievements. In the 1980s she was active in the establishment of a U.S. Peace Institute and has become known for her workshops on imaging a positive future.

Since the 1940s, Ruth Gleissberg worked in various movements for progressive social change in the Federal Republic of Germany. In 1975 she joined WILPF and has been a leader at the section and international levels. (Photograph by Joseph Cimmino)

Sadie Hughley (*left*) and Pat Samuels look on as Kay Camp and Le Thi Tuyen of the North Vietnamese Women's Union sign a women's peace treaty, Hanoi, January 1971. (Kay Camp)

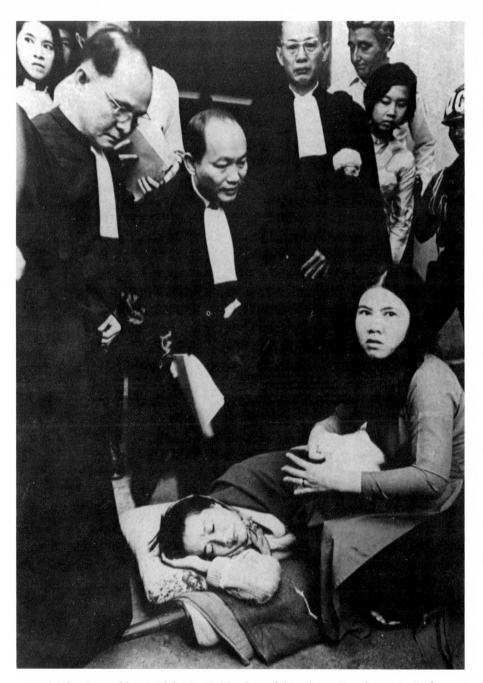

At the time of her trial for "activities harmful to the national security" of the Thieu government in 1971, Ngo Ba Thanh was in critical condition from asthma and exhaustion. Brought into court on a stretcher, she is shown here under the scrutiny of the trial judges, who did postpone the trial but returned Thanh to prison despite a physician's plea that she be taken to a civilian hospital for treatment. (Swarthmore College Peace Collection)

Janet Bruin has been the editor of WILPF's international newsletter, *Pax et Libertas,* since 1978. Bruin was largely responsible for resurrecting the defunct Swiss section of WILPF, which she coordinated in 1984 while living in Zurich.
(Courtesy of Joseph Cimmino)

In October 1975 the WILPF Executive Committee met in Hamburg and hammered out a new and meaningful position on the Middle East.
(WILPF)

Else Pickvance, a British war tax resister and longtime WILPF member, is shown here at an auction at which she retrieved an antique chest confiscated by her government for tax collection purposes.
(*Birmingham Mail and Post Ltd.*)

From Portuguese aristocrat to women's peace movement organizer in the Netherlands, Carlota Lopes da Silva experienced a transformation that exemplifies the league's vision of changing world priorities. In 1986 da Silva was elected as an international vice-president of WILPF after helping to reestablish a Dutch WILPF section. (Courtesy of Joseph Cimmino)

Nearly a million people from many countries marched in New York City on June 12, 1982, during the United Nations Second Special Session on Disarmament. (WILPF)

Irene Eckert, pictured here in 1986 with her daughter Yesmin, coordinated WILPF's STAR demonstration of ten thousand women in Brussels, March 1983. (Courtesy of Joseph Cimmino)

Olga Bianchi has been instrumental in expanding the WILPF section in Costa Rica. She was elected WILPF international vice-president in 1986. (Photograph by Joseph Cimmino)

The Danish Ida Harsloff, a coordinator of the league's international summer schools, is shown here at the World Congress of Women in Moscow, 1987.

On International Women's Day, March 8, 1983, ten thousand women converged on NATO headquarters in Brussels to protest the pending new missile deployments, climaxing WILPF's STAR campaign. (WILPF)

An organizer of rural women in Kenya since her youth, Angela Gethi first learned of WILPF in the peace tent at the 1985 United Nations women's conference in Nairobi. Since then she has become an active international member and has been organizing a new section in Kenya. (Photograph by Joseph Cimmino)

Mildred Scott Olmsted joined WILPF just after the end of World War I and was executive director of its U.S. section for forty-three years, working closely with Jane Addams and other WILPF founders. In 1986, Olmsted celebrated her ninety-fifth birthday with a banquet hosted by the U.S. section. She is shown here (*center*) with Eleanor Smeal of the National Organization for Women (*left*) and Anne Ivey, president of U.S. WILPF. (WILPF)

Executive Committee officially disbanded the group after its policies of hardened nationalism became totally at odds with the league's position.

That same year, Libby Frank made contact with Maya Zahavi, a woman active in another Israeli peace group, and cultivated an association which gave birth to a new Israel WILPF section in 1983.

It should be noted that there has never been consensus within the league's membership on the Middle East, and the subject is still hotly discussed at nearly every international gathering. However, paralysis has evolved into action, and in many countries the WILPF section has been one of the few peace groups even talking about the difficult dynamics of a Middle East peace. Having heard from all the sections on this matter, Edith Ballantyne reflected:

> I think it is true that there has never been agreement in the league—even quite far back there were those who were against partitioning Palestine. On the other hand, in the 1930s there were those who felt that the Jews had a right to a homeland there. After the war, with the creation of Israel, there was much more polarization on the issue. When Israel declared itself a state, I think the majority of WILPF members were in favor of that. They were never very clear on the Palestinians—to my knowledge, they never came out and said Palestinians had a right to their own state. Yet, a strong sector of the league—including many Jewish members—were very critical of Israeli policy and definitely defended the rights of Palestinians. By that time we had a Lebanese section, and Lebanon was becoming more and more drawn into the whole Palestinian issue because their [the Palestinians'] presence was beginning to affect life there for everyone. And when our Lebanese section acquired Palestinian members, there was really a confrontation within the league.
>
> So Libby and I were sent on the mission, and as a result we made a report and proposed a policy statement that was accepted. There were quite a lot of members on the Executive Committee who perhaps didn't vote against it but were very skeptical and critical about it. But some sections began to do a lot of work and education based on it: to try and show that the Palestinians were people too. Because of what they had chosen to do to call attention to their situation—bombings, hijackings, and so on—they

were seen as terrorists and as not having any real rights. Actually, by 1975 they had dropped a lot of those tactics. They did develop an army, but they also organized on many levels to get diplomatic recognition. For the league, it came down to this: these Palestinians are there, they have rights too and therefore accommodations must be made for coexistence. So the only way to do it is to sit down and negotiate to settle the disputes. But not all members accepted it and we lost quite a few members over it, particularly in the United States.

What to me was always rather striking was that many of those who were skeptical of the Palestinians talked about their violence, but they could see it only on one side. They saw Israel's violence as self-defense, when in fact Israel was a state, with state power, a power that it used very violently. Well, I condemn all violence too, but I just felt like you can't blame the victim all the time.[11]

The rift and the resolution were summarized by Lucy Haessler, a longtime member from the United States: "It's an issue that has divided us, though the debate on a solution of the 'Palestinian problem' has died down very much. We lost a few members, and then many came back. WILPF has taken plenty of controversial stands and survived them."[12]

Old and New Approaches

In a decade devoted to promoting women, amid a rising groundswell of support for disarmament and with an ardent feminist as its president, WILPF began to focus more on educating and involving women in the complex, forbidding field of disarmament. Because of its close ties with the UN and its conviction that UN negotiations should be monitored, its approach was slow, scholarly, often tedious, taking place in a predominantly male environment. It involved following lengthy UN negotiating procedures, submitting written testimony, and learning about abhorrent terminology such as "megatonnage" and "throw weight." This studious approach was in sharp contrast to the passionate, impetuous actions of new women's peace groups that were starting to emerge about 1980, although, certainly, there were always WILPF members who participated in both kinds of activities and WILPF as an international body encouraged this dual approach.

In Europe, the nuclear threat became a catalyst for a new wave of feminism which was manifested in a women's peace movement. This phenomenon soon spread to the United States, where WILPF women were often the ones who took the lead in planning creative new women's peace actions.

Perhaps the most striking example of all the new initiatives was the women's peace encampment at Greenham Common Royal Air Force Base, 100 kilometers outside London. On September 5, 1981, forty women and four men marched from Cardiff, Wales, to set up a women's camp in front of the base in order to block entry of the new cruise missiles. Over the following years women kept the camp alive, enduring physical and psychological abuse, barren living conditions, and constant evictions to maintain a witness against first the entry and later the tests and trial runs of the missiles. Soon Greenham women and others like them were engaging in dramatic, risky, and, to a great extent, leaderless actions almost daily, sparking the imaginations of women all over Europe.

After WILPF leaders saw the energy and activism of the Copenhagen mid-decade women's conference, it did not take them long to broaden their own tactics. In November 1981 they made a move to join forces with the newly blossoming women's peace movement by sponsoring a meeting in Amsterdam called "Women of Europe in Action for Peace." With the cooperation of two of the newer Dutch groups—Women for Peace and Women against Nuclear Weapons—the league assembled five hundred women from twenty-five countries to discuss nuclear war and detente.

Unfortunately, the climate of detente that had characterized the last half of the 1970s was fading fast in the new tide of political conservatism that was engulfing the United States and Western Europe, aggravated by the Soviet invasion of Afghanistan in late 1979 and illustrated in the election of hard-core conservative leaders such as Ronald Reagan in the United States and Margaret Thatcher in Great Britain.

"If you want to work against nuclear weapons in Europe, you

first have to work against cold war feelings," insisted Adrienne van Melle, a Dutch theologian who was an organizer of the Amsterdam conference and a founder of both the Dutch Women for Peace group and the revived WILPF section there, which came into being in 1983.[13] Since 1967, van Melle has organized tours of theology students to the Soviet Union and other East-bloc countries to combat what she calls "fear of the unknown."

She recalled that a concrete contribution which the league made to the new generation of peace activists assembled in Amsterdam was to counter this fear. It did this through its long-standing association with women's groups in Eastern Europe, van Melle remembered: " Many West European women found that this meeting offered them their first opportunity to talk to women from the Soviet Union, the GDR, Czechoslovakia, Poland and Hungary. It was encouraging that in spite of all the different opinions, a common denominator became clear: the will of all these women to engage themselves in the struggle for disarmament and peace."[14]

Of course, there were varying ideas on *how* to reach these goals. But the East-West contact gave many women new to the issue a heightened understanding of the myriad of sensitive political and psychological factors fueling the arms race. The positive outcome of the conference represented a first step toward a unity of approach between the new women's peace movement and the established ranks of WILPF, as illustrated in the meeting's concluding statement that study and action "must go side by side." The range of follow-up plans—from monitoring disarmament negotiations to organizing women's peace demonstrations for March 8, International Women's Day—reflected that perspective. A combination of study and action had always been characteristic of WILPF, but the *type* of action was new for many WILPF women— more militant, more blatantly prowoman, and less sedate than the letter-writing and lobbying drives typically undertaken by the older and particularly the European members. Some WILPF women were skeptical of the antimale sentiment that prevailed in many of the emerging women's peace groups. They shrank from the idea of Lesbianism.[15] However, getting to know one another in person did much to dispel their suspicions and pointed up the need for mutual support despite differences. And for the Greenham women, for instance, the conference was their first opportunity to get their story to an international audience.

Edith Ballantyne was an idea person behind the Amsterdam meeting and has consistently mediated between varying approaches. She said this of her experience:

> There are a lot of men in the peace movement, but I think women have suddenly taken some confidence and come to the fore. They have brought some very creative ideas. Most of these ideas have been for protest, which has really been very effective because it couldn't be ignored; it gained attention. But that's different from the long-term peace activities. The league, being a rather structured and old organization with specific aims, has a program of long-term work. It is less an organization of protest than of working within certain structures to bring about certain changes. It's not very spectacular, it's an ongoing thing, and it's hard to measure any kind of success. That doesn't mean that the league hasn't also demonstrated, but that's not its main activity. We join often but we do not organize that many protests. We tend to continue to write letters, send delegations, work with the UN, and so on.
>
> Bringing together that and the protest movement is not easy. That's why we've tried to bring women from these groups to Geneva, to at least introduce them to the UN, dull as it is. And to some extent, it's worked. I think some of the women have seen that it's all right to climb over the fence at the Soviet mission and such, but you have to work with the governments too because that's where the decisions are made. It's something that's at least given us as the league a role in the eyes of some of these movements.[16]

Throughout the 1980s WILPF has continued its efforts to bring together the two approaches and to promote cooperation. One method of realizing that objective has been the WILPF summer schools, which were resurrected in 1981, bringing new faces and ideas into the league and often educating relative newcomers to peacemaking on topics such as peace education and the world economic crisis.[17] The league has also embraced more of the politics of protest in its own tactics. Both of these moves have brought more young women into WILPF.

Stop the Arms Race!

Probably the league's most imaginative idea in years grew out of the politics of protest: the STAR (Stop the Arms Race) campaign, launched on March 8, International Women's Day, 1982, with the slogan "One million women can stop the arms race. Be one in a million." Over the following twelve months women in nearly every WILPF section, particularly in the United States and Europe, worked to enroll a million women in the STAR campaign. They distributed cards printed with the STAR message on street corners and through every available avenue, such as women's centers, bookstores, and radio stations. WILPF women in each country decided on their own demands and designed their own STAR cards, which included both regional and national concerns. The Sri Lanka WILPF, for example, included a plea to shut down U.S. bases in the Indian Ocean, while the British WILPF included a call to halt the basing of Trident submarines in British harbors. However, they all demanded a halt to any new nuclear missiles in Europe; the issue of the cruise and Pershing missiles formed the centerpiece of the STAR campaign.[18]

The STAR campaign attracted women far beyond the ranks of WILPF, especially in the countries of central Europe. Women in the Netherlands printed STAR posters in four languages and sent them out to other countries to help finance and promote the project. The Dutch organizer Adrienne van Melle remembered: "Some people will sign things without knowing what they are, so we got them not just to sign the cards but to pay two guilders. We made it clear that if they are wearing this button, they must also be trying to get other women involved."[19]

By that year, an urgent fear of nuclear war had overtaken masses of people in both the United States and Europe, primarily due to frightening new developments in nuclear weaponry planned by the Reagan administration in the United States. Correspondingly, the disarmament movement was in full flower. While the movement's focus in Europe, of course, was on stopping the cruise and Pershing deployments, the concept of a nuclear weapons freeze had suddenly caught the public's interest in cities and tiny rural communities all across the United States. Though obviously not a new idea, the freeze captured the enthusiasm of many Americans because of its simplicity and bilateral nature (meaning it dealt with Soviet as well as U.S. weapons). Another appeal was its forthright style of presentation: initiatives from small communities that built up to local, state, and ultimately federal government endorsements.

In June 1982 the UN General Assembly convened its Second Special Session devoted to Disarmament (SSD 2), and by this time all manner of groups both in the United States and worldwide had been organizing for months. On June 12, 1982, the largest crowd in recent history—nearly one million people of many nationalities, ages, and political persuasions—marched from the United Nations to Central Park in New York City to call for a nuclear freeze, cuts in military budgets, and nuclear disarmament. Surrounding the event, as Kay Camp wrote in its aftermath, was "a month-long veritable festival for disarmament involving thousands swirling about the UN with marches, cultural events, lectures, conferences, balloon launchings, dove releasings, receptions, petition presentations, etc."[20] Perhaps the most dramatic action came on June 14 when 1,600 people were hauled off to jail for blockading the embassies of the four major nuclear powers: the United States, the Soviet Union, China, and France.

But the protests were to little avail. In spite of them and a host of impassioned pleas to the superpowers by small and nonaligned nations, no new concrete actions toward disarmament were taken at the session. A no-first-use-of-nuclear-weapons pledge by the Soviets was little consolation in the face of bellicose words from President Reagan in his address to the UN. A poorly funded World Disarmament Campaign under UN auspices was the session's only tangible outcome, and it was opposed by the Reagan administration. However, the nuclear freeze concept, though debunked by the U.S. president, did become a household word during this time and found its way onto the UN agenda.

In addition to helping organize the rally and mobilizing members to attend both that and the special session, WILPF sponsored a world women's peace conference held at Barnard College in New York City one week before the opening of SSD 2. The main conference, organized by the international WILPF, was actually piggybacked by a second, smaller gathering with a more openly feminist bent, entitled "A Global Feminist Disarmament Meeting." That event was convened by the U.S. section of WILPF and the American Friends Service Committee after some women from the two groups observed that none of the other events for SSD 2 were specifically feminist-oriented. Although the differences between the two conferences were primarily those of style and semantics (most of the same people attended both), the mere fact that there were two conferences instead of one illustrated the continuing reluctance to embrace feminism by WILPF as an international body.

Out of the global feminist meeting came an idea which galvanized thousands of American women in the following year: the first U.S. women's peace encampment, modeled after the Greenham women's camp. The camp was at Seneca Falls, New York, which seemed the perfect spot to link the women's and peace movements, having once been the setting of a historic 1848 women's rights convention and now the storage depot for U.S. cruise missiles headed for Europe.

The Economics of Peace

Another, perhaps equally significant result of the Barnard College conference was its gentle reminder that peace is more than nuclear disarmament. Like many other activists in Europe and North America, WILPF women were caught up in the fervor of the new peace movement, whose clear emphasis was disarmament. But at this conference, over and over, the stories told by Third World women living under conditions of apartheid, occupation, and famine prompted more comfortable WILPF members into remembering their organization's historic commitment to social and economic justice as integral to any true peace. For many Western middle-class women newer to the peace movement, however, this was a jarring realization—and one that would be more and more emphasized throughout the remainder of the international women's decade.

At its executive committee meeting that summer, the league was moved to alter its organizational aims with regard to the social and economic causes of war, stating the importance of social transformation and an end to exploitation as necessary components of peace. (See the Preface for the Aims and Principles of the WILPF constitution.) Ironically, WILPF was only restating what had been one of its founding principles, reflecting a view that the private profit goal of capitalism was a root cause of war and social injustice. In 1959, however, under pressure from cold war conservatism, the league had watered down its thinly veiled critique of capitalism.[21] A Danish member, Rigmor Risbjerg Thomsen, wrote this of the change in a 1982 memorandum to the Executive Committee:

> Disastrous trends within the League but also a beginning of detente might have been a cause for the alteration of the aims and principles. . . . the result was that the much-discussed Paragraph 3 of the aims was changed, and in my opinion rather weakened— the teeth were drawn. The paragraph became more presentable, aiming at an urbane and polite attitude to the rulers of society. From the fighting pioneers with their blood, sweat and tears, we became nice ladies, believing in the importance of friendly persuasiveness. Now we know that the optimism of 1959 was a beautiful dream and not in accordance with the reality of the future to come. It is easy, however, to be wise after the fact, and the Congress of 1959 surely did its best in order to consolidate the membership by not being too provocative and by supplying certain positive tendencies in world policy—and, in fact, we survived.[22]

Red-baiting

WILPF women were ready to become "fighting pioneers" again in countering the conservative trends of the 1980s—and those times had definitely arrived. In contrast to the cooperation the U.S. State Department had shown for WILPF's international conference in 1975 at the UN, this time there were more than three hundred visa denials for SSD 2 when the Reagan administration invoked a rarely implemented law to applicants thought to be too sympathetic to the Soviet Union.[23] About twenty of those applicants were seeking to attend the WILPF conference.

Government harassment was not new to the league. Its founders had endured public denunciation and questioning by national investigative agencies merely for calling themselves internationalists, and those that followed often had to answer similar charges. This was particularly true in the United States, whose Federal Bureau of Investigation had a voluminous file on the league's activities from the 1920s through the 1980s. Especially during politically conservative periods, WILPF often found itself on the defensive. In October 1982, for example, the *Washington Post,* a major U.S. newspaper, printed an editorial on U.S. peace activities in which it labeled WILPF a "Soviet international front."[24] After meetings of WILPF members and the *Post's* editorial board, the paper printed a backhanded apology and retraction—one which exonerated only the U.S. section and again blasted the international WILPF for even meeting with such groups as the Soviet Women's Committee. As always, it was the international aspect of WILPF work that governments and mainstream media found so threatening.

Moving into the Third World

In fact, the league was trying to strengthen that very aspect of its work by increasing involvement in Third World concerns. In the preceding five years it had established new sections in troubled, underdeveloped countries such as Ghana, Mauritius, and Sri Lanka. And in that time it had undertaken numerous projects seeking international justice. For instance, in June 1980, President Kay Camp stepped outside the ordinary bounds of WILPF concerns and defied U.S. government-imposed travel restrictions by participating in a mission to Iran during the U.S. hostage crisis there.

A January 1981 trip to Costa Rica, Nicaragua, Guatemala, and El Salvador by six WILPF women revealed firsthand the economic oppression of that region. In Costa Rica, the team met Erna Castro, a Quaker educator who was deeply moved by the meeting. "I was never quite the same after what they told me about the importance of working for peace," she remembered.[25] She and a handful of others formed a new section there later that year. The mission's reports of the educational, political, and social reforms instituted by the new revolutionary Sandinista government in Nicaragua—historically the poorest Central American country—prodded WILPF to act more decisively in support of the Sandinistas, whom the U.S. government was billing as Marxist totalitarians and destabilizing through covert intelligence acts. Over the next several years, that intervention in both Nicaragua and other Central American countries became a leading concern of the peace movement, and WILPF initiated projects to promote knowledge and understanding of the region's problems. However, it took time for such projects to evolve, as most WILPF energies were still consumed by the STAR campaign opposing the new missile deployments in Europe.

The Nuclear Shadow

The STAR campaign was very much an international project, giving new energy to WILPF sections in Europe. In the United States, WILPF was the organization largely responsible for keeping the cruise and Pershing missiles a central focus for U.S. peace groups, many of which had a tendency to immerse themselves solely in the nuclear freeze campaign.

Working with Belgian women's groups, WILPF organizers planned a mass event at NATO headquarters to climax the campaign in the spring of 1983. The manifestation was coordinated by a young WILPF organizer from West Berlin named Irene Eckert. On March 8, 1983, more than 10,000 women from all over Europe—and a planeload of 125 North Americans—congregated in Brussels to present their demands to NATO generals. In rallying women to attend, WILPF used the themes of the international women's decade to emphasize the links between the arms race and the economic crisis which was plaguing that region. In addition to the demonstration, groups of women called on the embassies of the five nuclear powers and of the Warsaw Pact nations, as well as on the NATO Secretariat. Edith Ballantyne wrote this shortly after the events:

> We were a large delegation and the room into which we were ushered was small. It was further crowded by a number of other NATO staff and a TV crew that was never introduced to us. Mr. van Campen [chef de cabinet to the secretary-general] remained standing during most of the half hour he accorded us. He addressed us as "my dear ladies." What Mr. van Campen said was a near-repeat of the 1979 meeting: "We will deploy."[26] The addition was "unless there is an acceptable outcome of the Geneva negotiations." To our question of what was considered an acceptable outcome, he would not reply. Everyone in our delegation left with the realization that NATO was determined to deploy the new missiles.[27]

The women's dismal predictions were correct. All over Europe, mass actions continued during the remainder of 1983, culminating on October 22 when hundreds of thousands gathered in London, Rome, Paris, The Hague, and Bonn. In fact, in the Federal Republic, where opposition was greatest, there were massive protests in several cities that October day and a human chain that stretched ninety kilometers from Stuttgart to Neu-Ulm, where the Pershing missiles were to be based. But on November 12 the first shipment of weapons arrived anyway, and in disgust the Soviets refused to name a date for resumption of the negotiations which had supposedly formed the second "track" in NATO's original "two track" decision to deploy and negotiate.

Deadly Connections

Within days of the October demonstrations in Europe, the U.S. government shocked the world, even its own allies, by invading the tiny Latin island nation of Grenada, allegedly to rescue a group of U.S. medical students. Later the Reagan administration admitted that it wished to prevent construction of a military airstrip, which it feared would be used by Cuban and Soviet planes. In fact, the invasion coincided with a coup which toppled the four-year-old independent socialist government of Maurice Bishop and installed a regime more sympathetic to U.S. capitalism.

That dramatic military overture by the U.S. administration, coupled with harsh rhetoric toward Nicaragua, caused WILPF members and other peace people to turn their attention to the troubled region of Central America. In conjunction with a group of other NGOs, WILPF ushered in 1984 by convening an International Conference on Nicaragua and for Peace in Central America. Edith Ballantyne chaired and the Nobel Peace Prize winner Adolfo Perez Esquivel of Argentina presided over the event, which was held in Lisbon, May 3–6. A women's speaking tour on Central America, hosted by twenty-one WILPF branches in the United States, was organized during the conference. And other WILPF sections increasingly incorporated Central American concerns into their various campaigns.

Start with a Test Ban!

While middle-class league members in the Western world had a commitment to justice that prompted them to act on issues such as these and other Third World struggles, they consistently kept disarmament as a priority as well. In terms of the arms race, 1983 had been an ominous year in more ways than the new missile deployments in Europe. In March of that year President Reagan made a speech describing his vision of a space-based "shield" over the United States to guard against incoming nuclear missiles. Now, it appeared, an arms race in outer space was imminent.

Undaunted, WILPF women launched a new disarmament project in 1984. For years, the league had pushed for a comprehensive test-ban treaty (CTB), a long-standing item on the U.S.-Soviet negotiating agenda. But in 1984 the WILPF Executive Committee voted to make the CTB a top priority item by initiating an international petition drive in which all sections would participate.

A nuclear test ban would be fairly simple to achieve, as verification measures existed to detect any significant violations of it. Also, a CTB would hamper new developments in the madly careening arms race, including parts of the space weapons system or "Strategic Defense Initiative" the Reagan administration was now devising. Less well known was the fact that the nuclear states had informally committed themselves to a test ban a number of years before in signing the Nuclear Non-Proliferation Treaty.

With the increased intensity of the nuclear arms race over the past few years, activists were desperate at least to slow its forward motion. For this reason, a number of other disarmament and environmental organizations joined the league in CTB campaigns, and the issue became a major focus for the U.S. disarmament movement in 1984–85. In September 1985, at the opening of the Nuclear Non-Proliferation Treaty review in Geneva, the WILPF and Greenpeace presented half a million petitions calling for an end to nuclear tests and a negotiated CTB.

Nairobi: Making the Connections

In the wake of the cruise and Pershing missile deployments, the reelection of Ronald Reagan in the United States in late 1984, and a burgeoning Third World debt crisis, the goals of the international women's decade seemed distant indeed as the decade drew to a close. But all over the world women were preparing for the "World Conference to Review and Appraise the Achievements of the UN Decade for Women: Equality, Development, and Peace," to be held in July 1985 in Nairobi, Kenya. There they would assess women's progress over the past ten years and map out a strategy for improving the status of women through the year 2000.

During the ten years after 1975, women of the Western world were becoming increasingly sensitive to and seeking more information about the concerns of Third World women. This process was occurring internally in the league, and WILPF was also trying to further it in the larger women's community by raising funds and sponsoring sessions that would gather more Third World input in planning for Nairobi. An example was the seminar held in Madras, India, in January 1985, entitled "Asian Women in Education and Development: Strategies to the Year 2000," the purpose of which was to solicit ideas from Asian women for the upcoming conference. Also, the Australian WILPF convened a Pacific women's conference in June 1985 to promote dialogue between white middle-class league members and minority and Pacific island women as well as in anticipation of Nairobi.

As with the past two conferences for the international women's decade, an NGO forum would parallel the official UN event; Edith Ballantyne chaired the NGO planning committee designated to deal with the theme of peace for that forum. With her facilitation, an idea emerged for a peace center that would be open for the duration of the forum, in which women could confront and discuss the tough issues which some of the conference planners were labeling "too political." Conference officials of the United States and its allies were threatening to boycott the event and withdraw funds from it if there were substantive discussions of apartheid, militarism, imperialism, or, particularly, the Palestinian question.

They did not carry out those threats, however, and despite their efforts, peace was a central topic in Nairobi, unlike the Mexico City conference which had opened the decade. This was a natural evolution which reflected the events and raised consciousness that had occurred in those ten years. And, for more than two years WILPF—particularly Edith Ballantyne—had worked patiently with a variety of constituencies to give the peace issue real force in Nairobi. The blue-and-white-striped peace tent which finally evolved was ablaze with lively discussion day and night—a symbol for the spirit of cooperation and connection that characterized the Nairobi events. An Australian WILPF member, Elizabeth Mattick, described it like this: "Here Soviet and American women pledged to work together. . . . here also Palestinian and Israeli women came together in search of ways to end the conflict. Thousands of women passed through the tent. And when there were emotional contributions, every fifth speaker was interrupted by a singer leading the audience in a peace song."[28]

In fact, the NGO forum all but overshadowed the official conference, drawing close to 14,000 women to Nairobi compared with 1,500 official conference attendees from 159 nations. With song, dance, crafts, theater, and other cultural exchanges as well as substantive discourse, the forum had an inescapable impact on the conference itself. Mattick recounted the events to her section in Australia: "As an observer for the WILPF, I attended some sessions of the UN conference at the Kenyatta Centre, which earlier some 9000 participants had crowded into for the opening of the forum. Here were the official delegations consisting of 1460 women and 400 men (two delegations having no women) . . . in a highly structured environment. Compared with the forum, the conference could only be described as dull. Indeed, many official delegates found it much more interesting to attend forum workshops."[29]

In the course of the international women's decade—and particularly through the Nairobi event itself—more and more women were realizing what Ballantyne had stressed throughout the planning process: "Some governments and even some NGO's warn against the "politicization" of the conference and forum and want to see only 'women's issues' discussed. We should understand that every women's issue is political. One cannot seriously discuss questions of health, education, employment, development, and all others without considering each in its political and economic realities and possibilities. Peace is a political issue above all and it is a women's issue."[30]

This debate went on and on in the official conference. As Margaret Papandreou, wife of the Greek prime minister, charged: "Why is it that the conference becomes 'politicized' when we talk about the rights of refugee women to a homeland or when we discuss violence experienced by women in South Africa?"[31] Those topics did in fact come up again and again. In spite of fiery exchanges, however, the conference did not end in a deadlock over the question of Zionism, as had its predecessor. The concluding tone was one of conciliation: in an eleventh-hour settlement, the conference agreed to a condemnation of all forms of oppression without specific reference to Zionism as such. The much-debated document "Nairobi Forward-Looking Strategies for the Advancement of Women" was adopted, setting forth recommendations for UN agencies and member states to "overcome the obstacles to the Decade's goals and objectives for the advancement of women" from 1986 to 2000. The implementation of those strategies must be evaluated in the year 2000, the women concluded.

The energy, enthusiasm, and good times generated in Nairobi went home with the participants, and thousands returned to their communities determined to make a difference. For WILPF members, there was an almost unanimous sense of renewed conviction. Having been so close to the entire event, Edith Ballantyne reflected on the significance of it all: "A conference like that is outstanding only in the experience itself: the learning, the exchange, working together with so many diverse people. In WILPF and groups like it, we always think we have so much to teach, but we found there that we have so much to learn, particularly from those who are deeply oppressed. They brought a reality to the discussions that helped make clear the links between equality, development, and peace. That helped women to rise above some very real differences and disagreements and seek accommodation."[32]

Other members echoed that sentiment. Kay Camp, for instance, recalled her experience in Nairobi as a very emotional one:

> I will never forget those strong and sturdy African women proudly displaying our button which proclaimed, "Listen to women for a change!" They were so quick to understand the connections. Many of them who had never heard of the comprehensive test ban couldn't wait to sign the petition when they learned it would stop new nuclear weapons' development. They knew instantaneously it would make a difference in their own heavily burdened lives. Along with the beauty of the complexion mix, the colorful range of styles, and the variety of languages came an overarching feeling of safety. I felt very secure among all those women. They were not strangers. They were myself in varying

guise. I was ready to turn the world over to them all and only wished that the input from their experience and spirit would translate into the new society during my time.[33]

Carlota Lopes de Silva of the Netherlands had a similar experience:

> It was for me a fantastic experience to have been in Nairobi. I think it's very important that we listen to the women of the third world. Those women know exactly how the world is: they know it is exactly like a jigsaw puzzle. I went every day two or three times to workshops, and it didn't matter what the subject of the workshop was. In all of them were women making the connections between militarism, feminism, exploitation. . . . they could see that all these things fit together.[34]

In coordinating the peace tent and other forum activities, WILPF members were able to take their organization's message to a broader group of women than ever before. Out of that effort came a new section in Kenya and a host of new recruits for existing sections. For the league, the experience of Nairobi only heightened recognition of how great was the need to expand its locus in the Third World in order to broaden its advocacy of real peace and freedom and to qualify as truly international. And for the women who attended, the Nairobi conference heightened their awareness of the world community of women in a most intimate way, prompting a deeper understanding of the interdependency of local and global problems, whether they be of a social, economic, political, or even personal nature.

5. Toward the Year 2000

"As women, we feel a peculiar moral passion of revolt against both the cruelty and the waste of war. As women, we are especially the custodians of the ages. We will no longer consent to its reckless destruction. . . . we demand that women be given a share in deciding between war and peace in all the courts of high debate—within the home, the school, the church, the industrial order and the state."[1] Those sentiments are strikingly similar to the ones expressed in Nairobi by 14,000 women. However, when the founders of WILPF wrote those words in 1915, the very idea of pacifism was shocking, let alone a peculiarly women's perspective on war and peace. When the founding women met at The Hague, their beliefs were shared by perhaps a few thousand others the world over, not many of whom were activists.

Seven decades later, WILPF is a very different organization from what it was in 1915. The league once composed practically the entire women's peace movement. Today it is a small organization that forms a significant piece of a much larger movement.

What did it mean in 1915 to "make" peace? To be peacemakers? For the women who went to The Hague, it meant risking public scorn, possibly death, defying the advice of even their own colleagues in the suffrage movement; it meant forsaking comfort, speaking and traveling ceaselessly in search of peaceful resolutions to conflict. And, from their strongly feminist perspective, it meant that being women gave them a special concern and responsibility for preserving life, a "peculiar moral passion."

From the start, WILPF women believed that peacemaking

meant not just eliminating wars and armaments but also achieving economic and social justice through structural changes in society— in the words of WILPF pioneer Jane Addams, "peace and bread."[2] Their approach also has traditionally combined study and action. In the ensuing seven decades, WILPF women have continued to take risks, to study and act tirelessly, but the environment in which they do so has changed considerably.

Historical Changes in Peacemaking

With today's burgeoning nuclear arsenals and international crises almost daily, the league's goals may seem even more remote than they were in the war-torn days of 1915. However, certain historical and cultural trends have actually helped the WILPF in its search to make peace in the world.

First, there are changes in attitudes. Though conflicts still rage across the globe, public perception of war and injustice is drastically different from what it was in 1915. Human cooperation and an end to wars are no longer seen as unattainable ideals.

The ninety-six-year-old WILPF matriarch Mildred Scott Olmsted said this of her experience in community peace work shortly after the end of World War I: "The general attitude [then] was 'the government knows best.' We were told we were starry-eyed, impractical, too idealistic, that there had always been wars and would always be wars. We had few tools to help us, no articles or literature. Anything we needed for our work we had to create for ourselves."[3]

In later decades, however, according to Olmsted, "more and more people are now beginning to recognize the interrelatedness of all social problems. Many more people are coming out more openly against war."[4] The technological ability to destroy the entire planet has likely been responsible for this change in thinking. In fact, peaceful coexistence is increasingly viewed as a practical necessity. For example, even President Ronald Reagan conceded in 1984, "A nuclear war cannot be won and must never be fought."[5] Reagan proceeded to negotiate with General Secretary Mikhail Gorbachev of the Soviet Union to eliminate an entire class of nuclear weapons (including the cruise and Pershing II missiles), and the Intermediate-range Nuclear Forces (INF) Treaty was signed on December 6, 1987. For WILPF, such a step represented the culmination of years of peacemaking efforts.

Second, the cries for justice from the Third World have become louder in recent years, and the rapid decolonization of the past three decades has forever altered world power configurations. Civil rights movements by oppressed minorities in the First World have had a similar impact. Today, nations once secure in their breadth of power find their authority challenged repeatedly. These uprisings have affected people's thinking too, as well as the perspectives of nongovernmental organizations like WILPF, giving them new allies and more hope. Many Third World and smaller nations which once had no voice in world affairs are now outspoken proponents of goals similar to those of peace and justice movements in the developed nations. In the 1980s a growing number of people link peace with economic justice, as WILPF has done since 1915.

Finally, the role of women in society has significantly expanded in these seven decades. The woman suffrage won in many countries in the early part of the century increased women's participation in politics. Though suffrage did not bring with it the permanent peace WILPF founders had envisioned, it did institute a process for increasing women's property, health, and other civil rights. Women thus gained more legitimacy in public life, giving them some voice in matters of policy and ethics. And, as the Nairobi conference at the end of the women's decade illustrated, women were once again using their unique voices in peacemaking, this time by the thousands and all over the world. These three enormous social changes, as well as a myriad of less sweeping ones, have generated corresponding organizational adjustments for the league.

Sustaining the Vision

Yet there is also a powerful continuity in WILPF which has enabled it to remain a viable organization over time. As the league enters its seventh decade, it continues to make peace through its enduring witness for disarmament and economic justice. The organization has consistently hoped for, worked for, and envisioned a better world. One of its primary means for doing so has been through support for the UN as the single organ able to facilitate global cooperation.

Perhaps equally important, the league continues to be an organization characterized internally by a deeply personal level of care and commitment even where ideas diverge and intense political differences appear. Its very ability to make creative shifts within its organizational boundaries in response to (or in anticipation of) outside changes is part of that continuity.

Since 1985, league members have begun looking toward the year 2000 as a goal for urgently needed changes in the world order, specifically for a hunger- and nuclear weapon-free twenty-first century. Meeting in congress during the summer of 1986, three hundred WILPF women from forty countries wholeheartedly endorsed this goal.[6] Gathering together once again in the Netherlands—this time not in The Hague but in nearby Zeist—members were hosted by the newly revived Dutch WILPF section. There they celebrated the passage of their seventieth year as an international organization. The program they adopted, "Toward a Nuclear Weapon- and Hunger-Free Twenty-first Century," used the forward-looking strategies set forth in Nairobi as an organizing tool for its implementation. Kay Camp was one of the first to put forward the year 2000 as a target date, and her work toward that end has greatly influenced the league's recent programs:

> I remember a few years ago you would never find the word "disarmament" in the paper and now it's there every day in some form or another. We've lived so long with the threat of nuclear holocaust that I think we're at a point of being ready to reject the nuclear system and maybe even the war system. So we have to start thinking about what's to take its place. It's always the question of security: that's what all people and all nations ultimately seek. So while we're all longing for a decentralization of power, we have to have a world where it can exist, in which everyone can be safe. It is my hope that a strengthened UN can give us a more

equitable and just economic system which will result in a more equal and just social system.[7]

Toward a United Nations

Advocacy for an international peacekeeping organ has always been high on the league's agenda, and the vision of a strong UN has been a consistent feature of its program. The women assembled at Zeist agreed that the need has never been greater. The outgoing international president, Carol Pendell, told the congress: "Today, the U.N. system has to be defended, not reformed. We must do so with lucidity and consistency. There is no alternative to the U.N. Our U.N. representatives will have to work harder still to inform our sections, and they to inform the membership, on the work of the U.N. and its Specialized Agencies and on the underlying reasons for the attacks against them. The United Nations is the one organization we have that can hold this explosive world together."[8]

WILPF's close work with the UN and its consultative status with UN bodies have helped it to maintain a unique identity in the growing array of peace, freedom, and women's groups in the progressive movement. For instance, the league remains the only First World women's peace group to hold consultative status with the UN's Economic and Social Council.

Sensitivity to Differences

The UN work has also been a significant unifying force for this organization with its disparate and geographically widespread membership. WILPF continues to promote and enlarge the UN's efforts; yet the league is not beset by the political obstacles which plague the UN. Political and cultural differences among League members are not as vast as those among UN member states and their representatives.

The points at which views do diverge among WILPF members are handled with care, as illustrated in this comment by Yvonne See, a French WILPF leader for more than four decades: "We have never been of the same opinion on everything. We have always discussed difficult issues on which we have been in firm disagreement. But we have always respected the minority point of view so nobody felt mistreated. We did not say, 'We are the majority, ten against seven, and we are right.' It was a good thing because it meant the seven could go on. They were not persuaded and yet wanted to continue working together. Of course we are all in accordance with the same aim and that is a great force. Yet there are many means by which to meet these aims."[9]

Perhaps because it is a women's group, WILPF has always placed a high value on interpersonal relations among its members, particularly among leaders at the international level, where the potential for misunderstanding is greatest. Eleonore Romberg of Munich, elected international president in 1986, had this to say of her experiences in this realm: "Even if you are discussing political issues, I think for a women's group it is [especially] important to realize and observe how people in the group are feeling. If someone at a meeting looks pale, go to her and say, 'Do you feel bad? What's happened to you?' Or if someone doesn't come for a while, telephone her. I try to take care and be interested in every person, in their personal lives. Of course it's not enough to keep on that level of personal needs, but it should be connected to our political work. I think women are more sensitive and we should become more sensitive still."[10] This cultivation of sensitivity to differences has on occasion made the league slow to act on difficult issues but ultimately enables members to find solutions because of their regard for one another.

With enough time and dialogue, the league has reached consensus on many difficult topics, one of which is nuclear power. The evolution of WILPF's position on this matter is described by Lucy Haessler:

> At these international gatherings there are always more U.S. women present because we have more money to travel. And we have had to be careful about certain issues where women from other cultures feel differently than we do: abortion, for example. But on the subject of nuclear power, there has been a coming together. I remember at my first international congress in Birmingham in '74, the U.S. people had to be quite diplomatic in

discussions of that topic. By 1977 when we met in Tokyo, it became evident in one huge workshop dealing with nuclear power and other energy issues that women from India and Japan had begun to share our concerns about the dangers. Women from some Third World countries were coming into this from a very different perspective; these were small sections concerned with survival issues such as health, medical care, and the status of women. Our message to them was "If you want to see your community build a nuclear power plant, these are the things you have to watch for: centralization, military contracts, creation of local jobs, peaceful use only, and safeguards." By the time the Congress in 1980 had a session on energy, there wasn't a single WILPF voice in favor of nuclear power. So this is the kind of thing we work through.[11]

As this example shows, there is usually enough common ground among members to create receptivity to certain political points of view even where there is not agreement. In the process, consensus is often reached. Not all discussions are resolved in a unified point of view, however, even over long periods of time.

WILPF and Nonviolence

The league's position on nonviolence is a good illustration of ideas remaining divergent. This issue, so central to WILPF's purpose, has been called more sharply into focus over the years, both in action and in searching debates. Particularly after the many movements for independence began in the Third World, league leaders were pressed to explore more deeply the relation of their own privileged race and class to their views on nonviolence. From the first, WILPF had a strong Quaker presence and a core of absolute pacifists. Yet, even among those members, the meaning of nonviolence in their own lives became a question along with increasing awareness of themselves as "haves in a world of have-nots," as Dorothy Hutchinson characterized them.

"We have said that we are not a pacifist organization but that we believe in nonviolence," said Kay Camp in a summary of the position WILPF settled on in 1971 after much internal dialogue. "It is important to uphold the principle of nonviolence but to ask where the violence begins. It is limiting and self-righteous to expect people living under extreme violence to remain nonviolent."[12]

The matter was ostensibly laid to rest at the 1971 congress in India. In practice, however, individual members have continued to hold very different ideas on the meaning of nonviolence; and various sections and branches have approached the topic differently in their activities. Edith Ballantyne's recollections of the India congress discussion reveal the need for such flexibility on this subject:

> Basically, the question was whether WILPF could support liberation movements that had taken up arms. Could we insist on complete nonviolent action in the face of extreme violence being used to oppress and dominate peoples and populations? The issue was not a new one and had cropped up in different contexts almost from the beginning of the organization. I was startled and disappointed by the discussion, which to me reflected muddled thinking and a lack of frankness. But I began to realize that it also showed sensitivity to the gulf that was there between the pure pacifists and nonpacifists in the league. That gulf was too wide to be overcome even with the carefully worded text that was finally voted on. The absolute pacifists were not at all pleased with the vote; yet the statement still stands and to my knowledge no one left the league because of it.
>
> But what really stands out in my memory is one night in the middle of all that, at dinner I sat with Helga Stene, who had been very involved in the Norwegian nonviolent resistance during the Nazi occupation. She was a pacifist, a very religious, committed woman. She was a hero, in a way, and I knew that this statement wasn't going to change her mind. Yet somehow she as a person decided how she could live with it. At no time did she threaten to leave WILPF or not do this or that. And I thought, well, that's the world we're in and we're all going to have to develop some tolerance of one another's positions. And while the league could have a position that might suit the majority, it also had to have room for the minority. Very often, when I get really heated, because I have strong opinions about things too, I think back to that discussion with Helga and think, well, I didn't agree with Helga, but it was possible to discuss and disagree and to continue to work for a better world. I found that something new in my life.[13]

In the 1980s, the terms of the league debate on this topic have shifted somewhat to focus more on nonviolence in the context of direct action. Nonviolent civil disobedience has become an increasingly common strategy in the disarmament movement, particularly among women. Correspondingly, WILPF members have discussed at length the relevance of their own and others' experiences of nonviolent direct actions to the movements they work in. Even in this context, there is a broad range of strongly held opinions.

In general, as Ballantyne pointed out, the best resolution of a topic as sensitive as this one has been to maintain a position flexible enough and encompassing enough to accommodate opposing viewpoints. The high degree of autonomy with which WILPF groups operate is helpful in allowing such differences to coexist; thus, an issue which could have split the organization has been peaceably resolved instead.

Organizational Coherence

A fairly well defined organizational structure has provided the framework for the league's coherence and longevity. WILPF has always had numerous clearly developed and actively functioning committees and individual jobs associated with various issues and UN functions. These range from local to regional to national to international. Mari Holmboe Ruge commented: "That is a strength of the WILPF: even if you're not able to see any result, you have a structure, positions to fill. So many people have given their strength to the antinuclear movement and now feel a certain degree of disheartening because we're not accomplishing much. I suppose every WILPF member would say she has her ups and downs. But you have to keep the organization going. It's there for better or worse."[14]

Ironically, that same structure which is loyally adhered to by some has also deterred many women from joining WILPF in recent years. Activists of the Western world who came of age during the women's liberation and alternative lifestyle movements of the past twenty years have charged that the structure is too confining, hierarchical, male, and traditional. According to Eleonore Romberg,

"The majority of young women we encounter hesitate to be in a membership organization with fees and structure. They prefer initiatives, where they are not so bounded. But without some kind of structure people get frustrated. Little by little more young women [are realizing] that a 'structure' need not be the ones we have experienced in a man's society."[15]

Although some have complained about it, there are—as Romberg emphasizes—good reasons for maintaining a certain level of structure and uniformity, particularly at the international level. Mari Ruge said on this topic:

> Of course it's easy to see the limitations of the structure, but we should be careful not to denounce it altogether because it does make for orderliness. You have to prepare yourself, do your homework, in a way. If twenty persons all want to speak, they know they must confine themselves to some kind of order. And it's been a training ground for the women who will attend these formal conferences, the UN and such as that. You can't turn these institutions around automatically: to participate, you must go through their way of doing things. And for those of us who don't speak English so well, it's useful to have a set procedure to enable us to speak at the international meetings.[16]

In fact, while organizational changes at the local level are more evident, even the international structure and procedures have evolved much in the past few years. They remain somewhat bureaucratic and rather formal, but far less so than was once the case. As Janet Bruin of Switzerland observed, "Sociologically, the life of an organization is often about eight years. To go beyond that, you have to have some degree of structure. I hate bureaucracy, I'll tell you that. But WILPF has the most gentle bureaucracy I've ever seen. There has to be some way of organizing. A total lack of it can lead to chaos. There are a lot of women coming from these unstructured organizations who feel comfortable with what they find in WILPF."[17]

In the 1970s and especially in the 1980s, many sections and branches began experimenting with new forms of process, decision making, and leadership. In the Dutch section, for example, presidents and vice-presidents have been replaced by a coordinating group. In Göteborg, Sweden, members have started electing three women to each leadership post to promote closer cooperation and less authority delegated to any one person.

Having participated in numerous WILPF meetings at every level, Edith Ballantyne reflected on the changes in structure:

> There's more informality [now], but it's been fought for and should never be taken for granted. And still the structure could be reduced further. In the UN, they realized a few years ago that so often, voting means nothing, though they're required to vote. But if there are important governments against a resolution, it can be meaningless even if it is passed. And thus, more effort is being made to work by consensus. That's true of the league too. When I first attended WILPF Executive Committee meetings, every little thing was moved, seconded, voted, and recorded. Now that's changed. It's better sometimes to discuss another two hours and find agreement rather than vote and have bad feelings and only partial implementation.[18]

While maintaining continuity with the league's traditional structure, WILPF women have relaxed the organization's boundaries to accommodate a changed social and cultural climate. The shifts described here are also partly a response to a more diverse and younger population coming into the league's ranks.

Embracing Diversity: The Essence of Internationalism

Among the women gathered in Zeist to celebrate the passage of the league's seventh decade were many young faces and many colored faces—a markedly more diverse group than those who had convened a mere two decades earlier at the fiftieth-anniversary congress. Over seventy years' time and especially in the last two decades, rapid social and cultural changes have released a greater degree of diversity on the world than ever before. Those changes have not significantly altered the league's aims, but they have affected its approach and the kinds of women who make up the membership. Embracing diversity has been an increasing challenge to WILPF in recent years. At its fifty-year mark WILPF was slow to take up that challenge, but the 1980s find the league responding to it vigorously.

Just as voices from the Third World prompted members to explore the issue of nonviolence from a new perspective, so have they pushed the league to expand its very understanding of internationalism. As a result, building bridges to cooperate with a greater variety of women has been of growing importance to WILPF.

This process was particularly evident at the 1986 congress: members had talked for years about the need to have more involvement from women of the Southern Hemisphere in order to be truly international. At last, in planning this congress, WILPF both sought and secured funds to bring twenty-one women from fifteen Third World countries for a seminar with European and North American members. Together they explored ways of broadening WILPF's relatively Western, white, middle-class orientation and programs, to make them more relevant to a greater spectrum of women. Four of the participants had comments on this matter, which reflected both the content of the seminar and new directions the league may take:

> We made an important step in opening the organization to Third World women in Nairobi and also in Zeist. I think the league is relevant to them since we are struggling for so many issues in common. WILPF still has a middle-class bias and orientation, so that makes it difficult for many Third World women to participate in many of our activities. Currencies are one problem, for example. We need to do more, maybe develop sister-section projects, or something else that would enable more participation and exchange.[19]
>
> Irene Eckert, Federal Republic of Germany
> (seminar participant, 1986)

> In my country there is much support for a philosophy like WILPF espouses. These international gatherings are good for exchanging views with people of many opinions on peace and justice questions. The links established are very useful because you can correspond with people of other countries with similar ideas. That kind of twinning is not necessarily for linking developed

and underdeveloped but for continuing networking and communication among us all.[20]

Angela Gethi, Kenya

One of our commitments [as Third World women] should be to work more internationally so that our problems are made known [to the developed world]. European and North American women are not to blame; they have the media against them. This is what attracts me to the league more than anything else, because I think you can do more effective work by working internationally. It is very difficult for European women to know what we are suffering. When I joined WILPF, for instance, it was very difficult to work in Costa Rica because in accordance with the international program, the members were getting signatures against nuclear tests, and the people would say, "We have bombs every day. Children are suffering and dying every day in poverty and hunger, and we care more about this than nuclear bombs." But now that Costa Rica is being remilitarized and people see that militarization involves their own lives and jobs and health, it is much easier to talk about war and peace issues.[21]

Olga Bianchi, Costa Rica

One of our biggest shortcomings is that our main strength is in Western Europe and North America in capitalist countries. Throughout WILPF's history there have been sections in developing countries that have come into and gone out of existence, as have some in Europe as well. Given that lack of consistent Third World input, there has been tremendous compensation on the part of our members by at least taking the perspectives of people in other parts of the world into account. I think this is very much lacking in other Western peace movements. Even given that WILPF does not really represent the entire world, the international focus has at least given WILPF members the feeling that there is a world out there. Emphasizing not just disarmament but its relationship to attaining a saner economic order, the importance of ending poverty and inequality, which historically WILPF has always acknowledged, can only make our statements more pertinent in parts of the world we have not really touched.[22]

Janet Bruin, Switzerland

Blending Generations

The process of outreach to younger women has also been of growing importance to WILPF. The league has always had a nucleus
of elderly women; Aletta Jacobs, Jane Addams, and many other originators were more than fifty when they went to The Hague.
Middle-aged and older women continued to form the bulk of the
league's membership over the years, as these memoirs of Elisabeth
Stahle, an elderly Swedish member, illustrate.

> When WILPF was founded in Sweden in 1919, we had a rather
> big group of well-educated women, many of them having aca-
> demic degrees, but who still had difficulty finding adequate jobs.
> They were often married and well cared for economically, and
> they felt a need to make use of their knowledge. So when the
> Swedish section opened this possibility they joined and contrib-
> uted highly in making the section grow, giving WILPF a reputa-
> tion from the very beginning of asking much from their members.
> And those women made others of their own generation inter-
> ested, while younger women felt ignorant and inexperienced in
> their company. I can speak from my own experience. When I
> joined in 1937, I was twenty-nine years old but nevertheless I felt
> very young the first time I went to a meeting with all those older
> women who were so familiar with the questions being discussed
> and so much more conscious of political and social problems than
> I was, since I had been married eight years and fully occupied by
> home and children. Only twenty years later did I become active
> in WILPF. I think that is a rather common experience. We get
> young women to become members, then they disappear for
> many years, but then they come back when their other social re-
> sponsibilities allow them to dedicate themselves more actively.[23]

In the league's first decades, small numbers of young women
always came along to broaden the membership ranks and lend another generation's viewpoint, often through the summer schools
and other youth outreach projects. This process was interrupted
after World War II, however, when a generation of young people
shunned political activity. By 1965 the organization was populated
predominantly by middle-aged and older women. Over the following two decades, other factors restricted even further the influx of
younger women.

For example, voluntarism, a practice which once brought many new members to WILPF and groups like it, has declined as increasing numbers of women have entered the labor force. Like Elisabeth Stahle, many of the women profiled in this research joined the league as young mothers at home raising children, a choice made less frequently by women in the 1980s. Kay Camp, a person for whom voluntarism became a career, said this of the change: "Voluntarism has to be done in one's spare hours nowadays. It shouldn't be a full-time job. But also, we're having more retirement years now and that's a source of new members that we haven't yet focused enough attention on."[24]

In fact, the league's embrace of diversity is not only international in character; it is also intergenerational. In the 1980s enough young women are coming into the league to lend to its programs and philosophies an added perspective that was largely absent after World War II, and it looks as if that trend is growing. WILPF's intergenerational nature has become one of its most compelling qualities and is almost certainly a key to the organization's longevity. This statement by Brigit Obermayer, a young woman who joined the Munich WILPF group in 1979, is fairly indicative of the sentiments of younger members: "At the beginning there were mostly older women in the group, and for my friend and me it was often difficult because we were forty years younger than the others. It took a long time to do it, but we did get more young members. We have one older member who is so young at heart that everyone enjoys working with her. And some of the older ones were in the Resistance during the Third Reich. I feel I have learned a lot from them. The important thing you learn is patience, never to give up."[25]

The woman she referred to as "young at heart" was Eleonore Romberg, who had come into the branch thirty years before as one of the only youthful women. Romberg, too, reflected on the process of meshing old and new:

> I'm a person who hasn't had difficulties with structures. But I've learned very much from the young women we work with in our branch. One thing is the mix of personal and political. When they asked me, "What do you think happiness is?" I would feel

crazy. I was thinking, we have to do a program, not discuss our happiness. And then I realized that maybe I push the members too much, that I must get more sensitive. So now in our meetings we learn from each other. It's so funny and it's so full of energy— the emotions and the strengths and the optimism, that message which is always there: these old women are fighters, so don't ever give up.[26]

The Future of WILPF

What has made WILPF "never give up" over such a long and tumultuous period of time? As the experiences of these two women indicate, the lessons of the organization's past are a rich resource for its future. The optimism, respect for others, and persistence displayed by one generation have helped to imbue the following generations with those same qualities. WILPF women continue to possess, as founder Jane Addams urged them to, "faith in new possibilities and the courage to implement them."

Some members today speculate that this persistence and the problem-solving it generates are special strengths of women. As Edith Ballantyne put it, "I think women never give up. Yet they are able to let things go. They don't have to have all or nothing. They are able to say, 'Well, all right, that's fine for now,' and then go right along working [for the larger goal]. I don't believe it's because they're biologically different but through their centuries of experience working in communities or as mothers. They've simply been pushed into certain situations where problems had to be solved."[27]

WILPF and Feminism

For Ballantyne and many others, these are recent discoveries. From the 1930s until well after the rebirth of the women's liberation movement in the 1970s, WILPF no longer emphasized that "peculiar moral passion" which had once propelled its founders and led them to equate women's rights with an end to war. In fact, the league remained a women's organization through part of that period largely to give women a forum in which to gain experience in the political and public arenas.

However, while WILPF has not always embraced the objectives and language of feminism, it has always worked for feminist values: cooperation, relationship, and community.[28] And it has consistently promoted women in leadership. In 1929, for example, of fifteen women delegates to the League of Nations' Tenth Assembly, seven of them were active WILPF members, and WILPF campaigned vigorously for the appointment of more women. In 1988 the staff at the Geneva headquarters continues to train interested members in the procedures and practices of the UN. Working outside and inside the world's policy-making structures to influence them, WILPF women have brought a perspective to twentieth-century world affairs that simply would not have been present had not a few women, representing half the world's population, continued to make themselves heard.

In the 1980s the league has begun to explore more deeply its rationale as a women's organization and to understand and heighten women's special contributions to peacemaking: the persistence Ballantyne attributed to women, for example. A pivotal choice in this process was the decision in 1982 to launch the Stop the Arms Race campaign, which sought to strengthen the women's peace movement by reaching a million women. In that action and others the league is slowly reincorporating and advancing the feminist orientation of its founding mothers.

This progression does not nor has it ever yielded a single organizational view of feminism, a concept which itself is open to interpretation. In WILPF's European and Third World sections, for example, there is not the same broad embrace of feminism by progressive women that is true in the United States. Even in 1987, many a WILPF member may oppose sexism, militarism, and discrimination, but still say, "Not me," when asked if she is a feminist. As Kay Camp noted, "If a feminist is any person who believes in equality for women, we would have a hard time finding non-feminist women in the peace movement. On the other hand, if a feminist is one who believes that the basic cause of all violence and injustice is rooted in the patriarchal system on which society is founded, feminism would lose some who feel that the genderless greed at the root of the economic system is at least as responsible."[29]

Many WILPF members' views on women and power lie somewhere between those two poles, as the following remarks illustrate.

> Because of culture, because we have been given the roles of taking care, and because we don't have political power, we're not in the system as much and we're freer to think about it critically.[30]
>
> Mari Holmboe Ruge, Norway

> I don't believe women are by nature, biologically, more peaceful than men. Still, in their development through the ages, women have acquired some qualities that have allowed them to be more direct in their contacts with other people. Not more peaceful. I can't help thinking of Margaret Thatcher and women like her, even some in the women's movement, who are so aggressive. But you can see in the development of the women's movement since 1975, we have a chance to have an effect on political life if we stick to it.[31]
>
> Ruth Gleissberg, Federal Republic of Germany

> It is my deep conviction that women can achieve a power that is different from that of men. Women have never had power, at least not the power we know now as ruling the world. We are not in the military-industrial complex, we are not in politics and we are certainly not in big business. We are kept away from power. I think and I hope that if women did have more power, they would act in a different way from the way power [systems] are now. But not if they are in a minority position in a man's world; only if our values and priorities were given an equal place.[32]
>
> Carlota Lopes da Silva, Netherlands

This excerpt from WILPF's STAR campaign literature elaborates on the kind of power Carlota Lopes da Silva referred to above: "Our experience as women helps us to understand the wholeness of body, mind, and soul. . . . We know that strength lies not in domination but in cooperation, living in harmony with ourselves, each other, and our environment. . . . Racism and sexism, the rape of the environment, and the threat of annihilation under which we live are all rooted in the will to dominate. And militarism represents this will in its most violent and virulent form."[33]

Conclusion

The league's sustained efforts toward a just reordering of priorities and toward redefining of power say, perhaps, more about its brand of feminism than any poll of the membership would reveal. Its women are fighters. A fierce loyalty to the goals of world peace and freedom—and to the organization itself—characterizes WILPF women and keeps them moving forward. They persist and find creative ways around enormous obstacles, and theirs is a struggle which employs not weapons but words and nonviolent actions.

In my view, feminism represents a vision of realizing not just women's creative potential but that of all people to make a more humane world, free of war and exploitation. Whatever the label, that is the objective for which WILPF has consistently worked, and it is with that vision that the league moves toward the year 2000. In an era facing the threat of nuclear destruction and world calamity, WILPF continues to exemplify the peaceful cooperation, hard work, and international community which it is pressing the world to embrace.

Profiles of Eighteen WILPF Women

 The pages that follow contain profiles of eighteen WILPF women compiled from several hours of conversation with each of them. Of the perhaps thirty thousand women who comprise the league, these eighteen lives reveal only a small glimpse of the broad spectrum of WILPF membership.

Yet these particular interviews were chosen for inclusion because they do typify certain characteristics of the organization. For instance, on the topics of feminism and nonviolence, both of which are integral to an understanding of WILPF, the comments of the women here reflect the wide range of views the league is able to incorporate. They also contain enough detail to reveal the subtleties behind a statement like "I am a pacifist" or "I am a feminist."

Most of the women interviewed here are leaders at the international level of WILPF, which is not the case with the vast majority of league members. This was unavoidable, since it was that very aspect of their work that made these eighteen women accessible to an author wishing to talk with women of many WILPF sections. As it was, not all sections were able to be represented here. It was simply not feasible to go into communities in fourteen or more countries and talk with a sample of rank-and-file members. But because the women interviewed are from fourteen nations, their profiles illuminate not just their individual personalities but the "personalities" of their sections as well. From the Olmsted, Camp, Pickvance, and Bianchi pieces, for example, one can surmise that Quakerism has been a significant force in several sections.

The profiles also speak to other organizational questions, such as what attracts people to the league. The women's responses to that question were varied; yet, from them some tentative conclusions can be drawn. For example, subjective experience of war often seems to move women to activism, and in particular, many of today's international WILPF leaders were prompted by the terrible consequences of World War II to become peace activists. Also, women have tended to become interested in the league through close and admired female associates, sometimes even their own mothers.

As for the type of woman the league attracts, these profiles reflect the mix of activists and academics in the membership, and they are a fairly representative sample of the professional status of WILPF members. Because the profiles are presented in chronological sequence according to the date of the women's entry into WILPF, they also depict some of the demographic changes that have taken place over time in the type of women joining the league.

The interviews are not uniform, though I conducted all of them myself except for the Olmsted piece, which contains portions of an earlier interview done by Mercedes Randall, and the Harsloff interview, which was conducted by Ellen Blosser at my request. Some of them focus more on personal experiences and views than others. In each case I emphasized what I took to be the subject's most unique qualities or bits of wisdom. One woman tells of her journey from apolitical aristocrat to internationalist, while another shares the lessons of organizing women in underdeveloped rural communities, and still another speaks of her decision to resist paying war taxes. The unifying thread of these interviews was a question which had originally drawn me to this project: "What keeps you going?"

Mildred Scott Olmsted

February 1972 and June 1985

Philadelphia Quaker Mildred Scott Olmsted is perhaps the oldest living matriarch of the Women's International League for Peace and Freedom. Born in 1891, she graduated from Smith College in 1912 and went to Europe during the latter days of World War I to do relief work with the Allied troops. There, she became a pacifist and first heard of the league. Back in the United States, working with Jane Addams and other early leaders, Mildred concerned herself with building the organization: she became executive director of the U.S. section, a post she held for forty-three years. In addition to that work, she raised three children, founded the social work department at Bryn Mawr Hospital, and served on the boards of numerous other progressive organizations and coalitions.

After World War II, when WILPF members' hopes for lasting peace lay in shreds and they met again in congress in 1946 to decide if the organization had a future, Mildred was one of the strongest and most eloquent advocates for continuing the work of the league. Over the years she participated in missions to Germany, the Balkans, and Turkey, as well as helped to organize in 1961 the seminars of the U.S. WILPF and Soviet women that continue today. Well into her nineties, Mildred has continued to be active in the league, attending U.S. board meetings, speaking to local groups, and soliciting new members with her unsinkable enthusiasm. In September 1986, the U.S. section honored her ninety-fifth birthday with a gala celebration.

I was brought up with the idea that I was going to be a lawyer. My father was one, and he had only daughters. But by the time I got to be a junior in college, he decided [law] really wasn't a place for women. Court work is the most interesting part of the law and women are at a disadvantage in a court, he always said. And as soon as he decided that, he wasn't prepared to put any more money into my education. But I knew I needed more education. And the settlement movement was just coming in. So in my senior year, when the settlement association offered a $1,500 fellowship for training in social work, I applied for it. I didn't hear for a while, but I did get it. So I got my training and went into settlement work in Philadelphia.

During the First World War, as one of the early second-generation social workers after such pioneers as Jane Addams and Florence Kelley, I was working in the military camps in this country in the War Camp Community Service.[1] After the Armistice in 1918, the military authorities decided morale needed building among the troops in Europe. [Working for the Young Men's Christian Association], I took charge of recreation work for the Allied servicemen who were going to the Sorbonne in Paris. We held dances and we were constantly feeding them. But I had different ideas about what the center should be, and one day I said to the young men, "Now that the war is over, wouldn't you like to know what it was all about?" They voted that they would like to, and so we arranged a talk for one Thursday evening.

I had read in the *Paris Herald* that Jane Addams was in Paris so I went to see her. I explained that these were all young college men who knew very little of the war except through their own experiences and asked her to start the discussion series. This was the first time I had met Miss Addams and I was delighted when she agreed to come. The boys were fascinated by everything she had to say about the causes of the war, and so they voted to go on with the series. [The series was canceled by an adviser to President Woodrow Wilson on the grounds that it was endangering the peace conference.]

I also opened the center to the conscientious objectors, whose headquarters were farther up the street. When the soldiers complained about their coming in and drinking our coffee, I insisted that they had as much right to be there and were as courageous as the soldiers. [The coordinator of the conscientious objectors' headquarters] urged me to transfer from the YMCA to the Society of Friends, who were working in the devastated areas. I agreed to, because I had been very much disillusioned by my work in the YMCA and in the whole military system. I saw a great deal of the war and what it had done to civilians. I [came from a fundamental-ist Baptist background] and was not yet a Quaker myself, though I did become one later.

We were sent down into Bavaria to organize all the child-feeding work there. Part of my job was going around visiting orphanages and deciding which should get food. It is almost un-believable what starvation will do to people. We had to check the food at every stage, and [still] it was stolen. You couldn't blame people. A few local women came to us and said, "Don't you need help?" Their service was invaluable. And they said to us, "What are the women of America doing for peace?" I had to admit I knew quite a great deal of what women in America were doing for war but not anything of what they were doing for peace. They said, "Don't you know about Miss Addams and the women at The Hague in 1915?" And they told me about what was to become the Women's International League for Peace and Freedom.

It was a little hard for the Germans to understand why the Quakers would come over and feed their starving children when they were their enemies, and at first they were afraid we were trying to convert them. Others wanted to know if we had been pro-German and we assured them we had not. We explained that we believed that all human lives were worth saving. They asked us if we would speak publicly to explain this. We held a very exciting public meeting, but I was devastated when I was put in the posi-tion of speaking for all my countrywomen and couldn't tell any-thing they had been doing for peace, whereas the German women who spoke were Gertrude Baer, Anita Augspurg, and Lida Gus-tava Heymann. I made up my mind then that when I got home, I would find out what women in America were doing for peace and try to join that organization.

But when I did get back to the States, I had great difficulty finding it. It wasn't in the telephone book and I couldn't find any-body who'd heard of it. Then one day I saw an announcement that a German woman, an English woman, and a Belgian woman were going to speak against war, and I thought to myself, this is it. I went to the meeting and joined on the spot. I've been with it ever since.

[Soon] they asked me to come and work for the WIL. That was the Pennsylvania branch. And I left my other job. When I got there, there was a broken desk and a pile of cards that I was supposed to address by hand. So I said, "You couldn't possibly afford to pay me." "Oh, yes, we know what you're getting and we're going to pay the same thing," they told me. When I started work, I found that the only plans they had to pay my salary were that three members had each said they would donate [enough for] one month. They thought, after that she can raise her own.

Well, we began going around talking peace. The general attitude was "the government knows best." We were told we were starry-eyed, impractical, too idealistic, that there had always been wars and would always be wars. We had few tools to help us, no articles or literature. Anything we needed for our work we had to create ourselves. I would travel from one community to another in Pennsylvania, and soon came to realize how isolated the peace people were. In one [place] it would be a librarian; in another it would be a teacher, perhaps a minister or a mother, all of them lonely, isolated, sometimes labeled as cranks. They were always delighted to discover that there were others like them in other communities and sometimes in their own. We would tell them about our organization and put them in touch with each other. I remember the head of the Women's Christian Temperance Union used to come to us for material. She would say, "Of course I can never mention you by name. That would never do. I'll just take your facts." So a lot of our work consisted of providing information for which we never got any publicity. Many were afraid of the consequences of associating with us.

In looking back at the early days, it is interesting how many programs that had their beginnings in the WIL have since developed into full-fledged organized movements. The WIL saw the connection between peace and freedom and minorities and the right to self-determination as all parts of one whole. But in those days others looked on those matters as totally unrelated. I always say that one of the greatest satisfactions in my older years is to see that more and more people are beginning to recognize the interrelatedness of all social problems.

Was the league strongly feminist at that time? And were you?

We were very feminist. It was the age of suffrage, you know. And they always pictured the suffragists as very unattractive. So I always made it a point to try and have attractive clothes to break that stereotype.

I had been an ardent suffragist myself, but I came very late into the movement. When I entered Smith College I think I was the only member of the freshman class who was a feminist. It used to irritate me so much that I was introduced as "our new little suffragette," because I didn't consider myself a suffragette but a suffragist. Suffragettes wanted direct action; they demonstrated and disrupted meetings and many of them went to prison. Suffragists worked state by state to change the law. We started a suffrage group at Smith, and to stimulate interest we encouraged an anti-suffrage group so people would come to our meetings. By the time I graduated there had been a great change of feeling toward women's suffrage.

When I came back to Philadelphia, I offered my services to suffrage people and was assigned to be a waitress in the suffrage tea room, which was how they raised money. Well, I had a regular social work job so I would dash over to the tea room at noon, don my waitress uniform, wait tables till two, and then dash back. I don't know how much good I did for suffrage, but I learned a great deal about the position of the working woman as a result of that experience.

I got into almost the last of the suffrage parades that were held in Philadelphia. When I announced to my family that I was going to march, my father said that if I did, I need not come home. I thought about it and came back and said, "This is a matter of conscience, and I have to do it." There were very large numbers of people in the parade and also watching. As we swung around City Hall, I saw my father in the crowd. I threw my head in the air and, ignoring him, marched straight on. Around another corner there were my mother and sisters. I was on the end of a line and my mother leaned forward and said, "Come home tonight." Not one word about it was spoken at dinner. Finally I asked my mother,

"What's happened to Father?" And she said, "He found it wasn't as bad as he thought." So that was my declaration of independence.

Women who worked for suffrage and believed in it went through very difficult periods of having fun poked at them. They had no rights, they were often spiritually separated from the menfolks in their family. One of their arguments was that women have a different point of view from men and that point of view ought to be expressed. They believed women were more interested in children, in education (at least the early parts of it), and in the care of the older and weaker of society. They also believed that women were much more concerned about war and the devastation of war, as they undoubtedly were and are today, I think.

During those early years, you worked fairly closely with Jane Addams, didn't you?

When I met Miss Addams for the second time, she remembered me but couldn't remember my name. She dubbed me "the lady from Philadelphia" and that's what she always called me. In my enthusiasm, at first as a volunteer and then as a staff worker trying to build the WIL from a very small organization into something more weighty, I was constantly taking ideas to her. The slogan of the WIL was "All women against all war," and one thing I wanted her to do was to issue a New Year's call to all women to take a stand against war. She looked me up and down and said, "I would never dream of doing it." I never could understand why she felt that way, but she would never take a position with great publicity. She was constantly attacked; she was called a Communist; she was called all kinds of things. But she would never allow us to answer, and she would never make a statement. She would always say, "The truth will out in time."

She had a strong feeling that the Americans must not be dominant in the WIL. Miss Addams had many devoted and wealthy followers, and she raised enough money to carry WILPF internationally every three years from one congress to the next. This was how the international was financed. After her death the financial situation became very serious. It was decided at that time that we would raise a fund in memory of her, and in 1953 we set up the Jane Addams Peace Association, the tax-exempt arm of the league.

Miss Addams also believed that the more peace organizations the better, and so she went onto the boards of all of them. I was interested in promoting our particular organization and could never understand why she wasn't willing to concentrate on the WIL alone. But she always said that each organization has its own interpretation and its own following and this spreads the word. She was always afraid the WIL would become too popular. She was very skeptical of popularity. She said that when an organization becomes too popular then people join it for other reasons than the work they can do in it. She said it should never be a mass organization. What she did want it to be was a group of thoughtful women who might influence the leaders of mass organizations. We used to say, "Don't worry, Miss Addams, as long as we take up all these unpopular questions, we'll never be too popular."

And you yourself were more of an organization person.

Yes. Some of us felt that we suffered very much from the fact that all our leaders were uninterested in building an organization. They were too busy spreading ideas. At one point there were so many problems in organizing that they set up a committee to go into that question. And they came out with the suggestion that the work be broken down into three units: policy and legislation, finance and projects, and organization and membership. For that they sent for me. The Pennsylvania branch generously released me half-time, and for six years I commuted to Washington and stayed half the week.

I assume there was a lot of public opposition to the work the league was doing.

It was at the time of our international congress in Washington in 1924 that public opposition first blazed out into the open. Some attacks on the WIL were stimulated by the American Legion and the Daughters of the American Revolution, and many by churches reluctant to divide their congregations, though you did find some members and ministers that were most courageous.

And long before the McCarthy era was something called the Red Network.[2] It was so inaccurate. I myself was listed in it, and all the things I was accused of were not things that I had done. Our headquarters in Washington were right opposite the War Department, as it was then appropriately called, and from time to time we were raided by the military. They would break in over weekends and steal our files or confuse our filing system, trying to get lists from them. They very much objected to the conference on chemical warfare we held after the First World War. [One general] attacked us by name on the radio, making all kinds of misstatements. We sat down and wrote him a letter pointing out all the errors. But this didn't make any difference. Then the military published the "Spider Web Chart" in which the WIL was shown with all its interlocking networks. They circulated that and the Red Network papers. We were forced to move out of our office because of all the pressure put upon our landlord.

We had been opposing conscription. At that time the military had an enormous [promotion] campaign, taking journalists and other professionals on cruises. Occasionally we would get someone who had been accidentally included in their cruises, and we would find out how much brainwashing they had done. I hate to call it that, but the military was definitely out to change the attitude of the public toward conscription and the growth of the military establishment. It is sad but interesting to see that the very things which we warned would happen if this was not checked are those things that have come to pass in the United States now. It has really been militarized. We had two great victories, however. One was heading off the war with Mexico, and the other was preventing the conscription of women.

Way back in 1934 our international congress stated that there must be basic changes in the economic system. This was picked up by the press, and we were attacked again and again on the grounds that what we advocated was an attack on property, whereas we urged only renunciation of privilege. It made a lot of trouble for the international.

And of course McCarthyism had a great effect because any organization which stood up for the recognition of Russia fell into disfavor. It wasn't that we believed in communism, but we believed in the right of self-government and self-determination. We saw that there would have to be great economic and political changes in the world, and we felt that different countries had a right to experiment with different forms.

But of course we lost people. Many members who were timid, or whose husbands' businesses were involved, felt that they couldn't afford to be connected with an organization which was under suspicion, even though they didn't believe anything was the matter with us.

And you saw personally some of the difficulties other sections faced, particularly in the Hitler era.

Yes, as a result of one of our congresses held after Hitler had come to power, I was taken aside by Gertrude Baer and Miss Balch. They asked whether I would perform a mission for the international, to go and visit the members of our German section [who] had not been able to come out and attend the congress. I was to go all alone and make contacts; I was given names and addresses and told how to do it. I had to memorize them all because it was dangerous to have them in writing. I arrived with picture postcards for my contacts, saying, "I bring greetings from your niece," which I delivered by hand. I remember [being] given instructions to go to the end of three tram lines, stand under a certain bridge and open a book. The moment I opened the book, someone joined me, and I was taken to a secret meeting of the WIL in the home of a woman doctor. They used only public telephones, and I was warned not to open my mouth of this if we passed anyone on the street. If anybody came to the door, the doctor immediately began lecturing on health foods and I kept my mouth shut. They sent me back with messages. One was, "Don't let it be known that there are any WIL members here because we've been trying to persuade the government it's an unimportant organization."

What's kept you with the league all these years?

Well, in the first place, it was larger than I was. It had a world viewpoint, and it put peace and freedom and nonviolence together, and they were all things I believed in. And most of the newer organizations don't go as far as we do. They're afraid of nuclear war, and that's a good beginning. But the world is outgrowing armaments; people are just discovering that, and WILPF is no longer the only one to see it.

I've always looked at things from the long viewpoint. There are ups and downs, depressions and peak periods. But I remain optimistic, because in my lifetime I've seen such changes. It's no longer just a few religious groups taking these positions. I think that more and more people in this modern world are saying the answer is to find some way of living together.

Inga Thorsson

July 1986

Inga Thorsson is one of the most publicly known women in WILPF. A lifelong politician in her native Sweden, she is also a rare example of women's leadership in the often male-headed United Nations. From 1973 to 1982 she was the only woman to head a government delegation to the UN Conference on Disarmament (CD).

In 1935, shortly before the outbreak of World War II, Inga joined the Swedish Social Democratic party (SPD), which proved to be the springboard for her political career. That same year she joined WILPF, and soon after, she served for several years as head of the Women's Young Front for Peace and Freedom, the Swedish WILPF's youth brigade. Over the next half a century Inga's interest in internationalism became a theme of her career: from member of Parliament to ambassador to Israel, she has consistently specialized in international affairs.

Although she remained a member of the league's Swedish section, she drifted away from active involvement in WILPF after

Hitler's defeat in Europe. However, at the time of the twenty-second WILPF congress in Göteborg (1983), her interest in the league was rekindled after she spoke at public events, and the congress elected her as WILPF's special adviser on disarmament and development.

Now in her seventies, Inga is a self-assured woman with a rather stern appearance, a dry wit, firm opinions on world affairs, and yet a gentle optimism that her years in politics have not managed to dim.

What initially attracted you to internationalism?

It was more or less a reaction to what was happening in Europe during those years. Very many young people in the countries surrounding Germany were worried. And in a young person's life there are always the personal influences of friends, teachers, and current events. In my case there were several teachers who stimulated my interest in international affairs. Also, in the late 1920s and early 1930s we had our first women parliamentarians. It was a political awakening among women in Sweden. These were a very talented group of women, mostly on the left side of politics, who acted in unison. Many of them were the same women who had gone to The Hague in 1915, and I had always admired their achievements, so I joined the league and the SPD when I was quite young. Two years later [1937] I attended my first international congress in Czechoslovakia, which had not yet been threatened by the Nazi regime. There I came to know all the famous international pioneering women.

However, very soon after that came the Second World War and it was impossible to keep up international contacts. About that time, I turned to Swedish politics.

Had your education been oriented in that direction?

No, actually I had two degrees, both in education. One was general and one was as a teacher of athletics. But I never used them for one hour! I entered politics instead. There I dedicated myself entirely to international issues.

Inga Thorsson

I understand you were quite instrumental in the convening of the UN Conference on the Human Environment.

I was always extremely interested in the environment, and was particularly engaged in this topic when I was with the UN Secretariat in the late 1960s [1967–70]. It was a general trend in those years in the various countries and UN bodies to take up that issue. I had learned enough about how the UN system worked to know that if each agency built up its own platform on environmental issues, there would be infighting that would be harmful. So I went to the secretary-general and suggested that we plan a central, UN-organized conference on the human environment; adopt a program of action; and divide the tasks among the various agencies. He thought it was a good idea, but the Secretariat can't make proposals. So I went to the Swedish delegation, and said, "Look here, we are much concerned about this in Sweden and it is an international concern as well, so why don't you propose such a conference?" And in 1968 they did. It was four years in the preparation.

People complain nothing happens out of these conferences—women, racism, the environment, you name it. But it takes time to create the political will to implement action. What these conferences did was to provide the intellectual awakening, make people aware of the problems and the linkages among all these problems. Now it's the obligation of the people to make governments understand that it's high time to follow up politically. The 1970s stand out to me as an extremely interesting decade—and it continues through the eighties. Unfortunately, there is some backlash because of reactionary regimes in some important countries of the world. Still, it's a process that can't be stopped, in my view.

Have you found that being a woman has created barriers you've had to overcome in your career?

It's difficult to say. I made many of my first career advances in the Social Democratic Women's League [an affiliate of the SPD]. There, women are listened to. But in holding public office it's certainly a factor. There has been an informal decision in the Swedish

Parliament to try and reach a 50 percent target of women parliamentarians. The general figure is 33 percent, and in some of the parties it is close to 40. All of the Nordic countries have a reasonably good record in this regard.

But when the government asked me in 1973 to chair the Swedish delegation to the CD, I don't think it was because they wanted a woman but because they knew I was deeply involved in the issue of disarmament. Once I was there, I didn't feel any problems whatsoever. It sounds a little boastful, but my male colleagues knew very well that not only was I a diplomat but an experienced politician, so I had a way of speaking out.

And I would never for a moment call myself more peace-minded than my male colleagues in the conference. That would be unfair. I don't believe women are better human beings than men, though of course no person, male or female, should be kept from doing whatever job he or she is capable of. However, it worries me that in so many countries women are now entering the armed services with great enthusiasm and delight. I hate to see that happen. I don't view that as equality, because I think it should be going in the other direction.

I'm very much against militarization because it puts values into young people's minds that are difficult to eradicate. I think, unfortunately, in some situations a resort to violence is inevitable. But the problem then becomes how to overcome the military climate that has been created. In country after country it has been shown that once arms are taken up—even to end oppression—it is difficult afterwards to get rid of that way of solving conflicts.

Yet you still consider yourself an optimist about the future of this world.

I have to be that way, because if I felt no resolution to all the conflicts could be achieved—that we would never have disarmament, a stable economy, or just social development in the world—how would I be able to fight for a lost cause? You must believe in what you are doing. I once read an article which I believe is true, stating that there are certain elements which keep people active for social change. One is enough anger at the evil in the world to keep you looking outward. Another is love: you have to be extremely attached to the people you want to save from danger. And the final one is hope: there is nothing worse than hopelessness.

And because I've seen tremendous growth in public opinion pressure for a more sensible world, I remain optimistic.

Yvonne See

August 1985

Yvonne See is a frail older woman who was obviously a great beauty in her youth and is still very striking. She is a small, slender person with finely etched features. A poet who lives in Paris, Yvonne uses language expansively and gestures to explain herself when she cannot find the appropriate English word for her descriptions.

Her involvement with the league goes back to World War II. Since then she has been active with the French section and for fifteen years served as WILPF's representative to UNESCO.

I came to the league because I'd had quite enough of war. That is the real reason, the first enormous reason. You know, my father had been in the war of 1914–18 because he was bound to—and then my husband, the war of 1939. We suffered very much from the [German] occupation.

In Paris?

Yes, but we couldn't stay in Paris because we are a Jewish family. So you know it was very difficult to live during those times in France. We had been in many places; we'd been in little villages in France. My children of course were very young at this moment.

How did you get involved with the league?

I've belonged to the league for so many years that it is difficult for me to answer. It was during the war that I met the president of the French section of the league in a little village in France where she was a refugee, along with my family and me. I found the idea of the league so beautiful, it corresponded so much to my beliefs, and I found Mme Gabrielle Duchene such a wonderful person, that I told her, "If I am alive after the war, I'll give you my name as a member." So I did. But you know in the first years I had many things to do; I had young children with me, and a husband. I attended some meetings, but I didn't do so much. Then I was elected by my friends as chairman of the French section. And I remained for many years the chairman. And at the same time, the international representative to UNESCO was Andrée Jouve, which she had been since 1947 when UNESCO began.

But she became nearly blind, and she asked me to help her. So I did. And, if I remember, in 1965 she asked to resign and that I should take her place, which I remained [in] for many years: 1965 to about 1980. I asked a friend of mine, Helene Berthoz, to help me in the first years, and then I asked the WILPF to name her in my place. But as we are bound to be more than one at UNESCO, even now I am often going around helping her because one thing happens in one hall while something else happens in another hall, so we must be two. And I am very interested by the work at UNESCO, especially in the preparatory meetings for symposiums. We are not very many in these little meetings, perhaps fifteen or twenty or even less, and there we can do really good work. Sometimes she or I have been coordinators of a symposium at UNESCO.

You were vice-chair of the league internationally at one time, weren't you?

In 1972 one vice-chair was missing because one took the place of the chairman. And they asked me to accept. I remember that I didn't want to accept because my English is not good and so it is difficult for me sometimes to present. But I was convinced. So I worked very hard during this time.

I think that I learned many things being in the league. First, I was bound to stick to the events, to know the facts. We must speak of real things that we know, or better not to speak at all. Of course, it helped me with the language too. I don't speak well but I understand and read English easily. Especially I remember at one of the congresses at Birmingham I was bound to make the opening speech, to speak in a public meeting. I was rather young at this moment—not that young, but rather young, and it was the first time I'd spoken in public in English. I had spoken sometimes in French but not very often. I was terribly moved, you know, because there were many, many people. I'd carefully prepared my speech and at the moment when I began to speak, a terrible storm broke out. And so people understood a little of it, but not all, but never mind. I had a great success, and so it showed me a new possibility.

And at UNESCO I have been speaking often, and that is rather difficult because we speak before people of very different opinions, from all religions, all cultures. So it came little by little. In the beginning I spoke very few words, but as time went by I had more confidence in myself and I knew better when to speak and when not to speak. Because you know I heard sometimes people speaking much too much, in my opinion, and I decided not to do that, not to say anything when you have nothing to say.

[Also] I've met people of many countries, and I've had so many contacts everywhere. Very often there are members of the league who come into my home to see me. And you know that really opens all the doors, and the ideas. On another side, I grew personally; you know, I like ideas, I like poetry, I am a poet. So it forced me to see reality. That was good for me because I was a little far from that, perhaps.

How large is the French section?

It's not very large. We are about three hundred, no more. Half in Paris and surroundings and half in the rest of France, especially in one or two provinces. We are working very much against nuclear tests in the Pacific. Very often we participate in demonstrations in the street. We are working very much too, when we can, for the liberation of political prisoners everywhere in the world. There's not a week when we don't write, we send aerograms here and there—to many countries right or left side. Amnesty [International] knows that we work generally for women, so when there are women prisoners, they always give us their names.

Do you consider yourself a feminist?

I frankly must say no. You know feminism has taken a very large development in the last years, in the younger generation. But I don't belong to the young generation, so it can be explained like that.

I consider women very well. If they'll do it, I think women can think and work in a very good way, so I am quite in admiration of women. But I can't say that I personally work very much for feminism. I quite agree with the ones who do. But I can't do everything. And, too, personally—because the personal life is something too— I have been living with my husband. He just died recently [1985]. So I had been accustomed to sharing my ideas with him—and with others: men and women, not only women.

Personally, I don't define that word "feminism" as many do. I think that feminism means for me being as a woman the best we can, in every sense of the word. In that sense, I am [a feminist], but of course if I had been bound to stay all the time at home doing the kitchen work—though I cook too—but nothing else, I should not like it at all. I had the chance to have an interesting life: I am something of a writer and a poet. I wrote theatrical plays which have been put on. And the league and family and many other things which make an interesting life. I think that I'm lucky in many ways, but I should like that every woman can blossom in her own way. I would like that women be educated everywhere, of course; that is the first thing. When we learn something, it's a pleasure, it's a gift. Every woman in every country ought to be able to read and to know something, but that's not the only thing. There's work, employment, many other matters.

I think that the league is taking a very good direction because it tries to know more of the Third World and that they know more of us too. But I'm sorry to say that when we speak of equality, for instance, it looks a little ridiculous when we see a woman starving and we here in our countries are doing interesting things. It's impossible to compare. So it's fine to speak of those beautiful words but they have to eat. Of course, I should like that it's a perfect world with equality, with justice, with all that. But we must realize that actually it's worse—you know what happens in so many African and Asian countries. And we say, "Oh, what can we do?" Well, I think each of us must do something, must do what we can, collectively and individually.

How do you keep from burning out, or getting disillusioned?

I think that we must never be hopeless. If we do we are lost. So many times, I've said to myself, I'm absolutely stupid to be tiring myself, working hard doing all that—why, why, why? When I see all the results in the world, why not let it be? I am old now, why be going on? But then I meet people who want to change the world, so I say to myself, no, I can't leave it to them as long as I can do something. When something is wrong, we must always try to correct what we can. Of course it's difficult sometimes to keep that hope, but nevertheless, I think there are some satisfactions to see that something good happens. I have told you that we try to get political prisoners released, and sometimes we receive letters from Amnesty, telling us the person has been liberated, or from the prisoners themselves. Oh, I feel better that day, you know?

Fujiko Isono

August 1985 and July 1986

Fujiko Isono is a Japanese scholar who has been affiliated with the league for about forty years, primarily on the international level, but also in the Japanese, British, and French sections. After establishing herself in the field of Japanese family studies, Fujiko decided that it was unwise to remain in the same field as her husband and turned her interests to Mongolian studies. Though maintaining an amicable partnership with her husband in Japan, she then spent a number of years working in Britain and France.

From Fujiko's life experiences, one might conclude that the

boundaries between "traditional" and "liberated" women are really quite blurred.

I was born in 1918, the last year of the First World War. When I was married, my husband's specialty was civil law, and he was most interested in the sociological side of family law. But it was impossible to do any scientific studies on Japanese society at that time, 1942, because it was still under a military government. So we went to Inner Mongolia to do field research on the customary laws of the nomadic peoples of Mongolia. Our study was cut short because of the Japanese surrender, and we were repatriated.

Actually, we had only been able to do this research because Inner Mongolia was under Japanese occupation. Though we thought at the time we weren't actually cooperating with the Japanese militarists, later I realized that as Japanese, we couldn't help being identified with the occupying people by those who were occupied—although personally, they treated us very nicely.

Then when I went back to Japan, it was under American occupation, and of course that was different from a full-time occupation. But still, this experience of being first the occupying and then the occupied made me very uncomfortable.

After the war, when we returned to Japan, there was a very drastic change in Japanese society. Because of the new civil code, the Japanese family system had been completely altered. There was a great deal of unhappiness and a lack of communication between parents and children during this time, as the parents had been educated when the morals were very different. The children, however, were taught to discuss matters, and when they did, the parents thought they were being disobedient. So both sides wanted affectionate relations but didn't get the responses they expected and there was misunderstanding.

I was interested in this because I myself had been a problem child. Starting in my teenage years, my mother, a very traditional woman, wanted me to be a very docile, "marriageable" Japanese lady, accomplished in housework. On the other hand, I started to read and got interested in English juvenile literature, Louisa May Alcott and such. I wanted my mother to be like Mrs. March in *Little*

Women. I was so influenced by the Western ideas of mother-daughter relationships that I thought my mother didn't love me at all. I was really the black sheep in the family. It was only when I grew up that I understood I was asking something impossible from her.

After the war, I saw my own experience happening on a nationwide level. I published one rather popular book for people worrying about this sort of thing and one handbook for students of sociology and social work. My degree was actually in English literature, but luckily that doesn't matter so much in Japan.

What prompted you to begin doing peace work?

Well, after the war I felt quite keenly about peace. Also, some time after the war ended my husband went back to Mongolia to attend a wedding. It was at that time that the Soviet Union declared war on Japan, and he was captured. He was missing completely for two and a half years, with no news or anything. Then all of a sudden he just turned up; he had been repatriated. There were so many women whose husbands never came back, so I felt perhaps a little guilty that mine did. Not guilty, but as if I wanted to do something for them.

Then Miss Tano Jodai, who was one of the earliest Japanese members of the league and was president of the university where I attended and later lectured, suggested I join the league. I admired her very much, and so I studied the constitution and found I agreed with many of the ideas. That was in 1952 or so. But I can't say I was really active; I only helped her with the correspondence. It wasn't until 1954 when I went to Liverpool on a fellowship that I actually became part of a local group. Then I became very much involved with the league.

I also think that the experience of having been in an occupied and occupying country had something to do with my work for peace. I remember once I was on my way to India; this was before the days of cheap airplanes and we were going there by boat. It was a British boat and so we stopped in Singapore and other colonial ports. These were the British colonies that had been occupied by Japanese troops. I had a British friend, a professor, who was eager for me to meet one of the local ladies in Singapore when we stopped there. But when I tried to contact her, she sent me a message that said, "I'm very sorry but I just cannot bring myself to meet a Japanese." I understood completely, and at that time it was driven into my mind and heart that even though I had felt I was different from the Japanese militarists, I couldn't claim to be dissociated from the things my country had done. And that is one thing which attracted me to the league—because we were speaking not for governments but to governments. Of course, under the military government there was no freedom of speech, but now we can speak.

Will you tell me about your work with Owen Lattimore?

While working on these family problems, I had decided it wasn't too wise for a husband and wife to be working in the same field for too long. It was about that same time I met Owen Lattimore, a specialist in China studies. Lattimore had been one of the main targets of McCarthyism in the United States. It's still a mystery as to why McCarthy singled out Lattimore except that he was a China specialist and was saying publicly that it was a mistake for the United States to get involved in the civil war between the Chinese Communists and Chiang Kai-shek. Knowing the Chinese peasantry, Lattimore knew the Communists had the popular support and Chiang Kai-shek did not. But this campaign carried out by McCarthy only succeeded in making Lattimore much more of a public policy figure than he really was.

Of course I had heard of him because during and after my stay in Mongolia, I had read all the books that I could find on Mongolia and he had written many of them. Anyway, after I met him, I was given this opportunity to work with him so I decided to go back to Mongolian studies, and together he and I translated the memoirs of one of the most prestigious of the Living Buddhas in Outer Mongolia. More recently, I was compiling Lattimore's China memoirs. So I have spent a number of years living in Britain and Paris working on these things.

And your husband is in Japan? You must have a very supportive husband.

He's quite understanding and supportive. He's retired now from full professorship but is still lecturing. When we meet, we talk about our respective work and interests.

It sounds very much as if you've lived your life as an independent woman. Would you consider yourself a feminist?

Of course the league started with feminism—women's emancipation, peace, and the economic conditions for peace that were represented by Jane Addams and Hull House in Chicago. It was that combination that attracted me to the league. But I think we have to realize—or remember—that feminism started among middle-class women who didn't have the same rights as their menfolks of the same class had. But at the same time lower-class men didn't have many of those rights either. So that is something we have to be careful of when we talk about feminism and equality: the question of where we draw the lines between discrimination against a class or race or sex.

I do think that in general women are always having a harder time than men, and I think women should be given equal opportunity. But I don't think that every woman should have to go out and work, especially mothers. As it is now, the men aren't paid enough, and most of the women have to supplement their income with their cheap labor. I would like to see a world in which women would not have to work until their children were at least three years old, and then they could work part-time.

Ida Harsloff

August 1986

Ida Harsloff is a weaver and an arts and crafts teacher who lives just outside Copenhagen with her two young sons and their father. Although she has lived with the same man since 1973, they have never married, as she does not believe in marriage as an institution. Instead, the couple have struggled for a partnership that allows each to maintain their individuality and to share equally in the parenting of their children.

Like a few other women interviewed for this book, Ida's connection to WILPF originated with her mother, who was active in the Danish section since before World War II. Coming into WILPF through a mother or other close female relative is apparently a fairly common way to do so.

Ida's own identity as a "WILPF'er" came much more recently: in 1984, after attending the league's international summer school at Cartigny, Switzerland, she became an organizer both of the summer schools and in her own community.

I was born into the WILPF, so without knowing it, I've been with it all my life because my mother was always active. They had lots of meetings in each others' homes, especially during the war [World War II]. I wasn't very old but it was fascinating and a little scary, listening to them. When I was thirteen or fourteen, my mother had young Germans coming up to Denmark for WILPF, as part of an exchange program to break down the enemy images. It was hard to find housing for them because we'd just been at war with Germany. That's my first conscious memory of being involved in peace work.

As soon as I could, I joined WILPF and started going to the annual section meetings. But I must say, boys interested me more at that time. So I didn't become really active until I was grown up and settled away from home in Copenhagen.

Then I started my own family and sort of got out of WILPF again. I think it had something to do with my mother being so active in WILPF as she was. It's always hard to have a clever and well-doing mother because you're always being compared. So, actually, I didn't become really active until she died, only two and a half years ago. My real life in WILPF started then.

Unfortunately, I think WILPF in Denmark hasn't really changed with the times. The questions they discussed when I was a child listening in on the meetings are more or less the same as they are talking about now. I think Danish WILPF has tried too hard to keep the image they had thirty years ago. You can't be a progressive peace movement and stay the same. That's why it's been difficult to get young people interested in WILPF. When you first join, unless you have a very strong opinion, you go in and do as they've always done.

So then, what prompted you to get more involved?

Obviously, since my mother had always done it, peace work was almost like reading and writing to me. But somehow it was always still a little abstract until I joined the [WILPF] summer school in Cartigny two years ago. There I met Anissa Najjar from Lebanon, who told me how her daughter was killed in a raid by the Israelis. And I talked to Sundari Ravindran, who told about her educational work with women in Madras [India]. We were all so eager to help and said, "What can we do?" She told us to look in our own backyards first—that they would ask for help when they needed it. That really taught me something: we're coming from the Nordic countries thinking we'll save everybody.

After that I *had* to do peace work: I couldn't help it. My participation at Cartigny was so inspiring to me, and then I was asked to help arrange the next summer school. I think the schools are so fantastic: the important thing is it all happens in a group where you, as a start, get to know each other. We have introductions that go really deep—not just your names, but really tell about yourself. So we try to get an understanding of each other in order to have a base. One needs to feel so much at home that she can cry or laugh without feeling shy or stupid, because quite a bit of what you hear is disturbing. To create that feeling of trust is important at the summer school because that's what you take home with you, and that's what makes you go on.

Other than your work with the summer schools internationally, what do you do locally?

In our little branch, we focus on getting people interested in what's going on in the world. We have a half-hour radio program on every week; not only from WILPF but quite often it's one of us who's speaking there. We give background on the Hiroshima and Nagasaki bombings, the nuclear tests at Mururua, women's peace camps and such as that. We've found out that if you talk to people about peace, they get scared. There are two reasons for this: first, they don't want to hear about these upsetting things, and second, they feel ashamed about all the things they don't know.

That first time I went to Cartigny, I felt I had to go home and crusade. So right away I went to my neighbor and said, "You must come with me to this WILPF meeting." She looked at me and said, "That's not for me. I've got enough to do with my family." And so I knew that was the wrong way. Then the next time there was a WILPF meeting, I said, "I've promised to bake a cake and I can't. Would you do it for me?" Then I came back and told her they'd loved the cake. And she said, "Who was there and what were they talking about?" And I told her, a teacher, a nurse, and they were talking about Greenham Common. So the next time I asked her to come, she did. I must say, she's not one of our most active members, but she did get interested, she knows what it's about and she's started reading. So I learned that you have to start where people are if you want to get them involved.

Would you classify the league as a feminist organization?

Certainly not in Denmark. I wish that it were, and I think maybe it is in some other countries. But here we've thrown away the "Women's" and are only the International League for Peace and Freedom. The reason we did it was thinking if we are going to accomplish anything, we have to do it with the men. And I actually think that I agreed with that idea at the time (1969), but I don't anymore. I seriously believe that the time of men is running out, and that now we have to find our own feminist way of living on this earth. Not that all women are angels, not at all. But we have a sensitivity that I find in very few men—and a belief that what we feel is right. That's one of the things that's needed in the world.

It's important to have organizations where only women come together. A whole lot of things start to happen when men are there as well. A lot of women shut up, and the ways they've been brought up start to get in their way. Having been brought up in a family where male dominance wasn't that big—my mother went off to peace conferences all over the world while my father took over the home—I know that if I can feel that inhibition, quite a lot of other women do too.

And your feelings on nonviolence? How do you feel about that?

Until I really got into peace work, I was an absolute pacifist, and I still believe things should be worked out without violence. But when I began to learn about South Africa, about Central America, I couldn't stand there and tell those people they shouldn't fight back. I'm very split on this. I don't believe in violence, but it's also very easy to sit in a country like Denmark and say you're a pacifist.

What keeps you with WILPF?

I think I'm actually more of an international WILPF'er than a Danish one. I like getting to know women from all over the world and the idea of being part of a worldwide organization: I hope someday we'll truly be that. Working from the same basic point of view in so many countries is like having an extra family. And in spite of the fact that I think WILPF in Denmark is a bit conservative and living in the past, I still believe it's the best organization around in giving out the information about what's going on in the world.

In my own life, I'm stronger than I'd imagined I'd be. I believe in myself more, and WILPF has helped in that. When you speak about things that mean something to you, it makes you grow stronger. I always wanted to be able to look in the mirror and feel okay about the way I've lived, and I feel that I can do that.

Anissa Najjar

July 1986

Anissa Najjar lives in Beirut, Lebanon, where her prominent Druze family dates back six centuries. She first made contact with the league because of its Middle East mission in the late 1950s. Since then she has struggled to focus the organization's attention on the plight of Palestinians in the region, and on the effects of the Arab-Israeli conflict on her country and those around it.

In June 1982 Anissa suffered from the aggression in a most brutal and personal way. While she was away in New York attending the UN Second Special Session on Disarmament for WILPF, her eldest daughter, Sana, Lebanon's first female agricultural engineer, was killed in a small village outside Beirut—the victim of an Israeli bombing raid. Understandably, Anissa is bitter toward Israel, but she maintains open dialogue with the league's Israeli members and adamantly encourages a Middle East peace settlement.

I was born in 1915. I was raised by my mother because my father died when I was small. He had served with the Allies in World War I. So my mother was always against war.

She was involved with the Arab Women's Federation, and she used to take me with her there when I was only eight years old. I had nothing to do but listen to what the women were discussing, so my feminism started from there.

Here in Lebanon we were always suffering from outside control. First we had the French mandate, then the British. So I've been complaining all my life. I was brought up in the national school, where we were able to speak out, unlike those brought up in the American or French schools, who were taught to be pro-U.S. or -French. But we were pro-Lebanon.

Being a Druze makes me an ardent defender of justice because we are raised like this. We belong to a religion that believes in the "culture of the mind": that logical reasoning is the right thing. We don't believe in superstition or miracles, just in one straight line between us and God. So the idea of justice comes from reason, and when I see a wrong being done, whether to me or to you, I must speak up. The Druze are known not to start fights but to defend themselves, but I myself am an absolute pacifist. All these years, I've spent negotiating among different groups and different points of view.

What attracted you to WILPF?

It was an international platform to speak out about all these injustices in Lebanon. I thought maybe they could help us. And it was appealing to me just to get support for my ideas.

When Madeline Bouchereau came to Lebanon in 1958, she got my name, and I had her meet with the members of several Lebanese women's organizations. [Bouchereau traveled through the Middle East on a fact-finding mission for the league.] Later when she wrote and asked me to form a section, I decided to do it. But there was a revolution here in 1959, and so we didn't get settled until 1960. There were about ten or twelve of us belonging in 1962 when I attended the WILPF congress in California—all Lebanese at that time, no Palestinians.

So you had been doing work with women in the community for some time?

Yes, ever since I was a child, really. Now I head the women's organizations of Lebanon; we are twenty-six societies. The first women's society was founded in 1850, and then later foreign societies such as the YWCA [Young Women's Christian Association] came in. At that time the men were always busy with politics and fighting the outside control; women were not engaged in politics in those days. So their work was social work: starting orphanages, kindergartens, homes for the aged. By 1930 women started to demand compulsory education from the British mandate, and that same year the Lebanese Arab Women's Federation came into being. The men didn't recognize women's social work as patching up the areas their politics missed until 1952, when they started the Ministry of Social Affairs. They didn't recognize us for this.

That's why we are feminists, because the men just think we automatically do all these things. When it comes to benefits, we get nothing. So now we are asking for several demands. For example, in the past a woman wasn't able to travel without the consent of her husband. And even up to now, a woman can only start a business with the consent of her husband; we are still fighting this one.

Now we are telling the men, "You have failed. You have only brought wars. Hand the reins to us and you will see that we will stop it."

When you say "we," do you mean WILPF members?

In a way. But every time you do something in the name of WILPF, they call you a Communist. So most of the time I speak for myself as an individual. When it's something that needs to be done as an organization, I say, "Village Welfare Society." We're the same people, mostly. We are the social work part of WILPF. In the past ten years the president of the Republic issued all these new regulations, and one says that all affiliates of international organizations are officially canceled. So we stopped speaking publicly of WILPF. We didn't want our permit canceled. Later on, they did cancel it, actually, but last year [1985] those regulations were overturned. And now we can speak as WILPF again.

And will you tell me a little bit about your section?

We have some Palestinian members, but we have no contact with the PLO and no direct contact with Palestinians in the occupied territories. We take the intellectual approach. We are only activists sometimes when it is needed, but we are always publishing something or talking to people. For example, I am organizing this women's march to the south to tell Israel to withdraw from Lebanon. There are many idealists in this organization. And I'm one of them.

Kay Camp

June 1985, April 1986, and April 1987

Kay Camp is a quiet, soft-spoken, and unpretentious person, but the intensity of her personality is reflected in her piercing gaze. Though she is small and thin, she gives the impression of sturdiness. Still, when she is sitting in the simple but elegant living room of her home near Philadelphia, it is hard to imagine her being dragged from the White House lawn by police. That was in 1975, when she took part in a protest against the Ford administration's continued military aid to Saigon.

In fact, Kay has been involved in a number of nonviolent direct actions and actual or potential arrests. She has traveled to conflict-torn areas such as Vietnam, Chile, and El Salvador, to name a few, on fact-finding missions for WILPF. And she has held a medley of leadership positions in the league, as well as having been responsible for helping to organize a number of new sections. During her two terms as international president and in subsequent writings and discussions, she has persistently challenged WILPF to examine its relationship to feminism. These activities and others have made her known to many WILPF members all over the world, and women in numerous interviews mentioned her as someone they deeply admired.

Perhaps because of her shyness or perhaps because of her other-centeredness, Kay finds it difficult to talk about her life and activities. It took many hours to draw from her the information presented here.

I was born just before they declared the armistice in World War I. So I grew up with the idea that peace is possible, and that's been very useful because it doesn't apply so much today. I had a very sheltered life growing up, a very happy childhood on the farm. I was pretty innocent right up through college about the ways of the world. It's traditional for sons of farmers to carry on the farmwork, and as I was an only child for six years, I fit right into that formula. My dad didn't make an issue of the fact that I was a girl, and nobody else did either. I just naturally took to the barns and the woods more than to dolls, books, and indoor activities. Later, when I went to a girls' school, it became important for me to demonstrate some advantages from my background because I felt like an outsider among the city girls. So because I could drive a truck, I was able to take them on rides all over the farm, which was quite a thrill for them and for me. So gradually I got the feeling I could do certain things well, although I was terribly, painfully shy and could hardly stand to speak in class, for example.

Yet now you've spoken out in the highest of places.

It's the power of the message. If I feel I have something to say, that overcomes my natural reticence. And though I never get over that anxiety, it has become easier through the years.

How did the message of peace come to hold such power for you?

World War II was such a devastating experience, one horror after another, including the need to be separated from my husband while raising our first-born child. Although we escaped without terrible sacrifices, I followed the news very closely and I remember every morning hearing the reports on the radio: how many U.S. bombers took off from Britain and what cities they'd dropped bombs on in Germany, how many tons of bombs, the extent to which the city below had been destroyed, and how many fewer planes had returned. It doesn't take much imagination to fill in the details of human suffering. So I determined even before the nuclear bomb was dropped that I had become at least philosophically a pacifist. And I responded to the only invitation I've ever answered over the radio or television, asking, "Would you like to help prevent World War III?" sent out by the United World Federalists.

I became a charter member. And over the years I spoke and helped organize for them, and for the Friends Peace Committee, though I was not yet a Quaker. Then one day I happened to pick up a copy of *Four Lights*, the U.S. WILPF publication, and immediately I thought, this is the organization for me. I joined in 1958. A few years later I helped form a local branch. Somehow I got involved in national board meetings, and since then it's been one thing after another.

I remember one day sitting in my kitchen with a good friend, a German who had suffered through the war and was a devoted pacifist. I was debating whether to take a teaching job (I was at home with my children at the time), run for the WILPF national board, or continue working with our local branch. She said, "You mean you have a chance to work nationally and you're thinking of not doing it?" That definitely influenced my decision to get into the national work, which led to the international. I never envisioned that, and I think it's made my life much more expansive than I ever thought it would be. But it's interesting too that after all these years I'm back to working with the local branch, though I'm still a member of the international Executive Committee. I think the local is the basis of why WILPF has lasted so long, because that's where much of our strength is.

What was it that drew you to WILPF?

It seemed such a natural place for me, I'm not sure I thought much about it. And I just loved the women I met there. To come to meetings and hear all these knowledgeable, articulate, and friendly women was an inspiration. I very much wanted to be a part of that. I certainly admired some of the older women—Dorothy Hutchinson, for example—so much so that when I was asked to be national president, it was overwhelming for me to try and see myself in an equal position with her. She was brilliant and fearless, although she later confessed to me that she too had to overcome a streak of shyness. That further motivated me to try to do the same.

And later you even ran for office in the U.S. government.

I had finished two terms as president of the section in 1971 and wasn't certain where I was going to apply my energy next. I had become quite an ardent feminist and was speaking about how women's input was needed by society, how women had to get involved in politics, and so on, and I talked myself right into jumping into a congressional race. Also, I was very concerned about Vietnam, and we were getting more engulfed there all the time. Our local congressman was a middle-of-the-roader who supported Nixon.

It was probably the most intensive ten months of my life. I announced in January and went to every little party precinct meeting to get the Democrats' support. I did get it, and I won the primary but not the general election. We got very good press, though we had to "educate" them to the fact that they shouldn't call me Mrs. William Camp.

Feminism is obviously very important to you. Will you tell me about your struggles with that, particularly within WILPF?

During the period of quiescence in the feminist movement, I think many women joined WILPF, as I did, because they felt comfortable, they felt that yes, there is a logic to women and peace, but without much understanding of their own motivation in doing so, and therefore, their own ability to contribute something special as women. I've wanted WILPF to articulate why we're important as women, what it means in terms of breaking down barriers: things we're pretty good at as women. I'm thinking of the fact that we're not as cowed by rules, nor by a system we've had no input in setting up in the first place. So we need to understand ourselves and our strengths in order to maximize them. And feminism includes the ability to think holistically, to relate to people across political and other barriers, to have no need to take over a situation we're put into but to just be part of it.

All of this was a gradual evolutionary process for me to awake to these ideas, but I know I was pretty certain of them by the time I held international office and I did make a plea that we take up this issue. I think it's being done, in some places more than others. I think as a whole, the organization is really examining the significance of the relationship between women and peace. And we constantly have to reiterate that it's a human world we're looking for, not just a balance of male and female but the flowering of our human potential. It's for all people, but women do have a special contribution to make. I get a little tired of hearing about women's role in the struggle; it's more than a role. Our contributions are really major.

And do you consider yourself a pacifist?

I do, and yet I have some problems with a pacifism that fails to understand or support people's need to take up arms in a situation that is itself violent. I support the African National Congress very much, for example. I think sometimes we pacifists tend to be pretty self-righteous and outside the problem. Violence is a very real, total, gripping thing, and what right do we have to tell others they should not take hostile actions when their own children are starving? I've met enough people around the world in that situation to be very conscious of it. First, we have to ask ourselves if we've done everything we can to promote nonviolent solutions before we condemn others. Not everyone has been exposed, as I have, for instance, to the philosophy of nonviolence and to the power of it. So we need to do a great deal more in that respect.

And I know you've put that philosophy into practice in quite a few acts of nonviolent civil disobedience. What led you to do that?

I guess I've always thought of it in a positive way, as "moral obedience." And that combines with a constant awareness that elected leaders are really only people like us, and we shouldn't be so intimidated by them. I respect law, I think we need it, and when it's democratically arrived at, I think it's a potent tool. But there are also many unjust laws that should be changed. Also, I do suffer from the need for approval so it's hard for me to do things that aren't popular, but I can put that aside when it's something I deeply believe needs to be done.

And when the point of a civil disobedience action is very clear, when conditions are right, I think it can be an effective organizing tool. It seems to be increasing these days. I know when I engage in it, I have always felt a great sense of satisfaction that this was the right thing to do.

How has your work for peace affected your personal life?

I've learned so much and met so many interesting people. I'd be quite unhappy if I didn't have some outlet for all I've seen in my travels and experiences. It's a terrible, complex problem that we face, and it's hard to convince oneself that a single person can have any impact on it at all. But for me, just as a matter of self-expression, it's essential.

On the other side, I probably would've gone back to teaching if

I had not gotten involved in politics, not that teaching isn't itself political work. So I've made my own choices, but I do feel some resentment. I had really hoped that by now things would be better; instead, they're worse. I always keep hoping there's this one little hump we have to get over when things will start to change: an election, an arms agreement. I keep waiting for us to get over that hump so I can go back to living a normal life. I'd really enjoy more reading, gardening, time with my children and grandchildren, and travel just for the fun of it. Each year I keep telling myself I'm going to cut back a bit. Well, it hasn't happened yet. But I think that one little step will happen someday, as soon as we get enough people working at it.

What keeps you going?

I've got a lot invested in it now, haven't I? It's become my career, and yet it's not a profession. But I've come to accept the fact that I don't have a job, though I do really work. In an informal way and on varied occasions I am teaching.

At times I get very discouraged, but I think basically I'm an optimist because I keep working at it. That's the evidence.

Edith Ballantyne

September 1985

For the better part of two decades, Edith Ballantyne has been known by many as the backbone of the Women's International League for Peace and Freedom. She came to the league's Geneva office in 1968 as a part-time volunteer who had spent the previous ten years as a housewife raising four children. From that modest beginning, Edith took an office that was little more than a post-office box and developed it into a flourishing international center. She became the league's international secretary-general and in 1976 was elected president of the Conference of Non-Governmental Organizations at the UN. Edith's active role in the UN's NGO community has given both the league and her, personally, a certain international prominence, and she has acquired quite a reputation as a mediator. Yet, she remains a rather unassuming and down-to-earth person who never avoids hard work.

My association with the league goes back to 1941 in Toronto, Canada. I was one of several thousand Sudetan refugees from Hitler nazism who was able to get out of Czechoslovakia under the 1938 Munich agreement the British made with Hitler. We were helped to get to England and from there were sent to British dominions. My family was among the first fifty to go to Canada in the spring of 1939. We entered as "landed immigrants."

The conditions of our "settling" were bad and highly exploitative. None of us were farmers, so of course we didn't last long in the north of British Columbia where we had been taken. So one by one we left. I followed my father and brother to Toronto in 1941 when I was eighteen and was placed as a maid/cook/child nurse in a mansion. I had very little knowledge of English—or of housekeeping, for that matter—or even exactly where I was in the city.

One day the doorbell rang and the woman who was standing there introduced herself as being from the Women's International League for Peace and Freedom. I found out later that the league in Canada, having always been concerned with civil liberties, had been following the situation of the refugees. They had a settlement house à la Jane Addams that they supported, and they were very anxious to get all the Sudetan Germans to come there and meet with them.

There I met many others like myself who had drifted to Toronto. Since my arrival, I had not been able to contact my father or my brother, but there they were that evening at the settlement house. The league women helped us all in every way possible. Some of the women really taught me English. They gave me lessons practically every day, and they also took up my whole working situation with my employer and eventually found other work for me so I could get out of this rather bad situation. Anyway, that is how I first got to know about the league. If it hadn't been for these women I don't know what would have happened to me. So I have a very special connection with the league, which is very personal.

I lost contact with them after I moved to Montreal in 1945. Then I married there and came over to Switzerland in 1948. I worked for about five years with the World Health Organization until the birth of my second child. So for the next fourteen or fifteen years I was at home looking after four children.

How did you get reconnected with WILPF?

When my youngest was about twelve, I decided to look around for something else to do; there was never really a question as to whether I would go back into the labor market with the educational costs of four children planning to go to university in Canada. By chance, really, I met Elisabeth Stahle, who was the secretary at the WILPF's Geneva office. So I came and helped a little bit here and there. Then they asked me to help with *Pax et Libertas*, and eventually they put me on a part-time salary. But I always looked on it as just filling in. They also had discussions going on about whether to keep the Geneva office, and I was asked whether it would be wise to move the office and, if not, how it might be structured to function better.

Ever since I had been helping out, I had been struck by how little the organization used its international office. It was getting nowhere near the value of its investment and was not at all developing its potential in filling its need for an effective international center. It needed that if it wanted to play a significant role in the peace movement and if it wanted to have an impact on the UN and the international nongovernmental community. Its own history showed how important a role the Maison Internationale had played between 1919 and World War II; for various reasons that role had diminished. WILPF had very small financial possibilities, and many of the league members, particularly the elected officers, had full-time careers in which WILPF was not number-one priority.

I presented proposals to the Executive Committee which included the establishment of an executive post and increased UN and NGO work out of the office. When they offered me the post in late 1969, I felt a little guilty and had mixed feelings about accepting it. But no one else materialized to take the job, so I carried on and began to build up the office, with the help of others, of course. Though I had originally drifted into it, the league's international work got hold of me and became a real commitment.

How did you manage to juggle your commitment to your husband and children and this increasing job responsibility?

Well, our children were pretty well grown by then. They had always shared in the housework, and they began to do more of that. Then one after the other left for university so that by 1975 my husband and I were alone. My husband had retired by then and worked only on short-term assignments. As he reduced his freelance work, he took on more responsibility for the house. He said that, after all, I had stayed home for fifteen years looking after the family so now he could do the same. I have a very supportive husband.

So you were basically by yourself at the office?

I had some voluntary help occasionally, but by and large I was alone for almost fourteen years. In 1972 the UN and NGO representation fell on the office here, too. So I began to follow the meetings as best I could. And I became very interested in that aspect of the work.

When I look back, I wonder, well, why did I become so oriented toward the UN and all the activities of the NGOs? I think it was partly because I saw that the WILPF could make a real contribution at that level and could also draw benefit from the cooperation. On many issues we had a clear position, but often we were able to also be the persons sort of in between the right and the left, as it were. We were often able to play a role—I wouldn't say mediators because we're not mediators. I think it's more being there as a link. We're not necessarily married to a particular phrase or a particular procedure. I think we very often see what the main goal is and then we try and find how we can get different people to come and work for the goal. And therefore I think we're much more flexible in our demands and willing to give a little in the interest of making a small advance to reach our ultimate aims. You know, women never give up. I think we're more patient, maybe more imaginative. As a mother you can't give up. When your children call, you respond to them and you keep responding until you find a solution to their problems. I think it's a skill women have learned in centuries of experience; we shouldn't look down on it, and we shouldn't lose it either, but put it into practice more in political life.

One thing about the league is how it has brought and held together women of many different backgrounds and opinions. You must have a lot of experience with the challenges sometimes involved in that.

I was born into a political family, very active in the Social Democratic party. For a number of years in Canada, I worked for what is the equivalent of the British Labor party, the Provincial Labor party. My first congress in the league—which was in India in 1971—I must say I was truly bewildered, because I was so used to having these very clear political positions, whereas in the league there were big arguments but once the vote was taken it was accepted by everyone. Maybe there were lots of people unhappy and they would continue to try and change the policies, but meanwhile that was it. I was not too comfortable with this; yet I was impressed with the way the women there were discussing the issues. I think for the first time I realized that the league obviously had to work differently than the political circles I was used to, in which there were fewer deep differences.

Very often when I myself get really heated, because I have very strong opinions about things too, I sort of think back to those discussions. Even though we disagreed, it was possible to discuss and to disagree still and to continue to work for a better world. I found that something new in my life. I think it is this ability—to work in the interest of the community and not to further our own personal aims—that has made it possible for the league to persevere and to be seen by the UN and others as an organization that can make a special contribution to international thinking. The UN may not take our advice or agree with us, but they rarely go ahead and do things without including us among the organizations whose opinions they seek.

What about your terms as president of CONGO and your role during the UN Decade for Women?

As I said, the NGO work has always interested me; it was also kind of a challenge for a women's peace organization to prove itself in that community. When it comes to decision-making places, women's voices are often not heard there. For instance, many of the permanent representatives accredited to the UN and who work in the NGO committees are women, but when it comes to elected offices, men are voted to them. I believe women have skills in bringing people together, and they are always willing to work hard so I thought we as women have to begin to assert ourselves and even introduce a notion of "affirmative action."

Well, I myself had worked hard in the NGO community for about six years. With groups such as the World Council of Churches and the World Federation of UN Associations, we worked for widening and strengthening the base of the NGO community, particularly for the full participation of organizations with strong constituencies in socialist countries. So then in 1976 I was asked to present myself as a candidate for presidency of CONGO. I was encouraged by many women representatives, but I was also seen with suspicion because of my effort for cooperation with groups close to socialist positions. But I was elected in a two-way competition and then reelected for a second three-year term in 1979. I think during my six years as president, the groundwork for closer NGO cooperation was laid. It was not easy at first, and many resisted the change. But bit by bit we put a new structure in place and began to work on improving the UN/NGO relationship.

The CONGO has a membership of about two hundred very diverse international organizations [out of a total of some eight hundred in consultative status with the UN Economic and Social

Council]. When we prepared the 1979 assembly, which I took chief responsibility for, I succeeded in getting the UN secretary-general to address the opening session. I believe that during that period the UN began to realize more fully the importance of NGOs, so circumstances helped us. They began to recognize that UN projects needed public support which the NGOs could help mobilize.

I had really not been sure if I should run again because it took a lot of time, and I realized I was neglecting the league's work to some extent. On the other hand, that period made contacts for the league that would not have otherwise been possible. [She was unanimously reelected.]

During my second term, a lot of my energy went into support of the mid-term conference of the UN Decade for Women. The CONGO board established a committee to plan and finance an NGO forum to be held in conjunction with the UN conference at Copenhagen in July 1980. As president you always work on two levels: one is to see that the forum runs properly, and then of course to make sure that the NGOs have adequate access to the UN conference and are being treated properly. That took a lot of my time, and when it became really difficult, they [the UN] offered that I should speak [to the conference] on behalf of the NGO community. We decided to accept this opportunity but not to speak on issues; rather, the main thing was to make them realize that they had to allow the individual NGOs to speak. And we all worked together on a statement that everyone could live with, but that wasn't so general as to be completely meaningless.

We were again very active in preparing for the world conference to mark the end of the Decade for Women, held in Nairobi in 1985. WILPF was a member of the planning committee for the NGO forum, and I was convener of the committee on peace. We worked to ensure that peace was given due attention both at the UN conference and at the forum. We proposed the formation of a peace center, which evolved into a "peace tent" for purely technical reasons. But it was the tent that caught the imagination of all and actually became the symbol of Nairobi. It was good to see the connections the vast majority of women in Nairobi made between peace, development, and equality.

What about the relationship between women and peace? What do you think about that?

When I first began to work for WILPF, the question of women's rights and equality were not issues dealt with separately in the league's program. We opposed and still oppose all forms of discrimination. The discussions, though, were whether WILPF should continue as a women's organization, and the answer usually was yes, because women still needed an organization in which they could gain experience, self-confidence, and so on.

There has been a change, largely forced by the growth of the feminist movement in the 1970s and 1980s. The women's decade helped bring us back to the strong feminist origin of WILPF. Many of us take participation in public and world affairs for granted even though we have to assert our rights as women constantly. It took me a while to realize this and to take proper note of what the feminists were saying. I was engrossed in working for the prevention of war and for justice in the broad economic and social sense, which concerns both men and women. I didn't pay much attention to the double discrimination most women suffer and that fighting this had a place in work for peace, particularly in a women's peace group. In my generation women had to work side by side with men in the resistance movement against Nazi occupation and later in the fight for justice for all peoples. Younger women had to remind us that the struggle for peace and justice must include the struggle to eliminate discrimination and violence against women because it is all part of the same fight. I have been making it my responsibility to get this message to my male colleagues in the peace movement.

Are you optimistic about the movement's chances for success?

I wouldn't say I'm optimistic, at least not all the time. But I have great faith in human beings. I see all the dangers, but then I've lived with these dangers all my life. And there are advances: look at the solidarity that exists in Latin America, in South Africa, on such a scale as we never saw before.

I guess I am optimistic. People made this world the way it is; people can change it.

Ruth Gleissberg

August 1985

At seventy-four, Ruth Gleissberg is a small, youthful-looking woman with twinkling gray eyes and a warm smile. She has been involved in social change activities for more than half a century, beginning in the early years of Hitler when as a German Jew she left her homeland and worked from England to strengthen what she saw as the "other" Germany.

Ruth came into the WILPF more recently, only in 1970. But since that time she has been a central figure in both the German section and the international, having been section liaison to the international for ten years and section secretary, as well as serving on the international Executive Committee and—more recently—beginning a German translation of *Pax et Libertas*, WILPF's quarterly international newspaper.

I'm a doctor's daughter. My father died in the First World War so I lived with my brother and with my mother. I finished high school at eighteen years of age, but I didn't go to university. Instead, I went into training to be a kindergarten teacher. That was a very important time for me in my development: it was 1931, I think. Just at the time when I finished that, Hitler came into power. And I'm half Jewish. I had participated in political work in a small socialist group which was trying to get the unity of the working class against Hitler, who was obviously getting stronger and stronger. We were left-wing socialists, I would say.

How did you come to socialism—through your family?

Not in the least. I was in a wonderful "free youth group." They were sort of socialists and I was very influenced by them when I was young and still in school. That was a start, I think. I even considered myself a communist—I didn't know what it was but [she laughs] I was very radical. Anyway, after the training was finished and the group was forbidden, naturally, a lot of them had to emigrate. And I got to know a German family that was also half Jewish with two small children. They had to emigrate to Britain and I was employed by them to look after the children. And that's how I got to Britain and worked with my same political group there. Many had emigrated but there were English groups as well. It was sort of a small party, socialism on ethical grounds, not Marxist. In my free time I was always at the office of this party. Then I married an Englishman so I was English afterwards, which was very useful after the war started. I was not one of those who were taken into camps. Many of our people were, of course.

I worked in an immigration office and later on I learned a little metalwork, became a metalworker, and worked in an aircraft factory all during the war. But I lived with my friends from the political group and spent all my free time with them. We organized meetings—all the immigrants from Czechoslovakia, Poland, and so on; together we organized meetings of all of them to show that there were different Germans from those who ruled the country at that time. We published quite a number of pamphlets on subjects such as anti-nazism, economic plans for the future of Germany, educational plans, and so on. Meanwhile I had been divorced from my husband and in my political group we were discussing our return to our home country because we felt there was a job to be done. After the war, I had some difficulty getting back home because of the British citizenship, though I was divorced. It was 1946, I think, when I returned.

In our socialist group we had decided not to start in Germany again but to become members of the Social Democratic party (SPD), to have as much unity as possible for the new political start in this politically destroyed country. So I worked there in this worker organization . . . in Hannover. After some years a friend of mine also came back from England to work on the newspaper of the SPD. He was a journalist and we married. So we went and lived in Bonn from then on. That was 1951.

He worked for the newspaper of the SPD. It's become a weekly;

it was a daily at the time. I was very active in the Bonn workers' organization. I was not employed by them but worked in the office without pay, voluntarily.

After some years, as you may know, the SPD decided—in an underhand way, I think—to agree to the rearmament of the Federal Republic. Both my husband and I were in complete opposition to that and so when he had the chance to start his own paper in Hamburg, we decided to go there. And that was called *Andere Zeitung* [The Other Paper].

In the beginning the SPD was quite in agreement, thought it was nice to have another socialist paper there, but very soon the line didn't suit them. And my husband was expelled from the party. And after [a] while I was expelled as well. Since I was in Hamburg, I had become active in a little socialist study group and then with a group called in English the West German Women's Peace Movement. That was 1956–57.

Since then, I have—with certain breaks—been working in the women's movement. During this time in the West German Women's Peace Movement, we had good contacts with women in the German Democratic Republic [GDR] and representatives from their women's organizations came and told us about their country and we went over when they had festivities there. So for quite a while I heard and saw quite a lot of the GDR. They came for meetings and spoke to audiences. This was in the time of the cold war, really: late 1950s, early 1960s. The GDR was still not recognized by the FRG. And at that time we were very much considered "leftists" and to be watched very carefully in this women's organization. The whole movement was being watched; of course the public was very distrustful, but it was mainly the authorities. For a while they had even forbidden movements to be active, you see. But we fought against that. This went on until about 1970, when we had a politically better time because we had an SPD government trying to get a decent relationship with the Eastern countries. And the whole atmosphere was different—more hopeful that with some development, we were moving away from the cold war. And the women's movement began to develop too.

How did you come to join WILPF?

In about 1970, I attended a national meeting as a representative of this other women's group. There was a Swiss woman who was giving a report about UNCTAD [UN Conference on Trade and Development] in Geneva, which she was following for WILPF. I was extremely interested by what she was saying and decided—as international things always were particularly interesting to me—to become a member of WILPF. I've worked since then with it. We have only about twenty-five members in Hamburg; it's quite a small group.

We have these international contacts, these UN contacts and so forth. Yet we have to work very hard to get individual members of peace groups interested in just this part of our work, and to come participate in our work. They are very interested in sort of joining a group for some action, a loose group, and then leaving it again—this very unstructured way of working together. And we are organized and sticking to it. So we have to find the few that agree it's necessary to work as we do. But it's not so easy, and that's why we are so few.

And we've started a little German-language supplement to *Pax et Libertas*. So when we get important information from the international in Geneva, I'm translating a lot, as you can imagine. I'm sort of publishing it for the Hamburg peace movement: it goes to thirty or forty organizations.

How did it become important to you to work with women?

We moved to Hamburg in 1955 and before that I had been mainly working in social work connected with political work. In Hamburg political life I had very little chance to really participate, in either social or political work. But I did have connections with women. It happened to me, I might say, that I got into this women's work. I can't say that it was a decision on my part.

How has it been different for you?

I think the real difference was I was sort of engaged all through my personality—that was only when I started with women. The other reason was I always had to do some political work in some way and this was the right thing. Peace is important to me.

What has kept you going as an activist all these years?

All these tasks are fascinating to me. I can't manage sometimes, but they are fascinating and I can't see anything that seems more important. And I would have a terribly bad conscience if I didn't give my little part to the question of peace. I'm very interested in the Third World, from the political angle, so I've tried to read as much as possible. I collect articles and so on. All this has come together in WILPF; more and more our tasks are in connection with the economic development of the world, our responsibilities to those parts we are constantly profiting from.

Else Pickvance

July 1986

Else Pickvance is a thin British woman in her seventies who has a look of both dignity and frailty. She is a tenacious Quaker pacifist and peace worker whose four adult children are all also active in the peace movement. In 1980 Else and her husband, Joseph, a conscientious objector during World War I, decided to take their beliefs one step further, resisting British tax law by withholding the portion of their national income taxes which goes to military purposes. They have continued to resist paying war taxes despite numerous government threats and attempts to force their compliance.

Else joined WILPF in the early 1970s and went on to become chair of the British section. More recently, she was Britain's international representative to the Executive Committee, a term she had just completed in mid-1986 at the time of this interview.

I've been doing peace work most of my life. Even as a school-girl my conscience wouldn't let me go to military displays. I think the roots of it lie in the fact that I had a German mother who married an Englishman just before the First World War, leaving behind her widowed mother. I couldn't help seeing what this separation because of the war was doing to her. And as I was growing up, my father was active for international understanding: understanding Germany and preventing another war were always part of the background conversation in our home.

Then as a student just before the Second World War, I signed the Peace Pledge, saying I would take no part in the war. That seemed to me the obvious thing to do. I joined the Society of Friends about that time too. At last I'd found a group whose ideas were as "strange" as my own, and I felt totally comfortable not only with their religious beliefs but also with their witness against war. Later I lost my brother in the war, and that was another thing that made me realize war is no way for society to resolve conflicts.

And how did you come to be in a peace group that was specifically for women?

In 1963 there was going to be a conference in Geneva on a partial test ban treaty, and groups of women decided to descend on Geneva from many sides. Somehow my name was submitted, and I was asked on about three days' notice if I would go with the British group. There was a newspaper appeal and money just poured in to pay for my trip. There were quite a lot of us, and we went about to the embassies and made a strong appeal. When we came back, everyone who had contributed wanted to know what had happened, and people who heard the report came to realize that women, as the creators of life, had something to say about peace. A lot of us were young mothers, and we felt we hadn't brought children into this world to fight one another. It was our very special peace witness as mothers. There were quite a few women's peace groups that sprang up at about that time, and our little group, Women for Peace, was pretty active for a long time. Later we decided it would be more sensible to join a larger organization, so we became a branch of WILPF. That was in the early 1970s.

At first I only went to branch meetings. Then I decided one year to go to [the British section's] annual council, and it was exciting to meet people from all over the country. Having a German mother myself, I was interested to find that a lot of the strongest members had an international background, often as refugees from Hitler or even longer ago. I've always felt that its international aspect was WILPF's strength and its distinction.

I understand you are a staunch pacifist.

Yes, I just can't believe it's ever right for people to take the responsibility of taking the lives of other people. I'm against capital punishment as well, and against corporal punishment in schools too. It's never been proven that violence was a successful way of settling disputes. The early Quakers made a declaration never to use weapons and they stuck to it. People may argue, "Render unto Caesar that which is Caesar's." But in defining what is Caesar's I believe no authority has the right to tell one man he must kill another man.

I'm quite willing to pay my taxes, but my husband and I have been trying for several years now to withhold the part of our income tax that we have calculated goes toward so-called "defense." For several years we sent it to the Ministry for Overseas Development instead. Then we discovered that when the checks came back from the bank, they'd simply been over-stamped and had gone into the income tax fund anyway. After that we decided not to send that portion of the money at all but to put it in a separate account and say to them, "You can have this money if you'll have it on our terms and use it for something positive and constructive, not for weapons."

Then last year [1985] we were taken to court for refusing this tax. At first it was a short case, but then they gave us a longer hearing because of all the evidence we had from international law which illustrates the illegality of nuclear weapons. We did have a sympathetic judge, but he ruled that tax law overrode international law and that we had to pay up.

Of course we didn't pay up. A few weeks passed and the bailiffs came and took a piece of our furniture, an antique chest, to sell. We had so many supportive friends that they bought it back for us at one hundred pounds. Then we sent the equivalent amount to Voluntary Service Overseas [VSO], a charity which receives nine pounds from the British government for every pound donated privately. So in the end the government had to pay out much more to the VSO than they collected.

We'll continue to withhold those taxes, and I only wish we'd done it sooner. If you feel it's the right thing to do, there's no stopping point. We'll go to prison if they make us do that, though probably they won't since my husband is seventy-five.

I can't give up doing what I believe is right. I'm convinced that people can change, and that lets me keep hoping.

Janet Bruin

September 1985

The daughter of trade-union organizers, Janet Bruin grew up in a Jewish middle-class neighborhood in Philadelphia. She is something of a free spirit, a quality that comes through in her energetic manner and sweeping gestures to illustrate whatever she is talking about. It does not seem surprising that she developed a passion for travel, languages, and other cultures at an early age.

After her marriage to a Swiss man, she moved to Zurich in 1978, where she established a practice in shiatsu massage and revived the then-defunct Swiss section of WILPF. That same year she took over the voluntary editorship of WILPF's quarterly, *Pax et Libertas*, which involved spending part of each month in Geneva, three hours away. Janet has since moved to Geneva and become a paid editor.

My mother was a member of WILPF ever since I can remember. I have a history of involvement in peace and justice work, mainly through my parents. When I was thirteen I went to my first demonstration: one on civil rights. Then at university I became involved in the movement against the Vietnam War. Later it was the women's liberation movement, and in 1973 it was the movement in solidarity with Chile.

I'd been traveling in Latin America, and just a few months after I came back to the United States, the Unidad Popular government was overthrown. I joined the Chile Committee in Philadelphia, and one day Vivian Schatz [a WILPF activist in Philadelphia] asked me if I'd like to join WILPF. I said sure, because I knew the league from childhood. And WILPF has really been my "home" for the past twelve years. I appreciate it so much because it has all the concerns I'd always been involved in, in one organization.

How did you come to be editor of Pax et Libertas?

In 1977 I went to the WILPF congress in Japan, since I was living in Japan that year. I made contact with Japanese WILPF before the congress and met up with the congress participants in Hiroshima during the commemoration of the atomic bombing that is held annually. I told Edith [Ballantyne] that I would be moving to Switzerland and that I'd like to get in touch with her there. Just by chance the Executive Committee met in Geneva in 1978, so I went. I was the youngest one there; I really felt like the baby of the organization.

But I knew at that point I wanted to work for peace in some major way in my own life. I was prepared to come to Geneva for some days each month and work in any way. They asked me if I'd like to edit *Pax* and I said, "Sure," even though I had no background in newspaper work! I'm a social worker by training. So I started from nothing.

Did it seem strange to you, being younger than the others?

Sort of. But I don't see age as so much of a problem now. There are young women coming into almost every section and for younger women, being in an organization with older ones who have had so many life and political experiences is great. I think it's the duty of any woman in this movement—no matter what her age—to see that new women are coming in: to keep the old, to keep the experience growing, keep our knowledge going further, but to also be sure we're getting new and young women. What I *would* like to see is the younger women having the possibilities, both financial and temporal, to participate as fully as the older, retired ones. Most younger people are students, young mothers, or working.

I hear you were largely responsible for reviving the Swiss section.

I have dual nationality—Swiss and U.S.—but it's very difficult for foreigners to organize in this country [Switzerland], and I'll always be perceived as a foreigner. So I was waiting to meet the right women. After the Swiss section had died out in 1975, the few women left from it didn't seem interested in getting something going because of their age and health. I was always looking for interested women, and then little by little, through my shiatsu practice and then especially through the STAR campaign in 1983, I met two women, one Swiss and one Greek, who were very interested in the league. After working with me on the STAR campaign, they said, "Okay, Janet, now it's time to organize a section." So since 1984 we're going as an independent organization, mostly in the German-speaking part.

What keeps you with WILPF as opposed to other organizations?

I sort of see WILPF as hanging together by chewing gum and miracles. It's kind of a remarkable organization: for years, we had *one* person in our international office. Given the political and historical conditions under which we've worked, and the financial difficulties, it's a miracle that we still exist. And I think it's a real tribute to women—to our vision, our stubbornness, and our love.

Do you consider yourself a feminist?

Of course! To me it comes down to something very basic. Women are an oppressed group. I call myself a feminist because I identify as a member of an oppressed group struggling for justice for our group. But justice for one group without justice for all is illusory, and WILPF has always recognized this. Our aims and principles contest all systems of exploitation, and the oppression of women—sexism—is one of those systems. Most people in the league agree that women are discriminated against and disadvantaged locally and in world society, and there can't be peace if such inequalities exist. And we're working to change that.

What keeps you from burning out?

I'm in the peace movement because I love life. I refuse to sit back and let this precious planet be destroyed. I take a lot of energy from knowing there is a worldwide movement of men and women who are working for a better world. It's been going on forever, it's a historical process. I've gotten so much from meeting women in the league who have been involved in these struggles—against fascism, colonialism, racism, and repression. Then, going to meetings like the Nairobi women's conference and seeing the commitment and determination of women all over the world gives me hope to go on.

Are you optimistic about the future?

I think we have to be extremely realistic. The dangers of nuclear war are greater than ever before; the economic problems in today's world are intense; debt, poverty, famine, and environmental destruction seem insurmountable. Yet there are solutions. The United Nations and the NGOs have formulated them, and it's up to us to see that they're realized. And more and more people are conscious than ever before. Each of us has a tremendous responsibility to mobilize in support of these solutions by activating people's sense of personal responsibility and love of life. To confront people with the dangers facing them without paralyzing them— that's a big job because those of us who have been with this for a while know these dangers are very real and that this earth could easily perish from nuclear war. I'll do everything I can to make sure it doesn't happen.

I'm hopeful that little by little other people will take action too. I think that's possible, and that's why I stay with it. Working together, each in our own community and each in our own country, we can do it. I'm sure.

Betty McIntosh

August 1985

Betty McIntosh looks as if she would be just as comfortable rolling out a pie crust as she would be sipping wine at an elegant reception. That combination of earthiness and sophistication springs naturally from nearly forty years of living in Western Australia. Betty is comfortable with the lifestyle that she and her husband, Senator Gordon McIntosh, have now, but it wasn't always that easy. In fact, it was the family's own experiences with discrimination that turned Betty into an activist and eventually led her to WILPF.

I'm from Scotland originally. I've been in Australia since 1950. I came as a newly married woman to Western Australia, which is a very isolated part of the world. Isolation was very evident in 1950, and coming from Scotland where one took an interest in international affairs, my impression when I first arrived was that I had fallen off the edge of the world. But I immediately plunged into working to combat the injustices that were being carried out—not cruelly, but innocently—by the Australian government and society. One of the injustices was that there was direct discrimination against refugees from Eastern and southern Europe. This was my introduction to taking up the cause of others to rectify injustices.

What motivated you to do that?

I think because I was a migrant myself I felt the isolation. There was also a certain discrimination against British migrants. There was an innate feeling in Australian people at that time that as a Scottish migrant you were very amusing but don't forget you are a migrant. My sympathy was greatest for a lot of the European migrants, who were not allowed to speak their own language and were very much discriminated against in every area of employment: many professional doctors, lawyers, teachers, came to Australia and were not even allowed to practice their profession without going back to university. If they happened to be over fifty, they found it especially difficult. It was these injustices that I spent my first twenty years in Australia trying to rectify.

How did you come into contact with WILPF?

This came during the 1960s. I became very conscious of the stockpiles of nuclear weapons and I was instrumental in bringing Dr. Linus Pauling to Australia to speak. There were only a few of us deciding to do this. We arranged large public meetings, which were overcrowded. There was no publicity, absolutely none in Australia. This was one of the areas in which I met a lot of the WILPF women. I got to know them from doing that and later the facts about the Vietnam War came out and again I was working against our government's involvement in the Vietnam War. I then got involved in the campaign to shelter these young men who decided to become conscientious objectors, and we had to move them from home to home.

My involvement with the WILPF grew closer and closer throughout this period, and even then I think why I resisted becoming a member is because WILPF in Australia has traditionally been academics who study situations. The result of those studies ends up in submissions to governments, of course, making facts known to other people. I was too much of an activist to sit down and study. But I adored the women involved, some of whom are quite famous. I think this is what even to this day frightens off a lot of people, and I often say to people whom I recruit to WILPF or just accept them as friends of WILPF, "There were the brilliant women right from the beginning of the league, and then there is me. Don't be afraid or inhibited by not having the academic qualifications of some of the women whom we project in our history as being so capable. We need all kinds of women and as long as you have common sense and sincerity, you will have exactly what is necessary."

So I knew WILPF women for a long time, but it wasn't until 1972 that I actually became active. Now I didn't become actively involved gradually. When they approached me about it, they said, "You must become a member of WILPF." And they made me president. So I got dropped in at the deep end and it was very wise of them.

You say "them." How large a group was it?

A very close-knit group of about thirty women. It was very wise of them because every one of them is a very strong personality. I hate to admit to having any virtues, but I think I am a very diplomatic person most of the time. I was the very person that they needed at that particular time. And it worked. I'm a great believer in the right person to be there at the right time.

I think it is important that we have broken into the community. We were really a catalyst for many of the movements that have followed in Australia, particularly Western Australia. In the early 1970s, WILPF played a big part in getting the cooperation of the trade unions in Australia to go to the [World] Court and try to stop the French atmospheric testing or at least take it underground. With two or three others we started People for Nuclear Disarmament in Western Australia. The United Nations Association joined the league. I feel that we did a lot to bring peace groups together.

But most of all I think being a lady—and I use the word "lady" pointedly—and having other ladies there, I represent acceptability into more conservative circles so I'll approach church groups, ladies' afternoon teas, and so on and ask them to come to hear some of our speakers. When organizations such as the YWCA [Young Women's Christian Association] adopted a peace policy, I'd get in touch with them and say, "Come and tell us about it." And the same with women candidates for office—this has worked very well. Practically every woman politician in Australia is a member of WILPF.

I think one thing we have in common with every other section is our optimism. I find a lot of young women in Australia are simply gravitating toward the league rather than our going out and looking for them. They've been in these spontaneous peace movements because they wanted spontaneous action. Now they're looking beyond the fear of a nuclear holocaust, thinking, "Maybe, just maybe, we can avert this and come through." So they're looking for answers. We see the age matter not as a problem but as a certain role that we play in the larger movement.

Would you classify yourself as a feminist?

I don't feel I want to drop other things I'm doing for the sake of pursuing feminism, and yet I have always been strongly in favor of women's rights and personally involved in a number of areas where recognition of women is very important. I myself have had the experience of taking on positions never held by a woman before, not because I'm a woman but because I could do the job better. So I didn't see why I should have to fall in line behind some man. In doing this, I got a lot of congratulations from feminists, which I wasn't really expecting. I'd just assumed that every female should be looking for justice, without realizing that some women have to first come together for moral support and that feeling of thrusting ahead. In any question of social injustice we have to have extremes to call the middle ground into focus, so therefore I'm all for the feminist movement for pulling public opinion over in that direction. But I think there's a difference between organized feminism and feeling the strength of feminism. I think when we use the term loosely, we do refer to organized feminism. And I've just never had the time to devote to that. I've simply lived my life and you can base your conclusions on that.

Also, Australia was a very male-dominated country and still is. So possibly I've moved more toward an interest in feminism than I would have elsewhere. I've always felt we've let far too much go to male domination, feeding the male ego so that then they've come to expect they know what to do. It's about time women took not control but at least an integral role in public life.

Marie-Therese Danielsson

How do you keep from getting depressed about the world situation and wanting to give up?

I think one does get depressed every now and then, but just as that happens, there's always some new glimpse of an area that— "well, perhaps we can do it this other way." I think that's a very feminist characteristic, compared to the quality most prevalent in males. Women can always see ways to get around. I don't mean deviously; it's almost a survival instinct. We always think, well, maybe if we did it this way, we would have more effect.

Anyhow, there isn't an alternative—we must keep going. There's always another injustice. Just when you think you've finished, you see something happening and you say,"Let's see what we can do about this one."

Marie-Therese Danielsson

July 1986

After living in Hitler-occupied France, Marie-Therese Danielsson fled 6,000 miles to the French Polynesian islands to escape the abhorrence of war and corruption. There she has lived for more than three decades with her Swedish anthropologist husband, Bengt. Together the two adopted the island way of life as their own and pieced together the history of Polynesian culture, which they published in several volumes along with numerous other books and articles.

But in the 1960s the French began nuclear tests on the islands, and again Marie-Therese saw what war and corruption can bring. The Danielssons were among the first to expose the terrible hazards of the testing and its effects on the fragile island culture. Their forceful writings and talks on the subject earned them the scorn of the French government, but the couple persisted.

In 1981 Marie-Therese organized a group of Polynesian women into a WILPF section to bring concerns about nuclear testing to a wider community of women. When I interviewed her at the 1986 WILPF congress, it was hard to believe she was sixty-three years old: with her ponytail, innocent demeanor, and restless energy, she could easily have been twenty or even thirty years younger.

I was born in France. My mother died at the end of the war [World War II], and I was left alone, the last of the family. The Germans had occupied the area where we lived from the first day of the war to the last, and we never had enough food. My mother was dying of cancer and could never get any medication to quiet her pain.

So after it was over I wanted to get as far away from Europe as possible. I met my husband in Peru in 1947, where I was a teacher and governess for a French diplomatic family. He was there studying the Amazon Indians. Before that, he had been to the atolls of Tahiti on board the *Kon-Tiki* raft, and he wanted to go back there, where the people had not been touched by European civilization.

During the war there had been no communication among the islands. There were 120 people living on Mururua Atoll when we arrived in 1949. We stayed there eighteen months that first time. When we went, we thought it would take three months to make our study. Then we discovered after three months we knew nothing!

It was a practical and sociological study of the population, so we grew to love the people. And I made do with little coconuts and fish, and then when a ship arrived, we got rice, flour, and tinned food. Sometimes it didn't come for two or three months, so then we had just the coconuts and fish. When you've been through a war, you don't think that's so terrible.

When Bengt became ill and I became pregnant, we went back to Tahiti and took a ship back to Europe. Six weeks to Europe with two cats and two turtles! In 1953 we came back to Polynesia and decided to stay.

How did you begin doing peace work?

We lived in Tahiti when the French nuclear tests began. As we had been working with the people, we knew how they might respond because we knew their social, political, and economic systems. And we thought that such a thing in such a place was terrible: they were not prepared for it. Until then it was the best of the French colonies because it had never truly been colonized. Very few people went to Tahiti back then; there was no money to be made there—no gold or oil or trees to cut down. It was far away, and even a letter took six months to get an answer. So the few people who did go there went because they liked the place. Only about a thousand French had arrived there by 1960, and they were mostly men who were married to Tahitian women. Most were older people, established before the war. We were among the only ones who came after the war and stayed.

But with the tests we could predict that many military people would come, and that would change the life of the people. The military would need workmen to get them to the small islands outside Tahiti. And people displaced from those islands would never go back. If people were working on the bases all the time, they would not have time to fish and grow their own food, so they would have to buy everything in the shops, and prices would go up. The French have a different way of life; they like to have possessions and live "well." So everything would change. That was easy to predict, but when we told people that they should resist, they said, "Oh, no, it would be wonderful to have all these things."

Some people were in opposition, of course. For example, the [Protestant] church came out very strongly against the tests from the beginning, and some political leaders as well. The tests were harmful and we have protested them from the start, but nothing did any good. It was incredible how the population was taken advantage of.

The tests began in 1966, and [Charles] de Gaulle attended the first one. That was the worst of all, the way they told everyone there was no danger. They said they would wait until the wind was blowing in the right direction, but when de Gaulle came on his big ship, they told him on the first day, "We can't do it today because the wind is blowing to the northwest." And he said okay, but the next day the wind was still in the wrong direction, and he said, "I can't wait any longer, I have to go back to France." So they set off the test anyway, and that was a very dirty one. There was fallout in

Australia and New Zealand. Their governments protested and South American countries protested. The situation became very difficult for the French, particularly after they lost their case on this at the World Court at The Hague. After that the tests were underground until 1974.

And how did you get connected with WILPF?

We lived so far away and were so isolated. In 1975 I was invited to a Pacific women's meeting organized by some women who had been to the International Women's Year Conference in Mexico City. We had no idea there was an international organization for women and peace, or anything like that, and after that we started receiving many newsletters and other information. We learned there would be another big conference in Copenhagen in 1980. There were five of us from Tahiti who went to that. We met other women and spoke of our problems, and one African woman [Daphne Ntiri, a WILPF member] said, "Come speak to WILPF." So we met Kay Camp. And then the Danish section asked us to a meeting. We went and we liked their way of doing things and decided we could learn from them.

So we came back home to organize a small group there—only four of us. It was very difficult. People thought we were talking too strongly against the tests. They weren't used to it. People there are frightened to speak up. It took me a long time myself to stand up and say something. It's not just women—it's the whole school system. You're not taught to put ideas together and express yourself. In French culture they don't learn that sort of thing.

But we managed to get started and to publish some articles. There were practical problems too. Most of the Polynesian women are black, have large families, and live quite far outside town. The communication is bad, sometimes I have to drive thirty to fifty kilometers to get an answer from a member. There are twelve or fifteen of us now. At the beginning some other French women (besides myself) wanted to come, but it didn't work out. The French have their ways and the Polynesians have theirs: it's hard to get together. I'm accepted because I have lived with them for so long.

And you've even become involved in local politics.

I've been a member of the municipal council since 1977. We had no municipalities until just a year or so before that. At that time, the mayor had died and there was going to be a new administration. So I proposed myself for the council. There was no party affiliation, which I liked. And I passed. At first we were only three women to twenty-seven men, but now we are five. It was only after World War II that French women got the vote, of course—the last European country to do so. So we've tried to really do something for women in the community.

But I never speak directly in the council about my work against the tests. However, each year at Christmas we give a gift to each schoolchild, as half the population is under twenty years old. And last year I asked that no war toys be given. The resolution didn't pass because of a technicality, but I'll try again this year!

The French have always tried to discredit my husband's and my work. They say, "Those WILPF people, they're crazy." But now that members of the council have come to know me, they listen to me and don't believe all the rumors.

What keeps you going?

Because we can't stop. As long as the nuclear tests continue in Polynesia, we have to keep fighting them. Two years ago I got depressed, but I'll never give up. Being together in this with my husband helps; with two together, if one gets depressed, the other can keep you going.

Harriet Otterloo

September 1985

Harriet Otterloo is a tall, imposing Swedish woman who can be a bit intimidating on first meeting. Harriet spent years in the women's liberation movement, and her strong feminist orientation is evident in her own life story. She came to WILPF in 1980 after having helped to found Swedish Women for Peace in her home city of Göteborg. Working as a primary organizer of the WILPF international congress held in Göteborg in 1983 got Harriet involved in WILPF at the international level, and in 1984 she and another Swedish member set out traveling, using their own savings, to make contact with WILPF branches all across the United States. Harriet is a woman of uncanny wit and initiative who became a medical doctor at the age of forty-one while raising four sons as a single mother.

I jumped off school when I was seventeen. I quit it and I promised myself never to go again, but one year later I had already returned. I went through a course to become a carpenter, so that was my first profession. Then I went to art school. I was a model for a time; I have worked in shops. During all this time I was working in the hospitals on the weekends because my other jobs were bad-paying. Then I married a Dutchman and moved to Holland. I was twenty-one then and living in Holland in the beginning of the 1960s. My oldest son was born there. And then we returned to Sweden in 1965 and I wanted more children.

I didn't want anyone else to take care of my kids. So to be able to have the babies and be home I had to work or to study in the evenings. I gave some courses in English for women who knew less than I did. After that I went to university and studied the Dutch language, and I studied the history of women and of Africa.

I had four children in seven years, and I started medical school when I was thirty-five. I was divorced during that first year. I have been to school for thirty-five years; there's not so very much I can study anymore. [Yet] if the time comes when I don't want to be a doctor, I'll have to decide if I'm going to study economics or theology.

So you don't plan to remain a doctor?

I don't know. It depends. I'm a middle-aged woman, and not so attractive. There can come a day when it would be difficult for me to get a job in medicine. There are a lot of doctors in West Germany without jobs, and in Denmark. We are still good in Sweden, but because of my work in WILPF and the peace movement, I couldn't take a four-year contract as is usually done in Sweden. If I did, I couldn't work so much in the peace movement as I do today. But I'm not afraid; I can go back and do some of the other kinds of jobs.

How did you get interested in WILPF?

I've been a member of WILPF since the early 1970s, but only a passive member till 1980. Then I became the chairwoman of the Göteborg branch, and since then I have spent all my free time in and for WILPF. I didn't hear about WILPF, I read about it. I did study women's history at the university. If you study women's history, it seems that every important woman has been a member of WILPF, especially in Sweden but even outside it.

How did you go from passive to active?

It happened one day I was stopped in the street by Ragnhild Svensson [another Swedish member who later became branch secretary]. We had met before; I didn't remember her but she did remember me, and she stopped me. She said, "Harriet, I want you to become the chairwoman of the WILPF Göteborg branch; otherwise, it will die." So I accepted out of respect for the women who had been working before us. But I also said that I would accept only if they could find two more women who were not yet fifty. And they did. When we entered the league in Göteborg and started to be active, I think that the youngest one was seventy-eight years old, and there were not very many members. On paper it was about forty, but it was six or eight who kept it together and were mostly just talking about the old times. I had met them before because I had been into an organization or, actually, a school called Kvinnliga medborgarskolan pa Fogelstad [the female citizen's school at Fogelstad]. It was a school which was started in 1925 just to educate women how to use their possibility to vote. We [Swedish women] were allowed to vote in 1921 so one of our famous women started that school. It was those same women who started WILPF in Sweden. Every woman who had any idea about what women's lives should be like was there. So I had met some of the older WILPF members there.

I was the chairwoman of Göteborg [branch] for four years, and I was vice-chairwoman of the Swedish section for one year. But I couldn't do anything as section vice-president that I couldn't do as president of the branch. So I withdrew from the seat. And then we had the congress in Göteborg in 1983 and I think the reason I was chosen as international treasurer was they had heard me talk about money and nobody else wanted to be the treasurer. Nobody knew me: that is a problem we have with the international, I think. We have to choose officers every three years and we don't know the people whom we are going to elect.

I have never been talking about money before I became active in WILPF. The women there have taught me quite a lot about women and economy. The first thing I learned is that women usually think that money is dirty; they want to have everything cheap or free. They're so idealistic. But you've got to prioritize. We need people who understand that the work we are doing is important and that we need money because everything in our society costs money. So I said, "Okay, if you want peace for ten crowns you pay ten crowns but if you want more peace, you have to pay more." And it seems to be a good thing to say because most all women do pay more. We have the highest dues in all Scandinavia.

And how large is your branch now?

I think that the last time we counted them there were three hundred paying members. Between thirty and fifty are really active. Frankly, we have got a lot of young women now. WILPF has had, if you look to our history, very intellectual members, and that scares the head off most women. I think that is what we have changed in Göteborg: we have opened WILPF for everyone. We need all kinds of women in WILPF: we need the ones who run the businesses, the ones who clean the house, the ones who make the speeches, and so on. But we must also be aware that the one who cleans the house for some years may be the one who is giving the speeches in another period of her life.

Do you consider WILPF a feminist organization?

No, but it should be. The problem we have to deal with is to tell people what a feminist is. Feminists can love men; every feminist does have a father or a brother or son whom she loves. The best definition that I have heard is that a feminist is a person—man or woman—who believes that men and women should be equal and is working to make that happen. A lot of people think that you have to be a woman to be a feminist, but that is not so. One of the most positive things I saw in America was these male feminists.

If you use that definition, everyone will be a feminist if you ask them afterward. I think that in WILPF there is some misunderstanding because we often don't understand the words and what the words mean; naturally, this is because we are speaking in languages that are not our own. But it is also true that within our own languages, one word may not mean the same if you are in the working class or middle class or upper class or if you are in a different political party and so on.

One thing that we have to do is educate ourselves to believe in ourselves, our knowledge, and also to see that our way of life is worthwhile. If we don't see that the way of life women have with children and a household is fun, is interesting, what a lot of creativity it is, then we can never get men interested to take part in the job. If we just see it as a struggle and not worthwhile, why for God's sake should they do it then? It is so marvelous to have children when they are young and when they are teenagers, too, even if it is more trouble then. That is something that men should take part in because their life will be richer, and the society needs our experience.

What is it that keeps you going in this work?

Because I love life and I certainly love this earth. Of course I would love to have grandchildren and I would love to live together with my sons. But that is not as important. I don't care if there would be any of my family left, as long as I know we will save this globe—some people, some animals, some clean air, and some trees. That's what makes me fight: this world we have done our best to destroy. But still it is so beautiful and so worthwhile, and it is really our duty to do something now. It's a pity that a lot of people before haven't done it, but on the other hand, today we do have more knowledge and we do have more possibilities than people before us ever had. It is not the technology that's bad, it is how we use it. We have today so many good opportunities for communications—television, radio, telephone—that we can inform people all over the world at the same time. We are richer, if we would just learn to distribute, so that everyone can eat. There is such a lot of work to be done. The problem is that we pay for the wrong things.

I never think it is any one thing which turns a person around. But I do believe in something—you can call it God, or call it something else. But for me it is some kind of life energy which you find everywhere. And I have learned such a lot from my children, and still do.

Are you optimistic about the future of this world?

Of course I'm worried, but I am optimistic because it somehow seems to be the problem of the white man. We have such hubris—everything we do should always be the biggest and the best—even when we are simply going to the store, nothing should do but we should have the best bread. But nature has always been stronger than us: there have been a lot of big cultures before us that have had perhaps the same knowledge as us. If we go on this way, perhaps we will destroy part of the world, but if it isn't meant that this world should be destroyed, it will not be. It states in the Old Testament that as long as there were just one or two people who believed that there was something good in Sodom and Gomorrah, then it could stand by. So at least I'm doing that: standing by thinking that we will save the world. And there are a few more.

Carlota Lopes da Silva

August 1985

Carlota Lopes da Silva is a thoughtful and striking, almost flamboyant, woman who headed up the revival of the Dutch section of WILPF in 1983. Here is someone whose political and social views have made a 180–degree turn since her youth, and a strong commitment to internationalism has characterized her adult life. She was interviewed in Munich during the 1985 WILPF Executive Committee meeting, where she could usually be found in the middle of a group, deeply engrossed in conversation.

Carlota made her first contact with WILPF at the mid-decade women's conference in Copenhagen and since then has become increasingly immersed in the organization. In 1986 she was elected international vice-president.

I was born in Portugal of a very aristocratic family—with very little money, but so arrogant. I was not allowed to play with the common children in the streets because I was—the word that they used was *raci*. *Raci* is from the French, meaning someone of special high quality. At that time in Portugal there was a Fascist regime. I was born in 1932; a military dictatorship had been established in 1927. It was also at that time that Hitler had started in Germany.

My family was quite apolitical. They were not against or for; they didn't care anything for politics. I was educated by nuns. I remember when I was in my first classes at school; it was terrible. I was made to pray for the victory of Franco. So you can see how I had been integrated into the culture around me. But I was not unhappy, just innocent.

Then when I was nineteen I went to study to become a nurse. In this program I had to do an internship in the slums of Lisbon, and that was the strongest experience that you can imagine. That was the first time I had contact with life realities—poverty, disease, illiteracy. It was terrible, but at the same time those people had some force, some power, and they were so conscious. They knew much more than I knew about life. And I had a kind of "internal explosion." I refused to believe in anything any longer. I had this blow-up with the Catholic church; even with my family I had some problems. I went home only twice or three times a year because I was busy with my studies. And I started to try to get some real information, and I can assure you it was very difficult.

Why did you leave Portugal?

It was not a political reason for me personally, but for my husband, because in 1961 began the war in Angola. We heard that he would be called to go because my husband is a psychiatrist and would be needed because the soldiers were in very bad mental shape. We heard this before he was called so we left. So we were first in London, and now we have been living in Holland for twenty-one years. I am a Dutch citizen and my husband also.

So that's a little bit of my story. I left Portugal when I was thirty, ten years after I started my consciousness-raising. I am deeply convinced that when people start thinking about these things they never stop. The point is to start. People just choose not to start; instead they put labels and it is finished. If you start to think a little bit more fully, you see a bit more of the different shades of gray. Nothing is black and white.

It makes me very afraid that I can see what is in common between the United States today and Portugal when I was growing up. Always the Portuguese were "better" and there was the word "Portugism." Now Mr. Reagan is using "Americanism." I have nothing against American people, they are very nice, but when I see him with all these flags and speaking about all the special qualities of the American people—this nationalism, this thinking you are the best in all the world—that was exactly what I saw in Portugal.

Then when you begin to criticize our Western system, you are a "Communist." But it doesn't matter to me anymore. If you call me a Communist, OK. I'm not, but you can think it. I don't know if you know the story of the king of Denmark. When the Germans invaded Denmark, they asked all Jews to wear the Star of David. The next day the king himself wore that star and so did all the people. So I'm no longer afraid of what anyone calls me; I just put on the Star of David and go on.

Do you consider yourself a feminist?

Feminism for me is a deep conviction that women can achieve something different from men. Women have never had power, at least not the power we know now as ruling the world. We are not in the military-industrial complex. We are only a few in politics. We are certainly not in big business. We are kept away from power. And I am hoping that women have another approach to life. I cannot assure you that we are better or worse than men—I think it's very dangerous and a little like racism to say that. But I hope that if women could get more power, they would act in another way—but not if they are in a minority position in a man's world.

I think the league has a very good approach to this in the sense that I am a feminist but I am not antimen. I have worked with men in the political party, and I don't have any problem. But there are some women who have lots of problems in working in groups with men.

But if you choose as your priority to work for the emancipation of women in the fairly limited European or North American way, you don't have space in your life to think about women in the Third World and their problems. I think it is very important that we listen to women of the Third World.

So, some people in the league say, "Here we are sitting around talking about Third World problems, but we are all white and middle class." Well, I'm sure we cannot liberate these people; they have to liberate themselves. But the point is that when they do liberate themselves and we cannot get coffee anymore, that we will not complain and we will not make more problems for them.

What attracted you to WILPF?

Because it is an international organization, and I'm convinced that we will not survive if we don't find some way of making the

United Nations stronger. Maybe not as it is now; some things would have to be changed.

It is quite interesting; forty years ago was the end of the Second World War, the bomb of Hiroshima, and the beginning of the UN. I think these are the choices we have today. We can make the UN strong, choosing the very positive way: to get a world democracy—I don't mean world government, because that would be too much concentration of power. Or we choose the way of world fascism. That is unfortunately the direction we seem to be going in. Look at the priorities we choose globally: every day 45,000 children die of hunger, unnecessarily caused by malnutrition and disease. You can say it is not racism, but you can kill people in different ways. You can kill them as in Dachau [a Nazi concentration camp], or you can kill them by "remote control," and that is what we are doing today in Africa. These people are not white; therefore, they are not as valuable as 45,000 children in Europe or the U.S.A. This is fascism.

Are you optimistic about the future? What keeps you going?

I have such a stupid story, but if I can change in such a way as I did, anybody can do it. It is a question of a sparkle, and then you start thinking and you start looking for information. You start thinking big thoughts.

Irene Eckert

September 1986 and February 1988

Irene Eckert is a small, bespectacled woman in her mid-thirties. Her home is in West Berlin. She is a teacher by profession, as well as a historian and a writer. Irene's connection with WILPF began only in 1981, but her commitment to the league is obviously deep from the way she speaks about her work in it.

A child of the cold war period, Irene belongs to a generation who tried to break with their parents' heritage of nonresistance to or even collaboration with fascism. For her, growing up in a conservative Catholic province in the south of Germany, making that break forced her into constant direct confrontation with mainstream ideas, and she sharpened her wits in sheer self-defense. Today Irene speaks with passion but also with precision.

It is no surprise that she was attracted by WILPF when she discovered it to be a women's organization with a sincere and unbroken historical tradition of work for peace and justice. In our conversation, she reflected that the attraction was heightened by the fact that mothers, grandmothers, and great-grandmothers were all represented in the league, becoming figures with whom she could identify closely. Irene developed a fast loyalty to the league.

Despite very modest means, she manages to get to many WILPF international meetings, sometimes driving across large parts of Europe in order to do so. Irene has worked closely with the international officers for several years. In 1983 she coordinated the STAR gathering in Brussels, where, on behalf of WILPF and with virtually no local help, she made contacts and gained support for a rally of ten thousand women against the cruise and Pershing missile deployments.

When I first met Irene in 1985 at a WILPF Executive Committee meeting in Munich, she had just returned from a research trip to the WILPF archives in Boulder, Colorado, and she had enough materials in her pockets for several books and projects. At the time she was on a teaching fellowship in France that allowed her time to write.

Only a year later, however, at the time of this interview, Irene had slowed her pace a bit, having recently given birth to her first child, Yesmin, the youngest attendee at the league's twenty-third international congress. After several years of intensive organizing, writing, and speaking for disarmament, Irene was now experiencing the limitations of a professional woman who has family responsibilities. She noted that existing social structures make it very difficult for a woman in these circumstances to keep up her responsibilities to the global community.

What really opened my eyes to the peace movement was the decision by NATO to deploy new first-strike nuclear missiles on West German soil. I had started to be aware of peace issues when I was active in student organizations in the early 1970s and one of our slogans was *Baut schulen statt kasernen* [Build schools, not barracks]. And [in the late 1970s] I was working in the teachers' union and was already critical of the national defense policy. But the cruise and Pershing missile issue was what motivated me to get deeply involved in the peace movement. These were no longer defensive but offensive arms.

I first worked with an educational group in the Protestant church, in cooperation with the teachers' union. We worked on peace education, which was defined as political education to help students understand what these arms meant to our people. We developed kits, invited experts to speak, and held seminars.

How did you hear of WILPF?

In the summer of 1981 I followed the invitation of a colleague with whom I had worked on peace education. She was participating in the summer school held by WILPF in Cartigny [Switzerland]. I was on my way back from a holiday in southern France, and I thought, "Well, why not?"

It struck my imagination, and I was fascinated by meeting all these older women and women of different countries and of different political and ideological backgrounds. Yet here they were, getting along, discussing issues, working together. That was something I found overwhelming because I'd been beginning to understand that to live together, we needed to cooperate and stop fighting even among ourselves.

Becoming connected with WILPF also meant getting to know the UN. Till then I was not aware of the precious work being done in the UN and by the NGOs. I didn't even realize the importance of having a UN.

After that summer I went back to Berlin and started a new branch of WILPF there. And I tried to find out the historical roots of this organization I'd never heard of before. That November I participated in the conference WILPF held in Amsterdam ["Women of Europe in Action for Peace"]. And in 1982 I was sent to observe the UN Second Special Session on Disarmament as a delegate of the

German section. That really drew me more closely into WILPF work and what was going on at the UN.

Going back to Berlin, I decided to write about my experiences and to work more intensively for peace than I'd ever done before. It happened to be at a time when I had already decided to take two years off teaching, originally to work on a thesis. But I changed my focus and decided to become an expert on human and humane survival instead.

Back home I reported about the overwhelming experiences in the U.S.A. around the SSD 2, and about the major contributions of women, who seemed to be the backbone of the movement there. I was fascinated by the spirit of the June 12 rally and by the U.S. WILPF women who had initiated the STAR campaign. Time and again I felt inspired by the charm of these women, many of them much older than myself and yet supporting me in every sense of the word.

I had become acquainted with Edith Ballantyne and it was under her influence that I decided to volunteer at the international headquarters. [I was able] to benefit from her wonderful ability to focus on the issues that people have in common rather than on their differences. It was also she who gave me the courage to go to Brussels and set up the STAR office. When I was honored with the important job of coordinating the STAR campaign internationally and organizing the march and conference, I had little experience but a lot of enthusiasm and the knowledge that there was an international movement behind me. Overcoming feelings of personal incompetence, I went to Brussels because I was deeply convinced that 1983 was a crucial year in the life of humanity and that I had a duty to do whatever was within my power to do. I was able to carry out these tasks successfully only because time after time I received support from individuals and organizations in and outside Belgium.

Our presence in Brussels—a two-day international women's conference and a march and rally of ten thousand women—was a landmark in WILPF history. It showed the tremendous radius of women around our program ideas if only we go out and be active and inventive in ways to approach women and organizations. After working closely with a number of WILPF sections, I could see how appealing the league became at this vital moment in history when millions around the globe rallied against this deployment which was bringing us one step closer to nuclear annihilation. At that moment, WILPF was at its best because it had caught upon what was a major concern of the people and contributed its unique historical capability to build bridges among multifaceted women's groups who do not always realize how strong we can be if we act in unity, and to bring together women who had never before participated in any activities like that one. The media attention we received, after a long, hard struggle to be listened to, was tremendous. For one day we hit the news in the mainstream media internationally. Unfortunately, we didn't have the woman power and the necessary financial means to build on that success. In my mind it was a mistake to have abandoned the STAR campaign after Brussels and not to have found the means to stay in contact with all the groups and individuals who had paid us tribute.

Personally, Brussels helped me to see more clearly the [value of] coalition building, the need to work more on women's history, and to make visible the historical links between women's and peace issues.

That experience helped women to grow beyond themselves; it helped me to grow beyond myself, even though I was very tired after it was all over, and asking myself how I had managed. Yet I continued, and after a short break I went back to the international office to work up the STAR budget and to help plan for the Göteborg congress.

After that I went on a three-month speaking tour in the U.S.A. That too was very important for me as a person. I learned I was able to speak in front of many people, and it brought me together with many women of outstanding [character] and nurtured my wish to tell their stories, stories of the "other America," as we say, referring to democratic grassroots movements.

After that tour I had to do something about my job situation, but I continued to have close contact with the international office. At the time I focused more on my writing—on peace issues, women's issues, and the connections between them. In 1984 I had to begin a teaching job in France, where I was more than surprised to find an almost complete lack of a peace movement, compared to the Federal Republic.

You mentioned the connection between women's and peace issues. What do you mean by that?

As a woman, I feel personally affected by every dollar spent on conceiving, developing, and constructing weapons. That money is not available for child-care centers, for the employment of doctors, nurses, and teachers. Every pfennig spent on the military cannot be spent on human services, fields of massive employment of women. Every mark invested in machinery of annihilation cannot at the same time be spent on preserving life: on research into Sudden Infant Death Syndrome, for example. A society that prepares for fighting a war against a [vaguely] defined enemy necessarily creates structures of violence, and a violent society is violent against the weak ones first, namely women. Women are affected so much more profoundly by the arms race that there is a special need for us to struggle against it as women. We need to study more the history of our own ways of being: matriarchy, for instance. Were matriarchal societies more peaceful, and why? It seems to me very relevant to show the historical links between women and the peace movement, but also to [explore] the commitment of women to war and chauvinism and to analyze the motives for such self-negating attitudes among women.

In WILPF, there are many in our own ranks who don't know about the contributions to women's rights by women like Jane Addams, Lida Gustava Heymann, Gertrude Baer. It's not considered important enough. We need to become more aware of our own feminist heritage and what it means to approach all our programs from a female perspective.

[In the peace movement] there are enough mixed organizations [of women and men]. Sure, we need to learn to cooperate with one another, but first we must become still stronger as women.

What keeps you with the league?

I can't underline enough how much I owe to the older women in WILPF, especially in the U.S. section. My personal life has been so enriched by my political work. I was never so active as I have been since I came into WILPF. And it's helped me to overcome some of my European narrowness, to have a broader vision—all the traveling I've done, staying in the homes of women who work on these various issues. I might never have developed my interest in writing, in speaking.

Women have a tremendous potential that has not yet been fully thrown into this historic movement. Sometimes that thought keeps me going. Sometimes it's a woman like Edith Ballantyne, sometimes the support of my husband. These days it's very much my daughter. I feel a special responsibility for her, and if I transfer that to all the children of the world, as I try to, then I am simply not allowed to give up.

Olga Bianchi

August 1985

Olga Bianchi is a small woman with bright piercing eyes. She is originally from Chile, but was one of the thousands who fled after the 1973 coup which installed a military dictatorship. Upon being questioned about her experiences, Olga begins her story calmly. However, once drawn into conversation, her words tumble out rapidly, revealing her intensity.

She was interviewed during the WILPF Executive Committee meeting in 1985, at which she did not seem uncomfortable being one of the few Third World women present but offered opinions and suggestions in a friendly, helpful manner. The following year Olga was elected as one of the league's international vice-presidents.

I've lived in Costa Rica for eleven years; before that, I was a Chilean woman. The father of my sons was a professor, the head of the Philosophy Department at Chile University. In 1975, a year and a half after the Pinochet government was in, the police—the army—went in there and took him to a concentration camp. Heidelberg University and Frankfurt University did a very good campaign to liberate him, and he was liberated a year after, and he came here to Germany. He died in Heidelberg because he was so very ill in the concentration camp. I emigrated with my children to Costa Rica. I didn't go to Germany with him. When that happened, he asked me to take our children away. And I had my oldest son that was living in Costa Rica since 1973 so we went there.

Our sons never played with war toys. We were a very pacifist family. Now, I suppose, I am a peace worker, not anymore a pacifist. When the liberation from Somoza came in Nicaragua, my younger daughter said, "Mama, I'm going. Even if you did raise me as a pacifist, I'm going to take up arms to defend the Nicaraguan people." And she joined the Sandinista army because, she said, "I don't want other people to lose their fathers as I did." She was eighteen in that year. I was kind of scared but I thought it was her decision because my experience told me that you cannot be a pacifist, not in our countries, where we are getting assassinated every day. So she fought in Nicaragua. Now she is back in Costa Rica, but she was there, and I was very proud of her.

How did you find out about WILPF?

In Costa Rica I began to work with human rights. I was one of the founders in 1979 of the Commission for the Defense of the Human Rights of Central America. And now this year [1985] we have formed the Costa Rica human rights section because before that we didn't need it. But now Costa Rica is being militarized and we have a lot of problems, and repression is coming. I am also a founder of [a local] Amnesty International with another person. [At first] we had no place to gather. In Costa Rica we have a peace center that the Quakers run. They offer it to all organizations who are working for peace, so I went there two or three years ago, and WILPF was also there. So I became acquainted with WILPF women, and even though there were very few at that time, only twenty—now we are forty—they seemed very enthusiastic about it and I began to be interested. Two years ago I joined WILPF. It was difficult for them to work, but now I think it's much easier. In Costa Rica we have a very good health organization and educational programs; we're very proud of them. But now that Costa Rica is being militarized, they cut into this budget. We have an economic crisis because of the budget for arms. So it has been restraining the health and education [expenditures]. And now the Costa Ricans know that militarization involves their own lives and their own jobs and the health and education of their children. Now in the last months we have doubled our membership, and it was on account of this situation. Now it's much easier to speak to them about war because now they understand that.

How did the Costa Rican section get started?

Well it got started by the Quakers. We had a Costa Rican Quaker, Erna Castro, and she saw it was necessary because we have numerous organizations in Costa Rica, but they are [connected with the] political parties. So she thought they had to open a space for women to gather together even if they had different ideas. So with the Quakers she began this. They formed the Costa Rican section four years ago. At first it was she and three American women, also Quakers. Erna is a pacifist. Even though I'm not of the same idea, I admire her because she has dedicated all her life to that.

Are most section members pacifists?

Not now. We have increased the number, and the persons who have come in are peace workers, not pacifists. The first ones are really pacifist, but we get along very well although we are different. We have different positions but we work very well together. For instance, when it was the anniversary of the Nicaraguan revolution, we were invited to participate in an act of solidarity. And Erna was in accordance. So our statement was that we are against the intervention by other countries, we are for respecting the charter of the UN for self-determination, and we hope that this year you will have your peace. We asked persons to fast in solidarity, and we got a big group to fast for one day. Erna is against intervention, of course. She would like a peaceful resolution, but it is impossible. So she was with us, and it was her idea for the fast. It was a very good idea. I think we work quite well together, we support each other and we give a balance between each other. Because all persons who are in WILPF are very honest in their positions.

What kinds of projects does the section work on?

Now for the first time I think we will really have a program because we are really following what [was suggested by the Geneva office]. We also work very much with human rights because we have a lot of refugees from Guatemala and El Salvador. As there are no other WILPF sections in Central America, I feel I'm not only representing Costa Rica but Central America [on the WILPF Executive Committee]. And the situation in Central America is really awful. I don't know if I can give you some figures: the average income per person in Costa Rica is very high for Central America, and you know how much it is? It is less than seventeen dollars a month, and that's great because in Salvador they have less than four dollars a month. And in Costa Rica there's quite a big difference between rich and poor. All the countries of Central America are [so poor]; we're very well off here in comparison. It's a different world [from Europe and the United States]; they don't understand. For instance, maybe a common worker here [Munich] is really rich in comparison with us. That's very difficult for Europeans to understand.

Now we are doing a great campaign against militarization. In May [1985] the U.S. came in to train our police; and that's not going to be police, that's going to be military. In 1949 the army was abolished, now it's coming again with another name. So the peace center and WILPF went to all organizations—unions, churches, both Catholic and Protestant, all the political parties, everybody. And we made the Coalition for Peace, and WILPF holds a very important position in that. Because there were thirteen members of the House of Representatives of different parties that were against the military training of Costa Ricans, they made a national forum. And the coalition's first action was a silent vigil with posters, giving support to those representatives. We had that vigil the day the national forum started.

Do you consider yourselves feminists?

We consider ourselves feminists in the sense that we are equal to men, not that we must fight men. We must make them understand and respect our point of view and our participation in all things that were once "men's" affairs. We think it's our affair. There's a great feeling for that in Costa Rica.

Women are more peaceful than men, they're more concerned about peace. So I think it was a good idea to work on getting them [involved in politics]. I think if you want to have a political voice, it is important that they hear you in the House of Representatives, that they hear you everywhere.

What about women's rights in Costa Rica?

Well, the constitution in Costa Rica is very advanced. The women and the children have nearly all the rights, not the father. We don't work on women's rights as a separate issue but in conjunction with economic development. We do make lectures for women in the communities so they know what their rights are because the legislation is very good, but the women don't know some of the rights they have.

Are you all women?

Yes, but we have two meetings a month; one is only WILPF members and the other is a roundtable or a film, and there everybody takes their husbands or their boyfriends. So that activity is always with men.

This is the first time you've been to a WILPF executive meeting. How do you feel about being here?

It's very difficult for Europeans to understand what we are suffering, but there seems to be a feeling here of wanting to get in contact with us. I think that's very positive. That's attracted me to the league more than anything else because I think you can do more effective work internationally. We're very isolated and will continue being isolated. Unless we work internationally, we'll always have these problems.

You've been doing peace work for quite a few years. What keeps you going?

I don't want these things to keep happening in my country. So I think it's an obligation that you have. I think women within WILPF are thinking the same. We have to do something, we must do it, even if we get repression afterwards. I think it's an opportunity for women who don't want to be in one political party and who have an international view to come and join us, because we are of very different ideas and yet we all work very well together.

Angela Gethi

July 1986

Angela Gethi has been organizing women in her native Kenya all her adult life, but she had never heard of the WILPF until the international women's decade conference was held in Nairobi in 1985. There, impressed by what she learned about the league in the peace tent, she decided to start a WILPF group in Kenya.

An attractive, broad-faced woman in her early forties, Angela was one of the first women from her small village to attend college. She then became one of the first African women in her country to hold the post of community development officer. Angela's career has been devoted to organizing rural women into self-help groups to improve their daily lives.

Marriage and seven children did not stop her from pursuing her career: at the time she was starting her family, a woman who left her employment could not be assured of returning to it. In fact, Angela remembers that part of her life—juggling her roles as student, wife, mother, and professional—as most enjoyable, as well as a great challenge.

I was born in a village about 200 miles from Nairobi, the oldest of eight children. I was always keen to do something for my immediate community, partly because I wanted to prove to some of my villagers that it was worthwhile to educate a woman. My father was very much discouraged from educating me, and he went to a lot of trouble to help me get as far as I could in my education.

Anyway, I got interested in working with disadvantaged groups, particularly during the Mau Mau revolution. That was about the same time I left school, in 1956. There were many families left homeless and many children wandering about. So I got a job as a probation officer and helped these children to be committed to places of safety. It was through this experience that I got interested in continuing my education along these lines. On that basis I got a scholarship from my government to study community development in Britain. After that, I felt so much had been given to me by my own father and my own government that I wanted to see what I could do to help an average African woman do something for herself.

And what kinds of projects did you work on?

The way I have seen rural development work, it is the woman who really has to carry the burden of it. In many cases the man is moving between the rural home and the town in search of what he might call better employment and is leaving a lot of the farmwork to the woman. So she has to find ways of improving her lot. Women get together to organize themselves into self-help movements to improve their standards of living: in order to build better houses, buy essential goods or even in farmwork. This way they give encouragement to each other. Generally, their biggest concerns are schools for their children and better methods of getting water. The backbone of all things is the woman.

And do you still live in one of these villages?

I have lived in Nairobi for some time. But I don't lose sight of the rural community because my parents and parents-in-law are living in a rural area. And I'm also in touch with the women's self-help groups near my home.

What drew you to WILPF?

I feel WILPF is introducing a new element for women. It talks more about peace and human rights. I want to show women in my country through WILPF that peace can only come about when we as women aren't suffering from want. We must find ways and means of enabling women to provide enough food for their families. To them, this will bring peace. Through WILPF and this kind of education we are bound to create a more orderly society—helping a woman to get free of the harassing feeling (Will there be enough for next week?), equipping her with the appropriate technology to grow enough and to have a little time for herself as an individual.

I don't like it when a woman is so submissive in any society that she loses her identity. Women's identity must be felt in every nation, so we must get the women to come out in all their full colors and realize the contributions they can make. This acknowledgment has not yet been brought to the surface well enough.

There's very much support here [in Kenya] for the philosophy WILPF espouses. We have a small group of thirty women already interested, and we have in mind to hold seminars to introduce the ideas of the organization and to enroll more members.

My impression is that it's not necessarily the big numbers who change society but the committed few who continue day in and day out to carry out their tasks. This is what appeals to me about WILPF.

Appendix A

The Manifesto of 1915, Issued by Envoys of the International Congress of Women at The Hague to the Governments of Europe and the President of the United States

Here in America, on neutral soil, far removed from the stress of the conflict, we, envoys to the Governments from the International Congress of Women at The Hague, have come together to canvass the results of our missions. We put forth this statement as our united and deliberate conclusions.

At a time when the foreign offices of the great belligerents have been barred to each other, and the public mind of Europe has been fixed on the war offices for leadership, we have gone from capital to capital and conferred with the civil governments.

Our mission was to place before belligerent and neutral alike the resolutions of the International Congress of Women held at The Hague in April; especially to place before them the definite method of a conference of neutral nations as an agency of continuous mediation for the settlement of the war.

To carry out this mission two delegations were appointed, which included women of Great Britain, Hungary, Italy, the Netherlands, Sweden and the United States. One or other of these delegations was received by the governments in fourteen capitals: Berlin, Berne, Budapest, Christiana, Copenhagen, The Hague, Le Havre (Belgian Government), London, Paris, Petrograd, Rome, Stockholm, Vienna and Washington. We were received by the Prime Ministers and Foreign Ministers of the Powers, by the King of Norway, by the presidents of Switzerland and the United States, by the Pope and the Cardinal Secretary of State. In many capitals more than one audience was given, not merely to present our resolutions, but for a thorough discussion. In addition to the thirty-five governmental visits we met—everywhere—members of parliament and other leaders of public opinion.

We heard much the same words spoken in Downing Street as those spoken in Wilhelmstrasse, in Vienna as in Petrograd, in Budapest as in the Havre, where the Belgians have their temporary government.

Our visits to the war capitals convinced us that the belligerent governments would not be opposed to a conference of neutral nations; that while the belligerents have rejected offers of mediation by single neutral nations, and while no belligerent could ask for mediation, the creation of a continuous conference of neutral nations might provide the machinery which would lead to peace. We found that the neutrals on the other hand were concerned lest calling such a conference might be considered inopportune by one or other of the belligerents. Here our information from the belligerents themselves gave assurance that such initiative would not be resented. "My country would not find anything unfriendly in such action by the neutrals," was the assurance given us by the Foreign Minister of one of the great belligerents. "My Government would place no obstacle in the way of its institution," said the Minister of an opposing nation. "What are the neutrals waiting for?" said a third, whose name ranks high not only in his own country but all over the world.

It remained to put this clarifying intelligence before the neutral countries. As a result the plan of starting mediation through the agency of a continuous conference of the neutral nations is today being seriously discussed alike in the Cabinets of the belligerent and neutral countries and in the press of both.

We are in a position to quote some of the expressions of men high in the councils of the great nations as to the feasibility of the plan. "You are right," said one Minister, "that it would be of the greatest importance to finish the fight by early negotiation rather than by further military efforts, which would result in more and more destruction and irreparable loss." "Yours is the sanest proposal that has been brought to this office in the last six months," said the Prime Minister of one of the larger countries.

We were also in a position to canvass the objections that have been made to the proposal, testing it out severely in the judgment of those in the midst of the European conflict. It has been argued that it is not the time at present to start such a process of negotiation, and that no step should be taken until one or other party has a victory, or at least until some new military balance is struck. The answer we bring is that every delay makes more difficult the beginning of negotiations, more nations become involved, and the situation becomes more complicated; that when at times in the course of the war such a balance was struck, the neutrals were un-prepared to act. The opportunity passed. For the forces of peace to be unprepared when the hour comes is as irretrievable as for a military leader to be unready.

It has been argued that for such a conference to be called at any time when one side has met with some military advantage, would be to favor that side. The answer we bring is that the proposed conference would start mediation at a higher level than that of military advantage. As to the actual military situation, however, we quote a remark made to us by a Foreign Minister of one of the belligerent Powers: "Neither side is today strong enough to dictate terms, and neither side is so weakened that it has to accept humiliating terms."

It has been suggested that such a conference would bind the neutral governments cooperating in it. The answer we bring is that, as proposed, such a conference should consist of the ablest persons of the neutral coun-tries, assigned not to problems of their own governments, but to the com-mon service of a supreme crisis. The situation calls for a conference cast in a new and larger mold than those of conventional diplomacy, the govern-ments sending to it persons drawn from social, economic and scientific fields who have had genuine international experience.

As women, it was possible for us, from belligerent and neutral nations alike, to meet in the midst of war and to carry forward an interchange of question and answer between capitals which were barred to each other. It is now our duty to make articulate our convictions. We have been con-vinced that the governments of the belligerent nations would not be hos-tile to the institution of such a channel for good offices; and that the gov-ernments of the European neutrals we visited stand ready to cooperate with others in mediation. Reviewing the situation, we believe that of the five European neutral nations visited, three are ready to join in such a conference, and that two are deliberating the calling of such a conference. Of the intention of the United States we have as yet no evidence.

We are but the conveyors of evidence which is a challenge to action by the neutral governments visited—by Denmark, Holland, Norway, Swe-den, Switzerland and the United States. We in turn bear evidence of a rising desire and intention of vast companies of people in the neutral coun-tries to turn a barren disinterestedness into an active goodwill. In Sweden, for instance, more than 400 meetings were held in one day in different parts of the country, calling on the government to act.

The excruciating burden of responsibility for the hopeless continu-ance of this war no longer rests on the will of the belligerent nations alone.

It rests also on the will of those neutral governments and peoples who have been spared its shock but cannot, if they would, absolve themselves from their full responsibility for the continuance of war.

Signed by Jane Addams (United States); Emily G. Balch (United States); Aletta Jacobs (Holland); Chrystal Macmillan (Great Britain); Rosika Schwimmer (Austro-Hungary).

New York, October 15, 1915.

Appendix B

The Women Interviewed, with the Place and Date of Interview and Home Country if Different

Charlotte Adams, Chapel Hill, N.C., March 25, 1987.

Edith Ballantyne, Geneva, September 4, 1985.

Torun Bergendahl, Munich, August 15, 1985 (Sweden).

Olga Bianchi, Munich, August 19, 1985 (Costa Rica).

Janet Bruin, Geneva, September 8, 1985.

Kay Camp, King of Prussia, Pa., June 5, 1985; April 7, 1986; April 30, 1987.

Erna Castro, Wallingford, Pa., April 30, 1987 (Costa Rica).

Margaret Curwen, Zeist, Netherlands, July 26, 1986 (Britain).

Marie-Therese Danielsson, Zeist, Netherlands, July 27, 1986 (French Polynesia).

Irene Eckert, Pau, France and West Berlin, September 2, 1986 and February 29, 1988. (These interviews were conducted through the mail.)

Lois Evans, Munich, August 19, 1985 (Britain).

Libby Frank, Philadelphia, Pa., June 6, 1985.

Angela Gethi, Zeist, Netherlands, July 22, 1986 (Kenya).

Ruth Gleissberg, Munich, August 19, 1985.

Elizabeth Goffe, Munich, August 18, 1985 (British Wales).

Vivienne Goonewardene, Zeist, Netherlands, July 26, 1986 (Sri Lanka).

Lucy Haessler, Santa Cruz, Calif., March 17, 1986.

Erna P. Harris, Berkeley, Calif., March 28, 1986.

Ida Harsloff, Copenhagen, Denmark, August 5, 1986. (This interview was conducted by Ellen Blosser, a WILPF member from the United States.)

Fujiko Isono, Munich, August 16, 1985 and July 23, 1986 (Japan).

Kirsti Koltov, Munich, August 15, 1985 (Sweden).

Carlota Lopes da Silva, Munich, August 22, 1985 (Netherlands).

Naomi Marcus, Swarthmore, Pa., June 6, 1985.

Betty McIntosh, Munich, August 16, 1985 (Australia).

Anissa Najjar, Zeist, Netherlands, July 29, 1986 (Lebanon).
Anne Nelson, Munich, August 23, 1985 (United States).
Briget Obermayer, Munich, August 15, 1985.
Miriam Ohringer, Zeist, Netherlands, July 25, 1986.
Mildred Olmsted, Media, Pa., June 6, 1985. (Another interview was also
    used, courtesy of WILPF. The interview was conducted by Mercedes
    Randall in New York City in February 1972.)
Harriet Otterloo, Geneva, September 4, 1985 (Sweden).
Eleanor Otterness, Washington, D.C., January 1986.
Riita Pakaslahti, Munich, August 21, 1985 (Finland).
Else Pickvance, Munich and Zeist, Netherlands, August 19, 1985 and July
    24, 1986 (Britain).
Amelia Boynton Robinson, Tuskegee, Ala., June 19, 1986.
Eleonore Romberg, Munich, August 22, 1985.
Mari Holmboe Ruge, Munich, August 15, 1985 (Norway).
Phyllis Sanders, Philadelphia, June 7, 1985.
Renate Schaffer, Geneva, September 1, 1985 (Sweden).
Gonnie Scholten-van Itersen, Zeist, Netherlands, July 28, 1986.
Yvonne See, Munich, August 20, 1985 (France).
Reine Seidlitz, Zeist, Netherlands, July 27, 1986 (Switzerland).
Loranee Senaratne, Munich, August 23, 1985 (Sri Lanka).
Elisabeth Stahle, Stockholm, February 1986 and June 25, 1986. (The first
    interview was conducted by mail by the author; the second was con-
    ducted by Maggie Hennessey, program director of the U.S. section,
    on behalf of the author.)
Dolores Taller, Berkeley, Calif., March 25, 1986.
Rigmore Risbjerg Thomsen, Munich, August 21, 1985 (Denmark).
Inga Thorsson, Zeist, Netherlands, July 28, 1986 (Sweden).
Aiko Tokusue, Munich, August 22, 1985 (Japan).
Adrienne van Melle, Amsterdam, August 19, 1986.
Maya Zahavi, Zeist, Netherlands, July 22, 1986 (Israel).

Notes

Introduction

1. Jane Addams, *Peace and Bread in Time of War* (1922; reprint ed., Silver Spring, Md.: National Association of Social Workers Publications, 1983), 149.

2. Dorothy Hutchinson, speech presented at the Seventeenth Congress of the Women's International League for Peace and Freedom, Nyborg, Denmark, August 18, 1968, in *The Women's International League for Peace and Freedom, 1915–1978* (Sanford, N.C.: Microfilming Corporation of America, 1983), reel 24 (hereafter referred to as WILPF Papers).

3. Author's estimate.

1. The First Fifty Years

1. Kay Camp, interview with author, June 5, 1985.

2. Bayard Rustin, keynote address at the Sixteenth Congress of the Women's International League for Peace and Freedom, The Hague, July 26, 1965, WILPF Papers, reel 24.

3. Emmeline Pethick-Lawrence, *My Part in a Changing World* (London: Victor Gollancz, 1938), 307–8.

4. The most prominent prowar suffragettes were Emmeline Pankhurst and her daughter Christabel of Great Britain. The Pankhursts had already attained notoriety by introducing direct-action tactics into the suffrage movement. Another daughter, Sylvia, broke relations with her mother and sister to oppose the war. For further reading about the split, see Joan Montgomery Byles, "Women's Experience of World War One: Suffragists, Pacifists, and Poets," *Women's Studies International Forum* 8, no. 5 (1985): 473–79.

5. Chrystal Macmillan was a British suffragist and ISWA leader.

6. Crystal Eastman, "'Now I Dare to Do it': An Interview with Dr. Aletta Jacobs, Who Called the Woman's Peace Congress at The Hague," October 9, 1915, in *Crystal Eastman on Women and Revolution*, ed. Blanche Wiesen Cook (New York: Oxford University Press, 1978), 237–38.

7. Two other British women, Chrystal Macmillan and Kathleen Courtney, had come to The Hague earlier, giving Great Britain three delegates at the congress.

8. Pethick-Lawrence, *My Part in a Changing World*, 313–14.

9. See appendix A for more details.

10. Jane Addams, Emily Greene Balch, and Alice Hamilton, *Women at The Hague* (1915; reprint ed., New York: Garland Publishing, 1972), 1–19.

11. The original sections were in Austria, Belgium, Denmark, France, Germany, Great Britain and Ireland, Hungary, Italy, the Netherlands, Norway, Sweden, the United States, and Australia.

12. They were received by Prime Minister Cort van der Linden and Foreign Minister Loudon, in The Hague; Prime Minister Asquith and Foreign Minister Sir Edward Grey, in London; Reichskanzler von Bethmann-Hollweg and Foreign Minister von Jagow, in Berlin; Prime Minister Stuergkh and Foreign Minister Burian, in Vienna; Prime Minister Tisza, in Budapest; Prime Minister Salandra and Foreign Minister Sonino, in Rome; Prime Minister Viviani and Foreign Minister Delcasee, in Paris; Foreign Minister d'Avignon, in Le Havre; President Motta and Foreign Minister Hoffman, in Bern.

13. Addams, Balch, and Hamilton, *Women at The Hague*, 82–97.

14. Eastman, "'Now I Dare to Do It,'" 240.

15. Mildred Olmsted, interview with Mercedes Randall, February 1972, Mildred Scott Olmsted Papers, Swarthmore College Peace Collection (hereafter referred to as Olmsted Papers).

16. Mercedes Randall, *Beyond Nationalism: The Social Thought of Emily Greene Balch* (New York: Twayne Publishers, 1972), 206–11.

17. Paul Wasserman, ed., *Awards, Honors, and Prizes*, 2 vols., 5th ed. (Detroit: Gale Research, 1982), 2:52.

18. Olmsted interview with Randall, February, 1972, Olmsted Papers.

19. Rigmore Risbjerg Thomsen, interview with author, August 21, 1985.

20. Eleonore Romberg, interview with author, August 22, 1985.

21. Adrienne van Melle, interview with author, August 19, 1986.

22. Mari Holmboe Ruge, interview with author, August 15, 1985.

23. Dorothy Hutchinson to Elisabeth Stahle, April 2, 1966, WILPF Papers, reel 6.

24. Report of the French section to the Fifteenth Congress of the Women's International League for Peace and Freedom, Asilomar, Calif., 1962, in *Congress Report*, (Privately printed by WILPF, n.p., n.d.), 90.

25. Gertrude Baer, speech presented at the Fifteenth Congress of the Women's International League for Peace and Freedom, Asilomar, Calif., 1962, in *Congress Report*, (Privately printed by WILPF, n.p., n.d.), 53.

2. A New WILPF Decade

1. The women were all members of the U.S. section: Jo Graham, Beulah Johnson, Eleanor Davis, Rose Paull, and Annalee Stewart, who had been the section's president from 1946 to 1950 and its legislative director from 1949 to 1964.

2. WILPF Papers, reel 29.

3. Fujiko Isono, interview with author, August 16, 1985.

4. Dorothy Hutchinson et al. for the American Friends Service Committee, *Peace in Vietnam* (New York: Hill and Wang, 1966).

5. Aja Selander to Elisabeth Stahle, undated correspondence, WILPF Papers, reel 29.

6. Else Zeuthen, report on peaceful settlement of disputes to the Seventeenth Congress of the Women's International League for Peace and Freedom, Nyborg, Denmark, August 20, 1985, WILPF Papers, reel 24.

7. Amelia Boynton, interview with author, June 19, 1986.

8. Sheila Young to WILPF headquarters, n.d., WILPF Papers, reel 29.

9. Gertrude Baer, speech presented at "The Participation of Women in Public Life" seminar, Rome, Italy, October 1966, WILPF Papers, reel 29.

10. Dorothy Hutchinson, "WILPF and a Unified Peace Movement," *Pax et Libertas*, January-March 1966, 1–2.

11. Ibid.

12. Dorothy Hutchinson to Elisabeth Stahle, May 5, 1966, WILPF Papers, reel 6.

13. Mildred Olmsted, interview with author, June 6, 1985.

14. Frances Herring, interview with Women's Peace Oral History Project, Berkeley, Calif., April 2, 1985.

15. WILPF Papers, reel 96.

16. Lucy Haessler, interview with author, March 17, 1986.

3. A World in Turmoil

1. Martin Luther King, Jr., "Modern Man's Dilemma: The Nobel Lecture," *Pax et Libertas*, January–March 1965, 2.

2. "Some Findings on the Total Cost of Our Air War against North Vietnam," *I.F. Stone's Weekly* 16, no. 23 (November 18, 1968): 3.

3. Dorothy Hutchinson to Elisabeth Stahle, April 1968, in Lars Stahle, "Vara Gemensamma Ar vid WILPF's Internationella Huvudkontor" (Typescript, Stockholm, 1980), 45.

4. Isono interview, 1985.

5. Barby Ulmer, interview with Women's Peace Oral History Project, San Jose, Calif., April 27, 1984.

6. WILPF Papers, reel 24.

7. Kay Camp, interview with author, April 7, 1986.

8. Hutchinson, minutes of the Seventeenth Congress of the Women's International League for Peace and Freedom, Nyborg, Denmark, August 18–24, 1968, WILPF Papers, reel 24.

9. Kay Camp, interview with author, June 5, 1985.

10. *WILPF Circular Letter*, July 1969, WILPF Papers, reel 7.

11. Gertrude Baer, speech presented at the WILPF International Conference on Chemical and Bacteriological Warfare, London, November 1969, WILPF Papers, reel 29.

12. Ellen Holmgaard to Cornelia Weiss, August 26, 1969, WILPF Papers, reel 8.

13. Elisabeth Stahle, general secretary's report to the Seventeenth Congress of the Women's International League for Peace and Freedom, Nyborg, Denmark, August 18, 1968, WILPF Papers, reel 24.

14. Margaret Tims, *WILPF Circular Letter*, April 1968, WILPF Papers, reel 29.

15. Elise Boulding, *WILPF Circular Letter*, July 1969, WILPF Papers, reel 7.

16. Kay Camp, "Up with Women," *Peace and Freedom*, March 1970, 2.

17. Sybil Morrison, *WILPF Circular Letter*, September 1967, WILPF Papers, reel 29.

18. Dorothy Steffens to Elise Boulding, February 24, 1970, WILPF Papers, reel 7.

19. Congress brochure, 1970, WILPF Papers, reel 102.

20. Ibid.

21. Elise Boulding, introductory address at the Eighteenth Congress of the Women's International League for Peace and Freedom, New Delhi,

India, December 30, 1970, WILPF minutes, box 177, Geneva headquarters. (These documents are hereafter cited by box number and city.)

22. Edith Ballantyne to Dorothy Hutchinson, February 2, 1971, WILPF Papers, reel 7.

23. Elsie Simmons, "What Price Freedom?" *Pax et Libertas*, April–June 1970, 22.

24. Statement of the Eighteenth Congress of the Women's International League for Peace and Freedom, New Delhi, India, 1970–71, *Congress Report* (Geneva: WILPF, 1971), 31.

25. Isono interview, 1985.

26. Erna P. Harris, interview with author, March 28, 1986.

27. WILPF Executive Committee minutes, 1975, WILPF Papers, reel 8.

28. Hannah Bernheim-Rosenzweig to Edith Ballantyne, December 1, 1969, WILPF Papers, reel 79.

29. Johanne Reutz Gjermoe, report to the Eighteenth Congress of the Women's International League for Peace and Freedom, New Delhi, India, December 31, 1970, WILPF Papers, reel 79.

30. Sadie Hughley and Pat Samuels were the other members of the mission.

31. Kay Camp, "Report of Mission to Vietnam," *Pax et Libertas*, January-June 1971, 2–3.

32. They were Dorothy Steffens, executive director of the U.S. section, and Marii Hasegawa, the section's president and a Japanese-American who had first come to the WILPF after its campaign protesting the internment of Japanese-Americans during World War II.

33. Camp interview, 1986.

34. Accompanying Camp were Phyllis Sanders and Virginia Collins, both of the United States.

35. The team was composed of Kay Camp, Kay Cole, Peg McCarter, Evelyn Moss, Charlotte Ryan, and Pearl Shamis.

36. WILPF Papers, reel 8.

37. Kay Camp et al., *Chile: State of War, an Eyewitness Report* (Philadelphia: WILPF, 1974), 51.

38. Romberg interview, 1985. An interesting postcript to this story is that in 1983, upon turning sixty, Romberg told her school authorities that she was devoting herself to full-time peace activities and would no longer answer to anyone about it.

39. Kay Camp, letter to *Pax et Libertas*, September 1974, 16–18.

40. Kay Camp to Edith Ballantyne, August 18, 1974, WILPF Papers, reel 8.

4. The United Nations Decade for Women: Equality, Development, and Peace

1. UN report, issued in Copenhagen in 1980, on a study covering the previous five years, in Marcus Gee, "Assessing the Decade," *MacLean's*, July 29, 1985, 26.

2. Inga Thorsson, interview with author, July 28, 1986.

3. The WIDF is a large, socialist-oriented nongovernmental organization with members and chapters in many countries and headquarters in East Berlin.

4. *Summary of Findings*, WILPF leaflet reprinted from *Peace and Freedom*, May 1975.

5. Final document, UN Special Session on Disarmament 1, 1978, in Kay Camp, "Opportunity Lost: Disarmament Session a Disappointment," *Philadelphia Inquirer*, July 16, 1982.

6. Romberg interview, 1985.

7. Kay Camp, interview with author, April 4, 1987.

8. The mission had originally been planned to include the international vice-president, Prabha Rai, of the Indian section, but she was unable to get a travel visa because of her country's refusal of diplomatic relations with Israel.

9. Edith Ballantyne, interview with author, September 4, 1985.

10. WILPF Executive Committee minutes, 1975, WILPF Papers, reel 15.

11. Ballantyne interview, 1985.

12. Lucy Haessler, interview with Women's Peace Oral History Project, Stanford University, Calif., April 29, 1982.

13. Van Melle interview, 1986.

14. Adrienne van Melle, remarks in *Women of Europe in Action for Peace*, conference report, November 27–29, 1981 (Geneva: WILPF, n.d.).

15. The league's position on this issue has continued to be ambiguous. For further reading, see Shirley Powers's untitled essay in *Peace and Freedom*, October–November 1987, 3, as well as Holly Near, "Singing for Our Lives," and Mary Zepernick, "Carrying the WILPF Banner," *Peace and Freedom*, December 1987, 6 and 13.

16. Ballantyne interview, 1985.

17. These programs are now known as the Gertrude Baer Young Women's Summer Seminars, named to commemorate the WILPF pioneer who was once the league's youth referent and was always firmly dedicated to bringing in more young women.

18. The STAR messages also called for a U.S.–Soviet nuclear weapons freeze, a comprehensive test-ban treaty, a cut in military budgets, and support for UN disarmament efforts.

19. Van Melle interview, 1986.

20. Camp, "Opportunity Lost."

21. The 1959 revision of its constitution reads as follows: "the League seeks to remove such restrictions on freedom as impair human dignity and to establish by nonviolent means the conditions under which men and women may live in peace and justice free from fear of war and of want and of discrimination on grounds of sex, race, color, language, national, ethnic, or social origin, property, birth, or other status, political, religious, or other belief" (WILPF Papers, reel 23).

22. Rigmore Risbjerg Thomsen, 1982, memorandum to the WILPF Executive Committee, 1982, box 181, Geneva.

23. The applicants' countries of origin were Australia, Denmark, Finland, the German Democratic Republic, India, Jamaica, Japan, and the Soviet Union.

24. "Hot Words for the Freeze," editorial, *Washington Post*, October 6, 1982, 22A. For further reading on this incident, see also "Letters to the Editor" section, *Washington Post*, October 9, 1982, 18A; Robert McCloskey, "Ombudsman: The Editorials on the Peace Groups," *Washington Post*, October 12, 1982, 12A; Honorable Larry MacDonald, "Moscow's New Peace Offensive Revisited," *Congressional Record*, April 27, 1982, E1852; and "Smear Campaign against Peace Groups Intensifies," *On the Alert*, newsletter of the Campaign for Political Rights, Washington, D.C., October 1982, 1.

25. Erna Castro, interview with author, April 30, 1987.

26. A smaller WILPF delegation had previously met with NATO leaders during mass actions in Brussels shortly before the deployment decision was taken in December 1979.

27. Edith Ballantyne, in "International Women's Day, Brussels, March 1983," STAR campaign report (Geneva: WILPF, n.d.), 13–14.

28. Elizabeth Mattick, "Nairobi," report to the Australian section, 1985, box 6, Geneva, p.1.

29. Ibid., p.2.

30. Edith Ballantyne, speech presented at the Women and Peace Conference, Palais des Nations, Geneva, March 6–8, 1985, in *Women and Peace*, conference report (Geneva: WILPF, n.d.), 8.

31. Gee, "Assessing the Decade," 26.

32. Ballantyne interview, 1985.

33. Kay Camp, telephone conversation with author, February 22, 1988.

34. Carlota Lopes da Silva, interview with author, August 22, 1985.

5. Toward the Year 2000

1. Woman's Peace Party, platform statement, Washington, D.C., January 1915, WILPF Papers, reel 16.

2. Addams, *Peace and Bread in Time of War*.

3. Olmsted interview with Randall, February 1972, Olmsted Papers.

4. Ibid.

5. Ronald Reagan, 1984 State of the Union Address.

6. Members were present from twenty-two national sections; other participants were international members from countries with no section or invited guests.

7. Camp interview, 1987.

8. Carol Pendell, speech presented at the Twenty-third Congress of the Women's International League for Peace and Freedom, Zeist, Netherlands, 1986, in *Congress Report* (Privately printed by WILPF, n.p., 1986), 42.

9. Yvonne See, interview with author, August 20, 1985.

10. Romberg interview, 1985.

11. Haessler interview with Women's Peace Oral History Project, 1982.

12. Camp interview, 1985.

13. Ballantyne interview, 1985.

14. Ruge interview, 1985.

15. Romberg interview, 1985.

16. Ruge interview, 1985.

17. Janet Bruin, interview with author, September 8, 1985.

18. Ballantyne interview, 1985.

19. Irene Eckert, interview with author, September 2, 1986.

20. Angela Gethi, interview with author, July 22, 1986.

21. Olga Bianchi, interview with author, August 19, 1985.

22. Bruin interview, 1985.

23. Elisabeth Stahle to author, February 1986.

24. Camp interview, 1987.

25. Briget Obermayer, interview with author, August 15, 1985.

26. Romberg interview, 1985.

27. Ballantyne interview, 1985.

28. For further discussion, see Carol Gilligan, *In a Different Voice* (Cambridge, Mass.: Harvard University Press, 1982).

29. Kay Camp, "WILPF: Peace Women Consider Feminism," *Win*, March 15, 1983, 16.

30. Ruge interview, 1985.

31. Ruth Gleissberg, interview with author, August 19, 1985.

32. Lopes da Silva interview, 1985.

33. Camp, "Peace Women," 17.

Profiles of Eighteen WILPF Women

1. Florence Kelley was a colleague of Jane Addams who was also involved in early social welfare movements, as well as being a pacifist and a Quaker. One of the first women attorneys in the United States, she was instrumental in fighting for better working conditions for women and children.

2. The Red Network and the Spider Web Chart were documents allegedly compiled by the U.S. government detailing organizations and individuals that were supposed "sympathizers" of communism and/or the Soviet Union.

Bibliography

I include here the sources which have been most useful in the preparation of this book. Other writings were consulted, but those listed here are the ones from which I became familiar with the topic and formed my ideas. Therefore, they are the starting point to which I would direct any reader wishing to learn more about this subject. Because so many of the references used here are publications of the Women's International League for Peace and Freedom (WILPF), this bibliography is divided into two sections: General Sources and WILPF Publications and Papers. (For a listing of personal interviews, see appendix B.) Please note also that certain entire series are cited in the second section; I browsed through all of these publications in the course of my research and would suggest that any other researcher do the same in order to get an overview of the organization and its related topics.

General Sources

Addams, Jane; Balch, Emily Greene; and Hamilton, Alice. *Women at The Hague*. 1915. Reprint. New York: Garland Publishing, 1972.

Bonds, Joy; Emerman, Jimmy; John, Linda; Johnson, Penny; and Rupert, Paul. *Our Roots Are Still Alive: The Story of the Palestinian People*. 1977. Reprint. New York: Institute for Independent Social Journalism, 1981.

Camp, Kay. "Peace Women Consider Feminism." *Win*, March 15, 1983, 15–17.

Cooney, Robert, and Michalowski, Helen. *The Power of the People: Active Nonviolence in the United States*. 1977. Reprint. Philadelphia: New Society Publishers, 1987.

Detzer, Dorothy. *Appointment on the Hill*. New York: Henry Holt, 1948.

Eastman, Crystal. *Crystal Eastman on Women and Revolution*. Edited by Blanche Wiesen Cook. New York: Oxford University Press, 1978.

Gilligan, Carol. *In a Different Voice*. Cambridge, Mass.: Harvard University Press, 1982.

Herring, Frances. "To End the Arms Race, Not the Human Race." *Memo: A Quarterly Publication of WSP*, April 1970, 3–4.

Jones, Lynne, ed. *Keeping the Peace: Women's Handbook*. London: Women's Press, 1983.

Pethick-Lawrence, Emmeline. *My Part in a Changing World*. London: Victor Gollancz, 1938.

Randall, Mercedes. *Improper Bostonian: Emily Greene Balch*. New York: Twayne Publishers, 1964.

———. *Beyond Nationalism: The Social Thought of Emily Greene Balch*. New York: Twayne Publishers, 1972.

Stahle, Lars."Vara Gemensamma ar vid WILPF's Internationella Huvud-kontor." (Our common good is with WILPF's international headquarters). Stockholm, 1980. Typescript.

Wiltsher, Carol. *Most Dangerous Women*. London: Pandora Press, 1985.

Zaroulis, Nancy, and Sullivan, Gerald. *Who Spoke Up? American Protest against the War in Vietnam, 1963–1975*. Garden City, N.Y.: Double-day, 1984.

WILPF Publications and Papers

Bussey, Gertrude, and Tims, Margaret. *Pioneers for Peace: Women's International League for Peace and Freedom, 1915–1965*. 1965. Reprint. Oxford: Alden Press, 1980.

Camp, Kay; Cole, Kay; Mauss, Evelyn; McCarter, Peg; Ryan, Charlotte; and Shamis, Pearl. *Chile: State of War, an Eyewitness Report*. Philadelphia: WILPF, 1974.

Ducey, Mitchell. *The Women's International League for Peace and Freedom, 1915–1978*. Sanford, N.C.: Microfilming Corporation of America, 1983.

Holt, Betty. *Women for Peace and Freedom*. Wellington, New Zealand: WILPF, 1985.

International Women's Day, Brussels, March 1983. STAR campaign report. Geneva: WILPF, n.d.

Olmsted, Mildred Scott. Papers. Swarthmore College Peace Collection, Swarthmore, Pa.

Piper, Anne. *Herstory of the Women's Peace Movement*. Nottingham, England: Women's Peace Alliance, 1984.

Women and Peace. Conference report. March 6–8, 1985. Geneva: WILPF, n.d.

Women of Europe in Action for Peace. Conference report. November 27–29, 1981. Geneva: WILPF, n.d.

Women's International League for Peace and Freedom. Congress Reports, 1946–1986. Proceedings of triennial international congresses. Geneva: WILPF.

————. Papers. WILPF international headquarters, Geneva.

————. *Pax et Libertas*, January/March 1965–September 1987, Geneva.

————. *Peace and Freedom*, January 1970–January 1988, Philadelphia.

————. U.S. Section Records, 1919–present. Swarthmore College Peace Collection. Swarthmore, Pa.

Women's Peace Oral History Project. Stanford University Archives. Palo Alto, Calif.

Index